ECM Technology
What you need to know

Tom Jenkins

This book is dedicated to the staff, partners and customers of Open Text Corporation and its subsidiaries. This book is possible due to their combined efforts, innovation and collective vision.

We would like to thank the staff, users and partners of Open Text for their contributions to this book.

Special thanks go out to the writers: Elizabeth Chestney and Neil Wilson; contributors: Evelyn Astor-Hack, Jeremy Barnes, Virginia Bartosek, Dylan Barrell, Scott Bowen, Charles Carter, Michael Cybala, Lisa Dekker, Margaret Dobbin, Joe Dwyer, Peter Fischer, David Glazer, Roman Götter, Michael Heckner, Dan Hooper, Adam Howatson, Lynne Jackson, Peter Jelinski, Toby Jenkins, Carol Knoblauch, Agnes Kolkiewicz, Peter Lalonde, Marie Lindsay, Jennifer McCredie, Rich Maganini, Julie Mandell, Bill Morton, Jeff Murphy, John Myers, Tony Niederer, Paul O'Hagan, Marco Palatini Jr., Donna Pearson, Jens Rabe, Art Sarno, Dave Schubmehl, Jared Spataro, Renée Tremblay, Annemarie Vander Veen, Doug Varley, Chris Veator, Scott Welch; and graphic artists: Janet Catipi, Sabrina Prudham and David Rees.

Specific resources are accredited in the Bibliography and the User Case Study Bibliography.

Jenkins, Tom

Enterprise Content Management
Technology

Fifth Printing, July 2006
Printed in Canada

ISBN
0-9730662-5-3

$29.00 U.S.

Published by
Open Text Corporation
275 Frank Tompa Drive
Waterloo, Ontario, Canada
N2L 0A1

(519) 888-7111
info@opentext.com
www.opentext.com

In today's business world, ECM is about more than managing content. Society is now demanding higher standards for the accuracy and availability of content:

In the two years following 2001, more than 20 new laws were enacted throughout the world that impacted how organizations gather and disseminate information. Government reaction to events such as 9/11 and Enron have been to demand greater transparency in collaboration and content. Regulators are relying on recent advances in electronic content management technology to provide this greater transparency efficiently.

In the past few years, more regulations were passed in some industries than have been written in almost a century. From the Patriot Act to Sarbanes-Oxley and the Data Protection Act, government regulations are creating more secure living conditions for consumers. Across many industries, individuals and companies have already been penalized for not complying with these regulations and mismanaging critical business content.

In a business climate that demands structure and control, ECM creates a safe and transparent environment for organizations to foster innovation and growth. ECM leverages the power of the Internet to transform the way people interact. It creates secure and regulated environments, ensuring that protected content remains behind closed doors. At the same time, ECM unlocks the true potential of the enterprise by enabling people to transform content into knowledge, creating new possibilities and business opportunities.

This book tells you what you need to know about ECM and how it can help to transform your organization into a more knowledgeable and agile enterprise. It describes the creation of a new approach to data by some of the greatest minds in the world of information technology—a collective vision determined to solve the challenge of managing structured and unstructured information. Each chapter in the book focuses on a technology component of ECM, tracing its origins from early search technologies to ubiquitous computing, real-time collaboration and voice recognition. User stories are included in each chapter to illustrate ECM applications in action and paint the picture of an industry in the making. The end of the book explores ECM solutions and implementation and what the future of Enterprise Content Management holds.

I hope you enjoy this story about the discovery of new and exciting technologies and will be encouraged to make your own journey to bring ECM technology to your business.

Tom Jenkins

Open Text Corporation

CONTENTS

Part 1: The Business Case

Part 2: ECM Content Technologies

Part 3: ECM Collaboration Technologies

Part 4: ECM Solutions and Implementation

User Stories

Compliance Grid

Compliance Solutions Map	Gov	Pharma	Energy	Finance	Mfg	Services
Research	U.S. Army S 111	AG S 221	Energen S 231	UBS S 76	Holcim S 271	LMU S 205
Admin	Flor Hanford S 59	Aventis S 219	Vintage M 58	LVA M 142	Sony M 21	Translink T 119
Mfg	Northrop Grumman T 65	Genzyme T 238	Sasol M 98	Winterthur S 247	Arup S 269	Johnson S 74
Services	Calgary S 199	FSMB S 195	PG&E S 237	Shenandoah Life T 233	CAS S 279	Giant Eagle M 186
Enterprise	GD S 291	Roche S 215	South East Water M 158	EIB T 265	Distell S 6	ISO S 297
Extranet	FM S 167	Aventis S 219	Kerr-McGee M 216	OSFI T 54	DMJM S 267	LMU S 205

Company Name	Page Number
M = Methods Book	
S = Solutions Book	
T = Technology Book	

ROI Grid

Legend:
- M = Methods Book
- S = Solutions Book
- T = Technology Book
- Company Name
- Page Number

ROI Solutions Map	R&D	Admin	Mfg	Services	Sales	Executive	Enterprise	Extranet
Media	HBO T 29	CBC S 23	TWBG S 169	TSR S 173	EA T 201	TSR S 173	Standard T 223	20th C. Fox S 171
Gov	U.S. Army S 111	ILR S 185	Northrop Grumman M 200	DRC M 228	Lockheed T 164	Fluor Hanford S 59	USPTO T 68	USAF T 240
Edu	FOIC S 109	Broward T 225	Turner T 75	Emory U. S 209	LMU S 205	Clark S 207	Open U. T 220	Broward T 225
Pharma	AG S 221	Novo Nordisk M 134	Roche S 215	Aventis S 219	Novartis S 155	Roche S 215	Genzyme T 238	Novartis S 155
Energy	Murphy Oil S 235	PG&E S 237	South East Water M 158	Energen S 231	Sasol M 98	Shell S 229	Kerr-McGee M 216	Shell S 229
Finance	VERA T 58	LawPRO S 13	Alte Leipziger T 185	Barclays T 148	AGVA S 245	UBS S 76	Shenandoah T 233	Federated Investors M 178
Telco	HP S 47	Sony S 21	BT S 259	T-Systems M 92	Siemens S 85	C&W S 81	Motorola M 232	Cisco S 257
AEC	Miller T 167	M+W Zander T 177	Holcim S 271	DMJM M 267	Johnson S 74	Holcim S 271	Arup S 269	M+W Zander M 206
Auto	Volvo Aero S 121	BMW S 119	CAS S 279	Daimler T 7	Fiat S 281	Audi T 85	CAS S 279	BMW T 124
Mfg	Distell S 6	Reebok S 43	Miele S 123	Owens Corning T 145	Whirlpool T 205	Siemens S 85	Motorola S 83	Unilever M 170
Services	TRL M 164	Translink T 119	Dow Corning S 143	Mercer S 151	Swiss Air M 71	SKM S 40	CARE M 112	ISO S 297

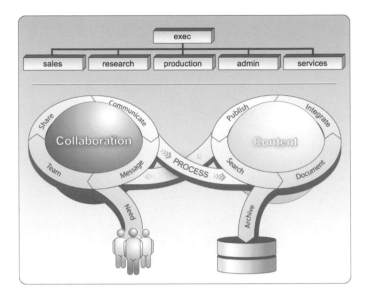

Figure 1.1: ECM Applications

The business needs for ECM and its benefits are identified in this chapter, along with its many departmental applications in a variety of industries.

Figure 1.1 displays a grid of applications by department. All ECM technologies and applications can be mapped to an organizational chart. The figure above shows a simplified representation of such an organizational chart to include Sales, Research, Production and Administration.

In some applications of ECM, such as Sarbanes-Oxley for regulatory compliance, multiple departments work within a single application, which is delivered by a common set of technologies. This type of cross-departmental application highlights the need for companies to invest in applications delivered by a common set of technologies. This chapter focuses on how ECM enables organizations to lower their total cost of ownership by delivering an enterprise data model and core applications that provide an infrastructure for additional business applications.

THE BUSINESS NEEDS

In order to succeed, companies need to know how to make use of the information and content that exists within and around their organizations. But what information should they know? How do they establish an infrastructure that enables them to understand their content?

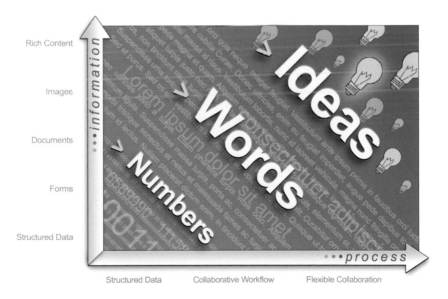

Figure 1.2: Working With Information

Companies that understand their content implement Enterprise Content Management (ECM) systems. Enterprise Content Management is a technology that provides a means to create, store, manage, secure, distribute and publish any digital content for enterprise use. ECM is not about numbers; it is about words. Much of the Information Technology (IT) industry in the past 50 years has focused on back-office databases and their management in Enterprise Resource Planning (ERP) systems. ECM is unique in that it was developed to manage the creation and consumption of growing amounts of non-numeric content such as documents, Web pages, spreadsheets, diagrams and images, largely affected by the rise in popularity of the Internet.

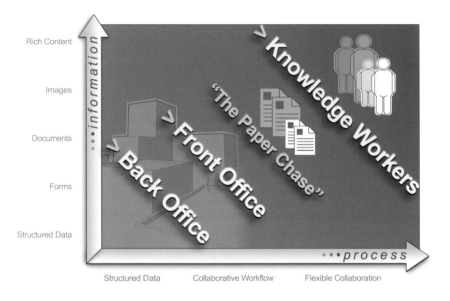

Figure 1.3: The Evolving Challenge

For ECM systems to be widely adopted, they need to emulate the way people work without disrupting their daily routines. This involves creating a digital place where people can work in much the same way they would work together in departments or at office locations. For ECM to be effective, it needs to automatically capture the content that is produced as a by-product of this work. The best ECM solutions deliver applications at the departmental level that integrate content management invisibly within the very act of collaboration. The transparent combination of content and collaboration benefits organizations tremendously by providing a place where simple ideas take root, are nurtured and finally mature into market-leading innovations. It is a critical point and one that we will explore in detail in this book.

People work together within a particular line of business or work group. Companies are normally organized by departments around these lines of business, such as sales or manufacturing or administration. Typical ECM applications are built to meet the content management needs of a particular department and are driven by a line of business manager with a particular productivity problem. These departmental solutions provide a shoe-in for larger enterprise installations.

ECM as a set of departmental applications is most effective when supported by a common data structure and a combined set of technologies. In other words, each departmental application typically requires the same basic technologies and infrastructure, but has a specific set of needs that are unique to that line of business. ECM systems that can be easily adapted to meet each department's unique needs, while maintaining a common data model, are inherently more flexible and future proof. Implementing ECM applications on a common data model results in lower total cost of ownership and faster implementation, leading to greater productivity and higher returns on technology investments.

Content-Based Applications

Let's consider group-level applications that are closely aligned to the way people work. The following represents a typical organization chart for a company:

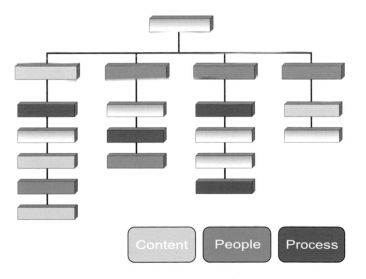

Figure 1.4: Typical Organization Chart

Companies consist of many separate departments—accounting and finance, legal, administration, marketing, sales, IT, research and development, and so on. Each department has its own needs and requirements for content management. ECM business solutions have been designed to meet many of these requirements and solve problems specific to a particular department. Typically, these solutions are driven by the need to improve efficiency or save money. Examples include: Purchase Order Processing, Invoicing, Project Management, Claims Processing, FDA Compliance, Product Lifecycle Management (PLM), and Sales Readiness, to mention a few.

ECM solutions often support core business functions. That is, if the solution were to be used inappropriately or did not exist, the business would not function. In the pharmaceutical business, for example, the development of new drugs must follow a regulated content management and approval process known as 21 CFR Part 11. The entire corporation is at risk if this process is not precisely followed. ECM business solutions for pharmaceutical companies must therefore support 21 CFR Part 11. Other industries such as financial services and healthcare have very similar needs controlled by their own industry regulations.

Figure 1.5: ECM Architecture Simplified

Once an application has been deployed at the departmental or group level, the IT department involved in implementing the first application can use the lessons learned to solve other content issues in other departments. While the first deployment may take place in the Sales department, the next deployment may occur in the Manufacturing area, and so on. Some of the most advanced ECM-enabled organizations in the world today have more than 20 distinct department-level applications supported by a common underlying suite of technologies and a common data model.

> DaimlerChrysler Financial Services

DaimlerChrysler
Financial Services

Operating at over 100 locations in 39 countries, and grossing $192.3M USD in 2004, DaimlerChrysler Financial Services is a global services provider within DaimlerChrysler, and one of the biggest financial services providers in the world.

The company's core business requires efficient contract management. The implementation of the ECM-based contract management solution at several subsidiaries has meant that for the first time all leasing contacts and related documents can be managed centrally, in accordance with industry regulations.

With the right information at their fingertips at all times, the staff of the DaimlerChrysler Financial Services call centre can now respond quickly to the many and varied customer requests. Response times are considerably shorter, and there has been a significant increase in the satisfaction of leasing customers. More than 320,000 electronic customer files are available, providing customer contract data at the touch of a button and guaranteeing that processing applications and insurance claims goes smoothly.

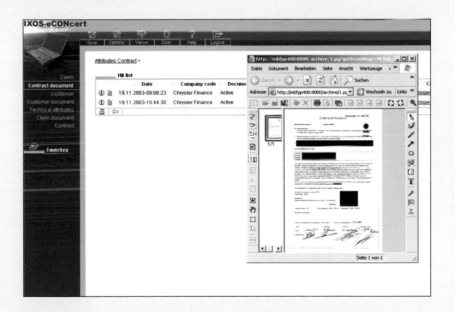

Figure 1.6: DaimlerChrysler's ECM-based Contract Management System

Figure 1.7: ECM Applications

Some of the solutions that have been developed for ECM include:

- Accounts payable administration
- Bid management
- Content management
- Court case management
- Customer care centers
- Customer due diligence
- Derivatives management
- Digital asset management
- Engineering change management
- Government publications management
- Vendor communications
- Human resources
- ISO 9000 quality assurance
- Managing marketing extranets
- Manufacturing processes
- New hire induction/Education
- New product development
- Policies and procedures
- Project collaboration
- Records management
- Vacation time management

As organizations move to leverage the same infrastructure for process improvements company wide, finding a solution often turns into a long-term strategic Enterprise Content Management solution. This involves deploying a complete series of applications across an entire organization. To make these applications simple to deploy and cost-effective to replicate, a common set of technologies with the same content model is required as an underlying infrastructure. This means the suite of technologies must be sufficient to deliver all applications across the enterprise.

There are hundreds of ECM solutions implemented in organizations in major industries throughout the world. This book profiles many of those ECM success stories.

As the deployments of ECM reach critical mass within major corporations, ECM applications are finding their way into every department. At the time of the writing of this book, there were more than 100 different kinds of applications using ECM technologies known to the author. On average a single enterprise-wide deployment of ECM involves more than 20 unique solutions, ranging from engineering departments using ECM applications for new product development to accounting departments using ECM to track changes to contract bid documents.

Inter-Departmental Requirements

In many applications that are critical to the operation of an organization, collaboration requires cross-departmental cooperation. In many companies, achieving this cooperation is the very basis for long term competitive advantage. For example, when planning and implementing New Product Development (NPD) within a research group, the interaction between this group and manufacturing and marketing is vital to the success of the project. This implies strong cross-functional cooperation and collaboration, and the sharing of critical documents from all three departments.

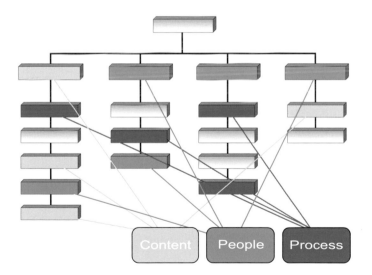

Figure 1.8: ECM Crosses Departments

The issue of cross-departmental functionality raises two important concerns for the ECM architecture. First, in order for multiple departments to collaborate or work together efficiently, both business and IT people outside of a particular department require infrastructure support. Secondly, an underlying common data model is required to allow people in different departments to share information contained in separate applications at a cost-effective rate. While it can be argued that some applications can be delivered within a department, most ECM applications need to be enterprise-wide in nature so that they can be accessed easily across departments. Otherwise, organizations are fragmented into isolated "islands of information" and critical content remains buried. Departmental implementations are limited in scope and will eventually be replaced by similar applications based on a broad underlying set of technologies that scale across the entire organization.

Industry Requirements

ECM customers are looking for a solution that provides a common technology for many different applications. Departmental applications have evolved to add elements that address specific vertical market needs. Many ECM vendors today are delivering solutions in specific industries based on their initial success in developing solutions in one or more markets. An organization's pain points are often specific to a particular industry, so customers prefer a vendor that has expertise in their industry. An ECM solution gains traction in an industry when one organization begins to use a solution and other organizations expect this solution to resolve their issues as well.

Within many industries, managing content is absolutely critical. Pharmaceutical companies are early adopters of ECM because managing documents is a regulatory requirement for doing business. We have seen how pharmaceutical organizations face stringent consensus standards. The New Drug Application (NDA) challenges organizations to provide detailed information about what happens during clinical tests, what the ingredients of a drug are, the results of test studies, how a drug behaves in the body and how a drug is manufactured, processed and packaged. The integrated document and records management, collaboration and workflow functionality of a comprehensive ECM solution enables pharmaceutical organizations to detail the lifecycle of a product from start to finish. Using a comprehensive ECM suite, pharmaceutical employees can seamlessly review new drug targets, deploy personnel and resources, manage drug discovery projects and accelerate time to market.

Pharmaceutical product development cycles—from conception to marketing—require on average four to ten years longer than in most other industries. Increasing the efficiency at which global development teams cooperate is critical in determining the speed at which new drugs can be readied for the market.

Roche's ECM-based platform for information sharing, entitled ShareWeb, supports the full lifecycle of global team projects. Providing a single point of access to training information, compliance programs and a broad range of documents, ECM helps improve efficiency at each stage of Roche's new product development cycles.

Since the launch of ShareWeb, access to documents is independent of formats, knowledge from previous projects is available and updated at all times, international teams can be assembled faster, and new team members are easily inaugurated. "ShareWeb brings the various countries in the Asia-Pacific region into one community," says Roche's Medical Director, Taiwan.

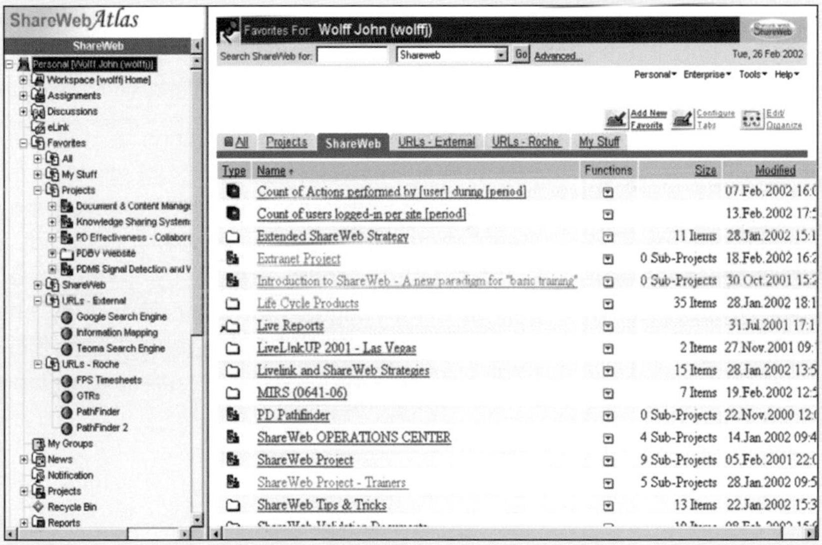

Figure 1.9: Roche's ShareWeb

Productivity Gains

ECM has its roots in document management. In the early eighties, the benefits of investing in a document management system were savings in print or paper costs and storage space and higher productivity. Today, ECM is evolving into a blend of proven technologies designed to solve a variety of content and process-centric problems. It follows that customer investment is moving from departmental solutions to an entire enterprise infrastructure that promises return on investment on many levels.

The key to success among earlier implementations has been the recognition of collaboration and its role in creating context for content. It is simply not enough to know that content exists without being aware of the situation (how, when and why) in which it was created. Collaboration provides this context since it records what was happening at the time of content creation. This provides far greater insight into the relevance of information.

The current trend in collaboration and content management is toward departmental or group level solutions. Currently, the Internet is still new and technically driven. In the future, companies will hide the technology beneath purpose-built solutions. Functionality will be there but it will be virtually transparent. Internet software will evolve and ECM will lead the evolution in collaboration by making solutions easier to use without having to know anything more about the Web than how to click on a hyperlink.

While many organizations still regard content management solutions as self-contained solutions, they will increasingly deploy technology with a larger ECM strategy in mind. Leading ECM solutions will evolve into comprehensive infrastructures offering fully integrated collaboration and content management functionality deployed at the departmental level and then rolled out to the entire enterprise. More and more customers will embrace an ECM approach that aligns with business needs on many levels. Companies will be encouraged to grow their ECM solution—whether it be improving corporate governance, streamlining processes or effectively managing content—as their business requirements evolve.

OSRAM, a subsidiary of Siemens AG, is one of the leading lamp manufacturers in the world. As customer demand increasingly required sophisticated materials and technology, OSRAM found its customers were asking very detailed questions about the lighting systems the company was producing.

To arm its sales force with detailed technical information, OSRAM's marketing department turned to Web-based document management and collaboration technology to develop the OSRAM Product Information System (OPIS). OPIS makes technical documents immediately available to all marketing and sales employees. New documents are fully indexed and searchable within 24 hours.

IDC calculated all costs associated with the project and was conservative in estimating the increased productivity for the sales and marketing staff and the savings in paper, distribution and telephone costs. These savings, combined with the low startup and deployment costs, provided a 201 percent return on OSRAM's OPIS investment.

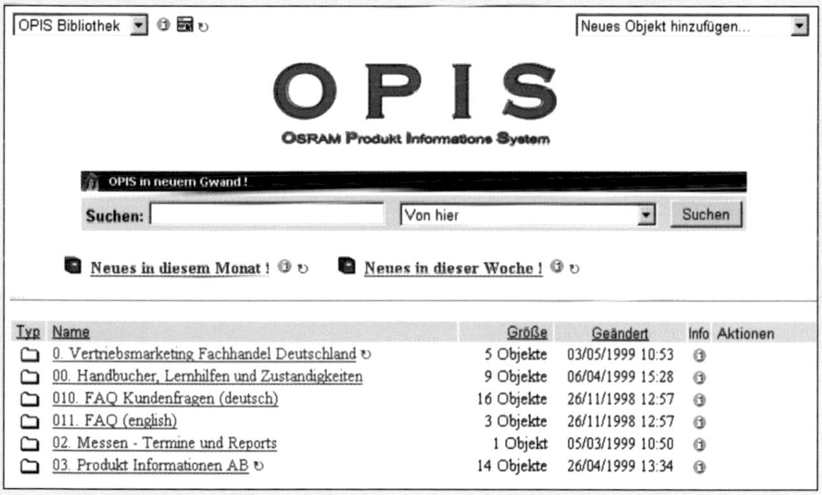

Figure 1.10: OSRAM's Product Information System

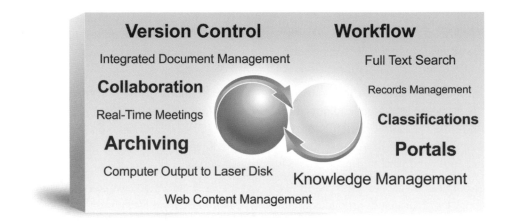

Figure 1.11: ECM Technologies

From a more academic standpoint, a new market is emerging that addresses the higher-level needs of the knowledge-intensive organization, namely, how to increase overall organizational effectiveness in a volatile business environment. In order to realize return on investment in technology—and to adhere to new regulations and legislation—organizations will move toward implementing an underlying infrastructure that supports many repositories and combines key applications.

Vendors will offer customized views and applications for specific departments and processes that are cross-industry applicable. The infrastructure will have to scale and support new technologies. Customers of ECM solutions will become interested in newer technologies and expanding these systems to support more content types, such as email and rich media files.

The aircraft industry demands rigorous standards in the storage of documents and data relating to all areas of the manufacturing, sales and support of aircraft and related products. Some documents and data must be kept for up to 50 and 60 years.

Airbus UK implemented a single repository data archiving and legacy document archiving solution to meet these standards and to ensure that the business and transactional data produced by its enterprise-wide ERP system could be stored in a cost-effective, yet readily accessible way.

"The integrated ECM system provides a simple yet effective solution to several of our objectives. The predicted growth of our ERP data had the potential to affect the responsiveness of the ERP system, and we had data in a number of legacy systems that we needed to transfer. The new solution is giving us the capability to achieve both of these aims with a single archive that integrates seamlessly with our ERP system," says Airbus UK's IS National Coordinator.

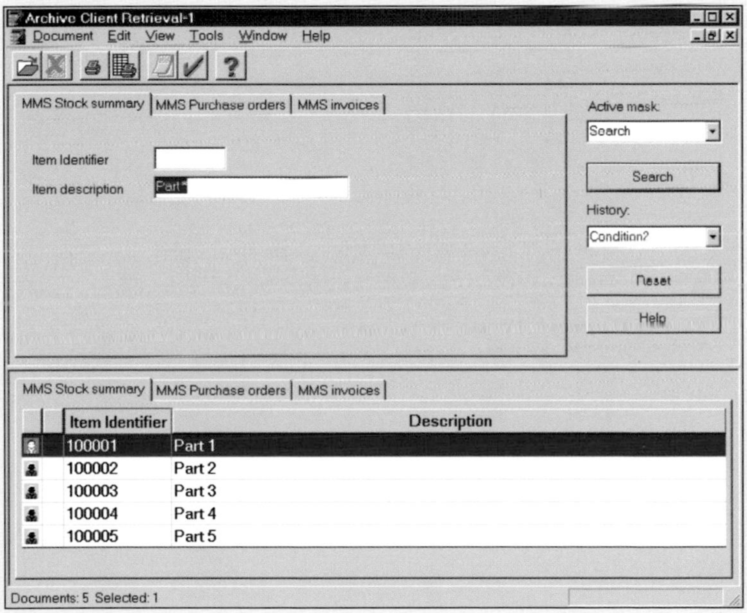

Figure 1.12: Airbus' Integrated ERP and ECM

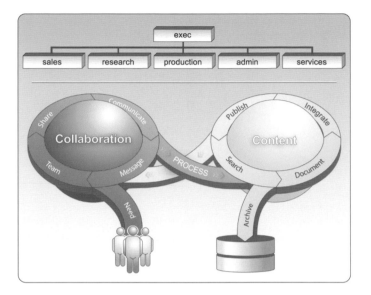

Figure 2.1: ECM Technologies

ECM technologies can be grouped into two categories: collaboration and content. Teams, Portals, Rich Media and Messaging are categorized as collaboration technologies. Document Management, Web Content Management, Document Lifecycle Management and Enterprise Application Extensions fall into the content category. Figure 2.1 represents these groupings.

While Chapter 1 discussed ECM applications in detail, this chapter will focus on ECM technologies. Chapter 2 explores the definition of ECM as a combined set of technologies and provides an overview of each technology.

ECM TECHNOLOGIES

During the twenty-first century, companies in the Enterprise Content Management market will dominate the Information Technology agenda as corporations seek to further advance with technology by managing content, people and processes.

We can trace the evolution of ECM from raw data and numbers to words by examining major developments made in the industry as early as the 1960s. At this time, companies such as Honeywell and IBM were major vendors. Their mainframe computer systems allowed for the automation of basic computations previously made by floors of workers.

In the 1970s, the mini-computer made automation more accessible and basic transactions a reality. During this time, Digital Equipment became a significant vendor.

In the 1980s, the introduction of the personal computer (PC) started the client-server revolution and personal productivity drove the creation of digital content. This content, created mostly by knowledge workers, complemented the automated generation of content that belonged in the mini-computer era. Intel and Microsoft became major vendors in this industry.

In the 1990s, Enterprise Resource Planning (ERP) programs further automated transactions within organizations, allowing the efficient management of numbers through a concept called a database. Companies such as SAP and Oracle were leading innovators in this industry.

	1970s	1980s	1990s	2000s
Who	IBM	Microsoft	SAP	Open Text
Why	Clerical Productivity	Personal Productivity	Departmental Productivity	Org. Compliance & Productivity
How	Data Processing	Email; Desktop Publishing	ERP	ECM
Computing Environment	Mainframe	Personal Computer	LAN	Ubiquitous Computing

Figure 2.2: Eras of Computing

ECM suites are made up of a number of technology pieces that work harmoniously to manage the complete lifecycle of electronic documents, from their creation to archive and eventual deletion. You can compare ECM suites with other suite-based software products, such as Microsoft® Office. Microsoft Office includes a number of different tools that work together to provide personal productivity for office workers. Likewise, ECM suites offer a set of tightly integrated facilities for searching, managing, distributing, publishing and archiving electronic documents.

Unlike Microsoft Office, ECM suites require little to no software to be installed on a personal computer. ECM software leverages Internet technology to deliver services to people, meaning that accessing the software requires only a Web browser, a username and a password.

ECM suites provide secure access, storage, publication and archiving of large volumes of business content. ECM allows organizations to manage the processes for working with different types of content, and track and control content changes. Content management is not confined to organizing computer directories, it involves exploiting your business know-how to avoid critical failures, to operate more efficiently and to become more productive and profitable.

Structured vs. Unstructured Information

To introduce the technologies that underpin ECM, it is necessary to understand the difference between structured and unstructured information and why managing unstructured information is such a challenge.

Structured data is based on numbers organized into tables. These database tables can be quickly manipulated to find data that refers to the numbers in the table. Unstructured data is not as easy to organize and retrieve. Words, an example of unstructured data, are organized into tables similar to an index found at the back of a book. Because the data model for words (unstructured data) is fundamentally different from the data model for numbers (structured data), the technologies that support each must differ.

Computers have fundamentally changed the way we work; most office workers today require a computer to do their jobs. Managing payroll, processing orders and invoices, inventory control and financial accounting all rely heavily on the numeric processing capabilities of computers. Computers are exceptional at crunching numbers, but the challenge for ECM applications is to use information technology to manage documents and pictures, or what are termed "unstructured data."

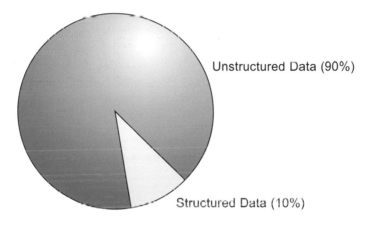

Unstructured Data (90%)

Structured Data (10%)

Figure 2.3: The Ratio of Structured Versus Unstructured
Data in an Organization

Individual productivity tools, such as word-processing systems, spreadsheets, presentation tools, Web editors and email have created an explosion of unstructured data that must be managed. Organizations are tasked with storing this information, making it accessible and ensuring that it is up to date and secure, and appropriately distributed, published and consumed.

Basic Principles of ECM

The quest for solutions to these problems created the ECM market. The remaining chapters in this book examine the technology components of ECM in great detail. The following provides an overview of the fundamental concepts behind each technology.

Search

It is not easy to search unstructured data; while numbers obey very rigid rules that can be easily interpreted by computer programs (one plus one always equals two), words and pictures have few formal rules and are open to different interpretations based on context. Take, for example, the task of cataloging a book called "Lemons." Should the book be cataloged in the section on cooking, fine arts or cars? Opening the book would immediately reveal to the reader the subject matter and therefore, the correct placement. Computers cannot read yet, so the challenge is to design a system that makes the same interpretations that we do. If this all sounds too theoretical, try searching the Web for "ECM." Search results will identify over 800,000 hits, including everything from software products to publishing companies, electronic countermeasures to espresso coffee machines and even the European Crystallographic Meeting in Durban, South Africa.

ECM systems manage huge amounts of unstructured data. Motorola, for example, manages over 4.8 terabytes of documents in their ECM repository. The electronic version of this book uses about 0.5 megabytes of disk space, so Motorola's repository would hold 88 million books like this one! ECM systems must not only manage huge amounts of data; they must also allow users to quickly find the documents they need. Modern search tools are able to "learn" concepts that allow them to automatically catalog documents, making them easier to find. Search technology also makes it possible to identify subject matter experts and readers with similar interests by tracking user behavior. Searching unstructured data is the first and one of the most fundamental disciplines of ECM.

Knowledge Management (KM)

Interest in KM may be a recent phenomenon but the concept and desire to preserve and apply knowledge is timeless. Formal processes for managing knowledge can be traced to the Fourth Century BC at the Great Library in Alexandria. The management of business records appears to have begun about 8000 BC in the Tigris-Euphrates Valley.

Knowledge management is the set of processes that govern the creation, dissemination and utilization of knowledge. It is a multi-disciplinary practice that draws from the theory and technology of artificial intelligence, expert systems, library science, document management, cognitive science, organizational dynamics and business analysis.

A large and complex organization, BT is a UK communications solutions provider. Functionally diverse and geographically dispersed, BT sought to gain competitive advantage by enabling an integrated communications network for every stage of product development, spanning from discovery to post-launch evaluation.

In order to enable collaboration on such a large and diverse scale, BT turned to ECM technology. Centralized knowledge management has enabled the organization to capture, store, and re-use its intellectual assets, providing its employees with easy and quick access to wide-scale information and expertise. In addition, BT has established virtual communities, or e-communities, to increase collaboration across the enterprise.

Currently, increased communication ensures the facilitation of common understanding, clearer company positioning and increased process visibility, while enhancing corporate governance. BT employees feel increasingly self-sufficient and productive, and consequently report higher job satisfaction. In brief, the ECM solution has enabled BT to leverage intellectual capital from across the enterprise and to achieve business assurance.

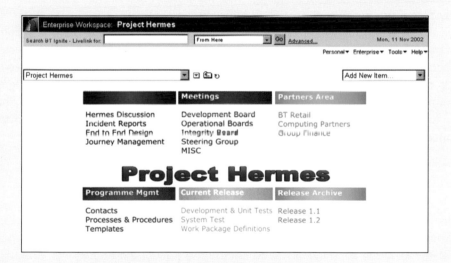

Figure 2.4: BT's Project Work Space

The practice originated in 1997 with publication of Thomas A. Stewart's groundbreaking book *Intellectual Capital*. Stewart was the first to clearly articulate how the Information Age changed the nature of wealth. In an economy based on knowledge, intellectual capital—the untapped, unmapped knowledge of organizations—was identified as a company's greatest competitive weapon. This capital is found in the talent of the people, the loyalty of customers, the value of product brands, copyrights, patents and other intellectual property. It is the collective knowledge embodied in a company's cultures, systems, management techniques and history. These vital assets, however identified, were not represented on a balance sheet—only rarely managed and almost never managed skillfully. Managing this corporate knowledge, or intellectual capital, became key to an organization's success.

The significant impact that knowledge management can have on corporate survival, competitiveness and compliance makes it a valuable component of ECM.

Document Management (DM)

We have all experienced the effect on a sentence as it is passed by word-of-mouth around a room full of people. Often, the sentence changes significantly from person to person and loses its original meaning. The same can happen with business critical documents that are mismanaged, often with disastrous consequences. Take for example NASA's embarrassment over a space telescope; its giant lens had been improperly ground because of a mix-up involving one team member working in centimeters, meters and kilograms while another was using inches, feet and pounds. As a result, the telescope was out of focus and inoperable. Another case involved confusion between different versions of an aircraft maintenance manual, which resulted in the cockpit window of a passenger aircraft falling out of the plane at 16,000 feet—the accident apparently caused by engineers using wrongly sized screws.

When a document is reviewed by a number of authors, it is easy to lose track of who has the most up-to-date version. Documents can get lost, deleted or fall into the wrong hands.

Document management systems allow businesses to control the production, storage, revision management and distribution of electronic documents, yielding greater efficiencies in the ability to reuse information and to control the flow of the documents. Managing electronic documents is a key technology of Enterprise Content Management.

Archiving and Document Lifecycle Management (DLM)

The accounting scandals at Enron Corporation made the world aware of the need for records management. When an employee of Andersen, Enron's outside auditor, admitted to destroying a "significant" number of documents related to the Enron

Dow Chemical is a leader in science and technology, providing innovative chemical, plastic and agricultural products and services to many essential consumer markets. With approximately 46,000 employees, Dow Chemical serves customers in more than 180 countries and a wide range of markets that are vital to human progress, including food, transportation, health and medicine, personal and homecare, and building and construction, among others.

The nature of Dow Chemical's business requires the company to keep impeccable accounts of all records. To that end, document lifecycle management technology has effectively consolidated Dow Chemical's records management activities, replacing three separate systems for managing both box storage of paper documents and indexes to millions of rolls of microfilm.

The company's solution features a "hold and freeze" functionality, as well as disposition and retention rules. Together, these features enable Dow Chemical to effectively manage corporate records, as well as legal, financial and tax information.

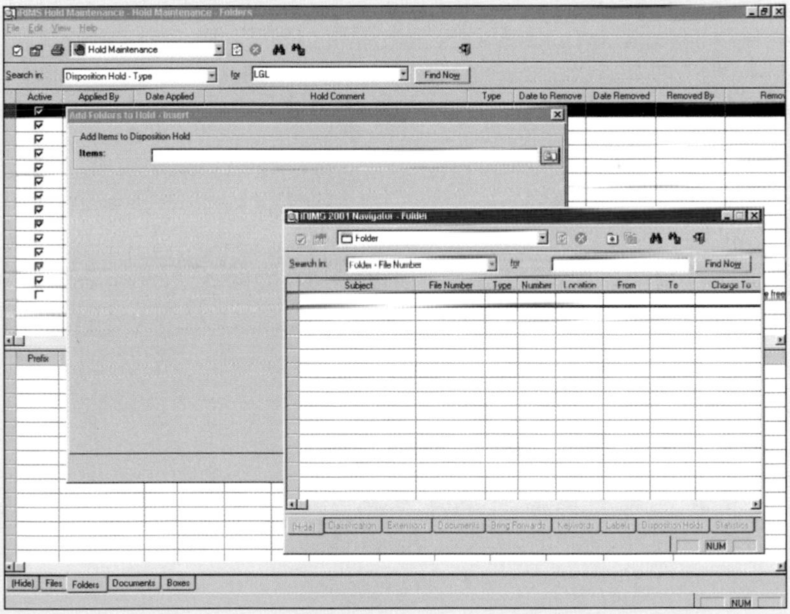

Figure 2.5: Dow Chemical's Records Management Solution

investigation, it made people wonder, "How could that possibly happen?" Whether the Andersen employee intentionally or accidentally shredded documents is a matter for the courts to decide; what is more relevant is that they were able to destroy the documents in the first place.

Everyone has experienced that sense of panic when a spreadsheet or document somehow gets deleted. No amount of screaming at the screen, banging on the keyboard or shaking the motherboard will bring it back. Now imagine that the document you lost contained proof of an accounting infraction or was the only copy of a sales agreement for a million-dollar order.

Records management is the discipline of managing records to meet operational needs, accountability requirements and community expectations. Records management software works by allowing you to attach rules to electronic documents. These rules tell the system when it is okay to delete documents or move them to a data archive, either physically in boxes or electronically on storage devices such as CD-ROMs.

Government offices are superb at record keeping. When we are born, when we are married, when we have children, when we get divorced and when we die, a record is created at a government office. The rules that determine when those records can be archived and deleted are stipulated in government regulations—records management systems often adhere to these standards, allowing companies to easily stay within the law.

With daily pressure to comply with regulations and changes to legislation, managing records and the lifecycle of documents have become crucial components of ECM.

Web Content Management (WCM)

How many Web sites does your company have? One? Twenty? These days, there are Web sites for every subject or product and many organizations host at least a dozen.

The first Web sites were created by computer geeks and academics. Because they were used mainly to share technical information, they were text-based and not very visually stimulating. The World Wide Web and its support for graphic images and animation moved the Internet into the realm of art, and graphic designers became the new Web Masters. Corporations soon discovered that Web sites could be more than just a place for casual visitors to browse; they could be used to sell products, attract investors, interact with customers and engage with suppliers.

In today's organization, every department wants representation on the corporate Web site: human resources wants to advertise job vacancies; marketing wants to promote events; sales wants to sell product; and investor relations wants to share financial data with shareholders. Furthermore, the CEO wants to have the site available in seven languages. Requests for site updates can overwhelm a single Web Master and create bottlenecks that result in information not being posted in a timely manner. The solution is to enable Web content to be owned and managed by individual content contributors.

Web Content Management (WCM) software was created to allow multiple content contributors to make changes to Web sites, removing typical Web Master bottlenecks. WCM systems conceal all internal workings of a Web page, allowing users with little or no technical experience to add and modify content. WCM enables data fragments to be easily reused, so that updating the company's logo involves changing only one or two files and the whole Web site is magically transformed.

The technology behind Web content management is very similar to the technology required to manage documents. Most ECM suites include Web content management capabilities.

Teams and Collaboration

We have quickly grown accustomed to being able to phone each other anywhere at any time and in a matter of seconds. Cell phones and mobile telephony are so entrenched in our daily lives that it is hard to imagine life before they existed. The Internet has also revolutionized our ability to connect with others. We send documents over the Web and drum our finger impatiently awaiting its delivery. Being able to connect so easily with our colleagues over the Internet has made it possible to work effectively in virtual teams, where geography is no longer a concern.

The Human Genome Project began in 1990 as a collaborative effort by research establishments around the globe to identify the 30,000 genes in human DNA. The project required the collaboration of scientists from many fields, including molecular biologists, engineers, physicists, chemists and mathematicians at the Department of Energy. Technology played a huge part in the project; the Genome Data Base (GDB) is the worldwide repository for genome mapping data. It was accessed by researchers around the world via the Internet to allow them to work together to share research and answer questions.The project successfully concluded in April, 2003. This achievement would not have been possible before the creation of the World Wide Web.

Global organizations are now able to capitalize on Web-based collaboration facilities to empower their workforces, working as virtual project teams to bring expertise from different areas and office locations to tackle business-critical problems. ECM systems include collaboration tools that enable the best minds within organizations to work together more efficiently—sharing information, capturing and preserving knowledge, managing collaborative processes and projects, and resolving issues.

Portals

The word "portal" immediately brings to mind science fiction movies or books in which a portal is depicted as a dimensional doorway in space that connects two or more worlds. Software portals are designed to perform a similar role by providing a place that connects multiple Web-based software applications. Portals are often the glue that pulls all of the various bits of an ECM suite together, providing a contextual shop window to underlying applications.

Portal technology was designed to make the user's life easier by providing all the tools needed in a single, unified Web page. Most of us use portal tools to make sense of the Internet; Yahoo!®, MSN®, and AOL® are all portals. They give us a way to get to places of interest very quickly, to book a vacation, check out the latest movie release or the stats of your favorite football team. Most portals also enable you to personalize your experience; My Yahoo!®, for instance, allows you to build your own home page by picking from your favorite places and pages on the Web.

Rich Media and Digital Asset Management

High-speed Internet connections now allow rich media types such as voice and video to be used over Internet connections. Software applications are rapidly emerging to take advantage of this technology for business use. Imagine sitting in traffic on your way to a business meeting and being able to have your email messages read out to you over your cell phone. Or picture yourself in an online meeting and being able to watch a presentation by a colleague overseas from the comfort of your home office. These are not pipe dreams; these technologies are a part of the way we do business today.

CARE Canada, a humanitarian organization fighting global poverty, uses collaborative technology to save lives. When CARE relief workers operating in Kosovo came across an uncharted minefield, they transmitted live video over the Internet back to CARE headquarters to update their pilots on safe locations to drop food and medical supplies.

As telephony networks develop to support unlimited bandwidth, rich media applications will become more popular and integral to conducting business. For this reason, the need to manage rich media within ECM applications is steadily increasing.

> HBO

HBO is America's most successful premium television network, offering rich digital media content, blockbuster movies, innovative original programming, provocative documentaries, concert events and championship boxing. HBO sought a solution that would allow them to easily access and share digital content both within HBO and the larger Time Warner family. The requirements for the overall system functionality and user experience entailed the system handling large volumes of content, as well as addressing disparate databases, workflows and use cases for each of the organizations.

HBO's Media Asset Management (MAM) implementation, now known as the HBO Digital Library System, encompassed all of HBO's digital photographs supporting such areas as marketing, promotions advertising and sales. These assets can range from location shots from HBO Films to a gallery of quality professional photos of HBO celebrities.

Part of their overall strategy was to ensure careful management of metadata. Assets are tagged with corresponding meta-data, such as contractual information, as early as possible to ensure that meta-data travels with the asset throughout its lifecycle. This meta-tagging process is enforced with an embedded workflow component. The HBO digital asset management system is accessed by all of the Regional Offices and currently holds more than 325,000 assets.

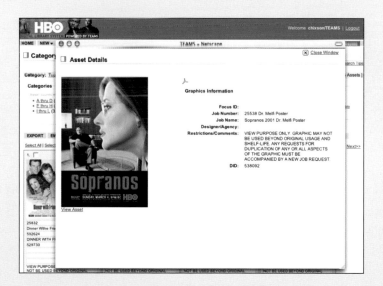

Figure 2.6: HBO's Media Asset Management Solution

Bringing all the Technologies Together

Enterprise Content Management (ECM) is an amalgamation of the different technologies previously discussed.

The component technologies that underpin ECM are shown in the grid below. The grid separates technologies that connect people with people, such as email systems, from technologies that connect people with information, such as search. We have also divided the vertical axis into applications that deal with structured business processes, such as document management, and those that deal with unstructured processes like Web conferencing.

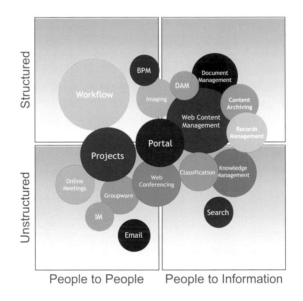

Figure 2.7: ECM Technologies

Making sense of all this technology is a challenge, so let's simplify the picture.

Everything on the left-hand side of the grid describes a technology that deals with working collaboratively. Collaboration technology links processes and individuals across the enterprise and creates a work environment where teams can share and circulate ideas, experiences and knowledge.

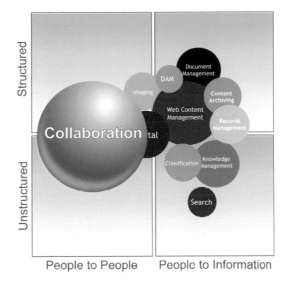

Figure 2.8: Collaboration Technologies

All the information, ideas and data created as a by-product of collaborative work need to be securely captured, managed and made available to others. The technologies on the right of the grid deal with all the content accumulated by business, such as memos, spreadsheets, reports, email messages, images, audio and video files, and transactional data.

Connecting the content and collaboration bubbles is the genius behind ECM software suites. With ECM, knowledge is automatically captured as a by-product of collaborative work and is transformed into invaluable corporate knowledge. This knowledge is information that enables action, or further collaboration. ECM enables you to effortlessly capture ideas generated during an online meeting or store plans and other documents created by virtual project teams. These knowledge assets are preserved in a secure knowledge repository where they can be easily accessed, shared and reused throughout an organization. The two areas are then interconnected by a key third area which is known as process.

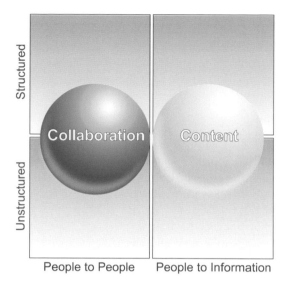

Figure 2.9: Content Technologies

The double bubble motif is used throughout the book to illustrate ECM's value proposition of combined collaboration, content and process.

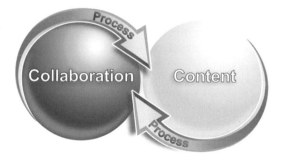

Figure 2.10: ECM Value Proposition

The core technologies of an ECM suite must work together to address a broad range of business needs. While it may be possible to buy each of the technology pieces separately, bringing the pieces together in a suite provides a more efficient way to access and use information across multiple applications—making it easier to move content from one application to another.

Workflow and Business Process Management (BPM)

Business Process Management is both a technology and an approach that connects people and content. BPM helps organizations combine content and collaboration to support structured and unstructured ways of working together.

In every organization, numerous business processes occur each day—from filling out a purchase request, to assigning documents for review and approval: the effectiveness of each and the overall efficiency of an organization depends on business process automation tools. BPM provides powerful tools for defining and reusing business logic, simplifying business process and helping employees coordinate effectively with both the organization and each other.

ECM solutions integrate with BPM systems to optimize business processes to improve performance. By linking processes with content creation, ECM enables organizations to exchange transactional information and respond more quickly to new or changing business requirements. BPM is a fundamental component of Enterprise Content Management.

Enterprise Application Extensions (EAE)

Enterprise applications, such as Enterprise Resource Planning (ERP) and Customer Relationship Management (CRM), effectively perform transaction-based processing. However, data residing in these applications is the result of work that has been completed and, in many cases, cannot effectively support other business processes. Many processes, like contract creation, still require collaborative efforts of employees in multiple departments. In order to maximize content's effectiveness, organizations need to connect content to the appropriate business processes and make it accessible to people participating in the process. Enterprise Application Extensions provide the underlying business structure that supports these business processes. Allocating unstructured content to business processes puts the information people need at their fingertips without requiring them to search across many systems for content.

ECM extends enterprise applications by providing links between key processes and transactional information. Making this information secure and accessible across a variety of processes helps companies lower costs and the risks associated with meeting data retention and disposal requirements.

ECM Solutions Framework

The diagram below shows the technologies that form the framework for ECM solutions. The framework provides a layer of ECM Lifecycle Management Services that link information workers to an Enterprise Library of information, which integrates content from multiple sources. The ECM Lifecycle Management Services include: Collaboration, Content and Process. Collaboration services support person-to-person interaction and facilitate cross-application collaboration, including community and project workspaces, discussion forums, blogs, FAQs and polls. Content services provide a single point of access to all content, either in Web-based portals or the desktop applications with which information workers are most familiar. The ECM Solutions Framework provides access to content across the enterprise and supports storing the content on any mix of storage devices from leading vendors. Business process services deliver a common framework for automating the routing of information and documents, entering information via forms and notifying information workers of critical tasks and events via email. The ECM Solutions Framework facilitates the smooth evolution of existing solutions, speeds development of new solutions and provides agility for the business to be responsive to change.

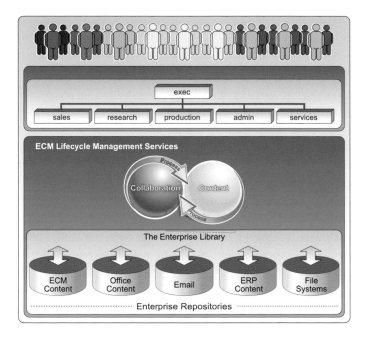

Figure 2.11: ECM Solutions Framework

Now that you are familiar with the fundamental technologies of Enterprise Content Management, we can begin the journey of discovery that led to the creation of a market. The remaining chapters of the book focus on specific areas of ECM technology. In them, you'll learn the history behind each technology and discover how organizations are using ECM technology today as the foundation for innovation, compliance and accelerated growth.

> Air Liquide

AIR LIQUIDE

Air Liquide, the world leader in industrial and medical gases, first adopted an ECM solution in 1999 within one of its French business entities to support its strategy for improving the efficiency and streamlining of its information systems.

By extending its original solution to incorporate all the affiliates and subsidiaries of the European branch of the Group, Air Liquide is ultimately putting knowledge management, content management and collaboration capabilities at the disposal of 12,000 users to optimize its processes for structuring and disseminating content, documentation and knowledge.

"The implementation of a single, unique platform for content and knowledge management will enable us to efficiently integrate silos of information and to facilitate the widespread standardization of best practices within the Air Liquide Group," says the Chief Information Officer of Air Liquide Group.

Figure 2.12: Air Liquide's User Interface

The Lifecycle of ECM

We all have jobs to do. And these jobs are tasks that are assigned to fulfill an identified **need**.

A typical first step is to assemble a dedicated project **team** to **share** the tasks that are required to solve the problem. Teams will then **communicate** with each other in order discuss and resource the project, resolve any issues and work together to deliver results.

After a team has been assembled, content or information relevant to the project must be gathered. To find related **documents**, team members could enter a document management system, using a portal and **search** technology.

Related content is typically exchanged using a **messaging** system, such as email. For the system to be effective, it should be integrated with ECM as a managed messaging environment.

The project team works on modifying documents and plans using a business **process** management system. The final document is approved as part of a workflow and prepared for redistribution and **integration** into various enterprise applications.

Content from the final document is redistributed and **published** to an organization's Web sites using a Web content management system.

Finally, the document can be tagged and **archived** using a records management system, as part of full document lifecycle management.

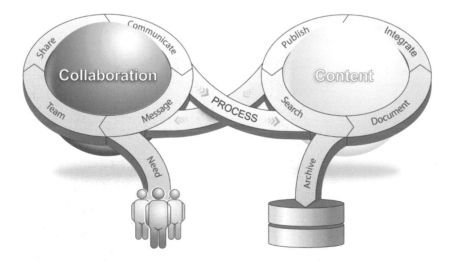

Figure 2.13: ECM Lifecycle Diagram

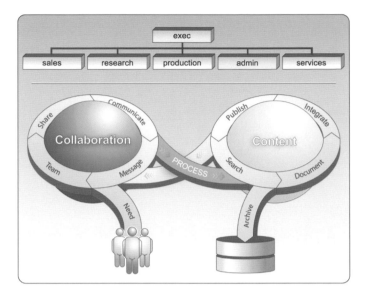

Figure 3.1: Compliance and Corporate Governance

Compliance and Corporate Governance is delivered across all of the departments within an ECM driven organization. This chapter outlines how ECM solutions are helping many of the world's leading companies address compliance and governance issues. User stories in this chapter demonstrate how organizations are using ECM solutions to comply with legislation, including the U.S. Government Paperwork Elimination Act (GPEA). In these stories, ECM enables organizations to not only achieve compliance, but improve business operations as well.

CHAPTER 3

COMPLIANCE AND CORPORATE GOVERNANCE

ECM solutions are playing a major role helping many of the world's leading companies streamline and accelerate compliance and corporate governance wherever they do business in the world.

In every industry and in all countries countless government regulations, industry standards and company procedures exist. How a company manages itself and its compliance efforts has a direct impact on shareholder value. Poor management and/or non-compliance can lead to lost business, financial penalties and even criminal charges. In some industries, failing an auditor's inspection can ultimately lead to a company being closed down until corrective action is taken.

Clearly, it is important for an organization to be well managed and compliant, but there is more to compliance than simply following rules. At the heart of each set of industry regulations and standards are the basic principles for doing good business—these principles are derived from the experience of *best practices, policies and procedures* for each industry and are often designed to prevent adversity from being repeated. To understand how ECM helps organizations manage compliance and governance, it is important to differentiate between the two concepts.

Compliance and Corporate Governance Defined

Today's business environment is more complex and regulated than ever before, and for good reason. Corporate issues involving fraudulent accounting, malfeasance and data quality issues are frequently in the news. CEOs and Boards of Directors are under public scrutiny and, as a result regulatory requirements have emerged to address these issues using commonly accepted principles of corporate governance.

Figure 3.2: Compliance and Corporate Governance

Each company has unique corporate governance activities. A company's business units, departments, operations, industry and geographic locations all define the environment in which it operates. These variables combine in a specific way to determine how the company can and, in the case of regulations, must operate.

Formally, corporate governance has been defined as "…the structure that is intended to make sure that the right questions get asked and that checks and balances are in place to make sure that the answers reflect what is best for the creation of long-term, sustainable value" (Robert A. Monks and Nell Minnow, Corporate Governance). Informally, corporate governance may be defined as how a company manages itself. A company's environment influences and determines governance activities. These include designing methods to direct, manage and control the company. These methods need to be communicated to necessary individuals. Additionally, these methods are improved over time to drive efficiency and cost savings or to respond to the changing needs of the business.

Compliance may then be defined as conforming to a rule. Types of compliance rules include:

• Government Legislation and Regulation

• Industry Standards

• Internal Company Policy and Procedures

A rule implies some sort of consequence for not following it, for example being non-compliant. Government entities created to enforce legislation, industry standard bodies or corporate directives are typical rule setting bodies. Furthermore, compliance with the rules can be required or voluntary. Figure 3.3 below depicts compliance types and typical corresponding consequences for being non-compliant.

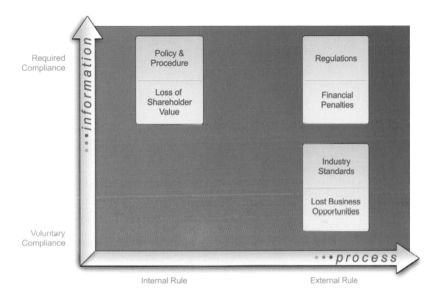

Figure 3.3: Compliance Continuum

In summary, it is important to identify that compliance needs to happen according to a defined rule (regulation, standard or policy) to have meaning, and that compliance is only one component of corporate governance.

Why Do Organizations Need Corporate Governance?

There are two key factors contributing to why organizations need to address governance: to mitigate risk and to optimize operations. The primary goal is to maintain and grow shareholder value. Poor governance exposes a company to unacceptable risks that can have significant or disastrous consequences.

In a growing number of industries, organizations are required to not only achieve regulatory compliance, but to prove compliance as well—and the penalties for non-compliance are severe.

> Fluor Hanford

Fluor Hanford

The Fluor Corporation has more than 2,000 engineering, construction, procurement and maintenance projects. Operating unit Fluor Hanford is a prime contractor to the Department of Energy (DOE) at the Hanford Site in Washington State. Hanford is one of the world's largest environmental cleanup projects. Correspondence between Fluor Hanford and DOE averages more than 2,000 letters per year, including attachments. Overall, the Hanford project involves millions of pages of records, including emails, documents, and various media such as photos, videos, and engineering drawings.

Fluor Hanford needed a solution to improve a labor-intensive, paper-based correspondence process. In addition to ease-of-use concerns, new regulations governing electronic records were also key drivers for moving to a new system.

By upgrading its enterprise content management (ECM) system to include correspondence workflow and records management, Fluor Hanford has been able to meet the new regulatory requirements.

The system also provides simple and secure records management tools, and a streamlined correspondence process. The Livelink ECM solution provides easy access to all project information, including records databases, schedules, and engineering drawings. With good access to project information, Fluor Hanford employees and project managers are better equipped to meet or beat cleanup milestones at the Hanford site.

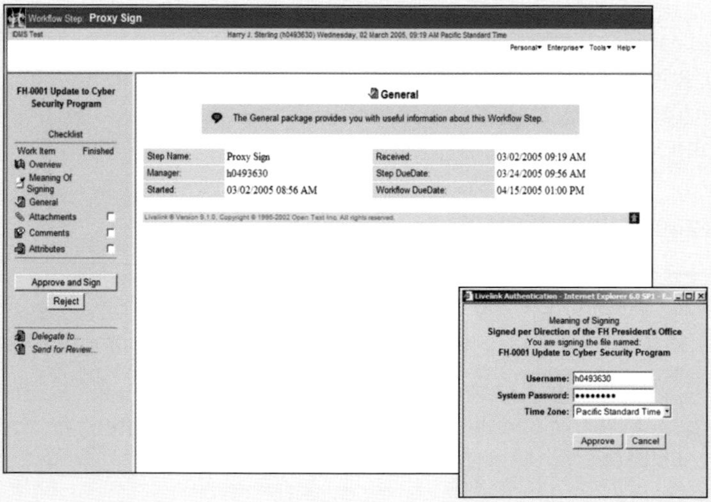

Figure 3.4: Digital Signatures are Used in a Correspondence Workflow at Fluor Hanford

But there are greater benefits associated with improved governance than simply mitigating risk and avoiding penalties. Regulations are based on demands that inherently describe optimal business operations; by meeting regulations, organizations are accordingly ensuring that their business processes adhere to industry-established best practices and procedures.

Corporations across the globe are wisely striving to learn from—rather than react to—the enormous governance failures of companies such as Enron and Parmalat. Each industry has its own regulators and regulations, but much can be learned from all regulations that can be applied to organizations in any industry.

ECM allows the systemizing of these processes and their underlying data so organizations can ensure that nothing important is omitted, and that everyone is aware of who is responsible for doing what, when, how, why and where. This helps ensure that everyone is not just "doing his or her thing" and that there is an order in the way the organization goes about its business, so that time, money and other resources are utilized efficiently.

Global Impact

Governance is impacting business on a global level. A representative sample of the various global regulations and regulatory bodies is shown in figure 3.5 below.

	USA and Canada	Europe and Rest of the World
Telecommunications	CRTC	CCITT, OFTEL
Financial Services	CFTC, FDIC, FRB, NAIC, NASD, OSFI, SEC	CCA, FSA, GICS, IMF
Engineering	APQP, QS	ISO9000, ISO14000
Government	DoD, PIPEDA, RDIMS	PRO, VERS
Pharmaceuticals	FDA, TPD	CPMP, EMEA
Healthcare	HIPAA	
Cross-Industry	COCO, OSHA, SEC, SOX	King II, KonTraG, Legge 321, LSF, Turnbull,

Figure 3.5: Who Sets the Regulations for Your Business?

A Platform for Compliance and Corporate Governance

Enterprise Content Management platforms play a key role in allowing organizations to provide the appropriate level of compliance and corporate governance in a cost-effective and efficient manner. Figure 3.6 provides a framework for how the components of ECM support the business requirements to ensure governance and compliance with the appropriate laws, regulations and court orders that form part of the environment in which an organization must conduct its business.

Figure 3.6: DLM Functionality is Core to Efficient Information Compliance

Although technology alone cannot satisfy compliance requirements, it can play a critical role when integrated into the proper processes and organizational structure.

ECM platforms assist in defining and supporting governance policies by providing capabilities to specify policies and allowing the organization to enforce and audit compliance with these policies. The following ECM technologies are key to helping organizations achieve compliance and manage corporate governance:

• Document Lifecycle Management

• Archiving and Records Management

• Accounting and Records Retention

- Enterprise Application Extensions

- Messaging and Email Management

- Rich Media and Digital Asset Management

- Web Content Management

- Search

Document Lifecycle Management (DLM)

Pertinent corporate information must be identified, captured and communicated in a form and timeframe that enables people to carry out their responsibilities. Effective communication must also occur in a broader sense, flowing down and across an organization, as well as to external parties, including customers, suppliers, regulators and shareholders. Compliance and governance necessitate the effective capture and dissemination of information. As part of an ECM solution, document lifecycle management plays a crucial role in helping organizations achieve compliance cost effectively. DLM delivers the ability to capture any type of electronic information and apply retention schedules to this information, ensuring that it is archived or deleted and physically destroyed. This capability is essential to organizations striving to achieve compliance. Permissions and auditing capabilities provide controlled access to critical information. An audit trail capture ensures that all access and actions are recorded to prevent unnecessary access to information that is subject to privacy regulations. Chapter 7 provides an in-depth discussion of DLM.

Archiving and Records Management (RM)

Maintaining impeccable records throughout their lifecycles can be a difficult task, especially in globally dispersed organizations with files that may need to be stored for decades. Companies are increasingly tasked with finding new ways to effectively preserve valuable data and ensure the destruction of obsolete records. In order to meet stringent regulatory standards, the tracking of all records throughout their lifecycles is becoming an increasingly complex activity that requires the integration of records management practices and procedures with collaboration and content management.

ECM platforms provide technology that allows organizations to specify types of information and the retention schedules associated to these types of information. A records management system enables an auditor or interested party to identify underlying reasons for a chosen policy. When policies change, the system keeps track of old policies, allowing interested parties to see the sequence and justifications for all changes over time. For more detailed information on archiving and records management functionality, see Chapter 7.

Every jurisdiction in the world has legislation that specifies what types of information must be retained by organizations and for how long. The Food and Drug Administration (FDA) specifies that clinical trials data must be retained for a period of 100 years, while SEC rule 17a specifies that all electronic communication between the client and the traders within a brokerage firm must be retained for three years. Many jurisdictions have standards that dictate what functionality records management systems provide. Examples of these include the Department of Defense's DoD 5015.2 specification, the Public Records Office (PRO) specification from the United Kingdom of Great Britain, and the Victorian Electronic Records Strategy (VERS) standard from the government of Australia. Agencies and organizations that fall under the influence or jurisdiction of one of these standards are advised—even required—to acquire a records management system which has been certified according to the appropriate standard.

Accounting and Records Retention

Following recent corporate scandals, financial records in accounting practices have become a core compliance requirement. Traditionally, organizations relied on the original paper files, invoices, receipts, order forms and more to validate finance practices and respond to litigation. While paper files may help organizations to comply with mandates, they also increase the possibility of error, inefficiency and corporate expense. In addition to requiring the time and resources to find critical documents, storing paper files often translates into enormous administrative overhead.

Even though organizations generally store financial documents for extended periods, they fail to fulfill many current regulations with long-term storage. Compliance necessitates that companies present requested financial records upon request, demonstrate how each record was used and show other records that contributed to a designated process.

ECM solutions can help organizations meet transaction-related and storage requirements by archiving all documents and storage in a central repository. By enabling organizations to produce images of original documents and linking these scanned records with related financial records, ECM helps organizations prove the accuracy of their financial records.

Enterprise Application Extensions (EAE)

An ECM system supports the scanning and storing of all accounting documents in their original state and in a format that cannot be altered. When integrated with an enterprise resource planning (ERP) system, ECM can link scanned financial records (such as invoices) and ERP-generated documents to the respective booking section in the ERP

> Federal Ministry of the Interior

Trainloads of paper, pencils and computers, and larger items like police cars and helicopters—goods and services worth over 250 billion euros—appear on the shopping list of Germany's public authorities every year. The public procurement process should above all be fast, economical and transparent.

That is why the Procurement Agency of the Federal Ministry of the Interior is creating an innovative alternative to traditional procurement practices. Called "Public Purch@sing Online," the project allows contracts for goods and services to be awarded via the Internet. The electronic Tendering Module helps to establish a clear system for managing the placement of contracts. Moreover, the module automatically assists staff by taking over certain procedural steps. This has been made possible by the development of a workflow system which not only performs document management, but also handles work operations.

The German Federal Government mandated that all federal authorities use electronic tendering and a one-stop eGovernment shop by the end of 2005. This means that companies seeking public contracts can find all the tendering notices for the contracts of the federal authorities on the Internet. The project brings the Procurement Agency into compliance with the EU Directive on electronic commerce.

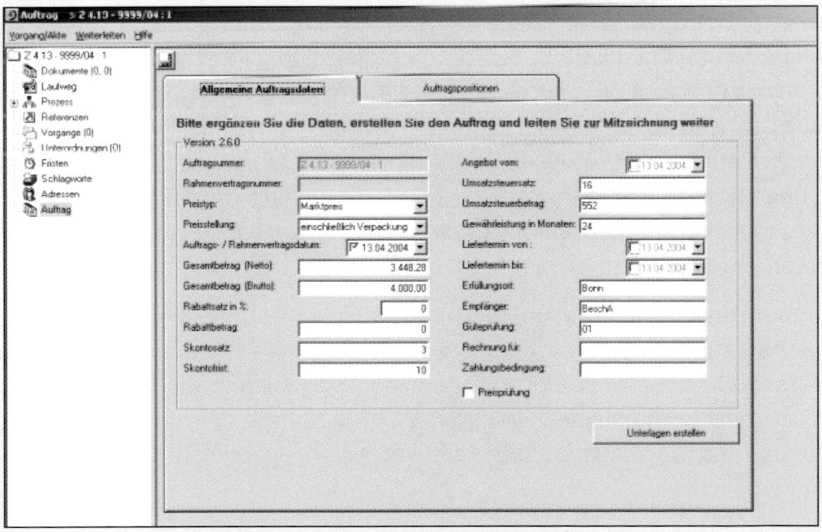

Figure 3.7: ECM Manages Online Procurement

system. If an auditor asks for a particular invoice, employees can access supporting documents to confirm the invoice's accuracy and justify its use. An audit trail traces the activity path for each requested document. When critical information is destroyed in compliance with corporate policy or regulations, an audit entry for the object in question can be presented as proof, in some instances allowing an organization to avoid spoliation penalties or summary judgments. Chapter 9 deals with EAE exclusively.

Messaging and Email Management

All records management legislation is concerned with the content of the information in question and not with the format in which it is stored, communicated or conveyed. Records management legislation covers all forms of electronic communication, such as email and instant messaging. However, due to the unprecedented rate at which email has been adopted by organizations and the sheer volume of communication that occurs through this medium, email represents one of the largest information and risk management problems today. Many organizations have been subject to large losses because they lacked an effective email management system. ECM platforms provide the functionality organizations need to reduce risk and maintain compliance with any regulations that apply specifically to email. Email management is discussed in greater detail in Chapter 13.

Rich Media and Digital Asset Management (DAM)

Compliance and corporate governance necessitate the communication of appropriate policies, obligations and standard operating procedures to all employees responsible for the implementation of these policies. An ECM platform delivers rich media training formats including synchronized voice, video, text and presentations. As well as supporting these formats, the system automatically captures all necessary data required as proof that employees have been trained and certified. This is essential to organizations in industries like financial services and pharmaceuticals, where non-compliance can mean the collapse of the entire organization.

The Investment Dealers Association of Canada's Policy Number 6 lays out the guidelines for the ongoing training and certification of employees. Under these guidelines, firms are required to develop compliance training and maintain the proof of successful completion of training in employee records. ECM platforms can be used to automate both the process and the documentation for certification, enabling organizations to lower the costs of compliance.

> **Mitsubishi Automotive Engineering** MAE

Organizations that want to not only survive but thrive in the automotive industry must manage knowledge processes. Committed to quality products and service, Mitsubishi Automotive Engineering was one of the first companies in Japan to recognize the value of implementing an integrated collaboration and content management solution.

Since 1999, ECM has been helping Mitsubishi to gain and maintain ISO certification enterprise wide, providing its customers with a quality assurance that gives the organization an edge over competitors. Online processes and controls have saved Mitsubishi paper costs, approximately U.S. $190,000, as well as time and resources.

"One of the main reasons we chose ECM was to facilitate the achievement of ISO 9001 and ISO 14001 certification... we were able to enhance and expand the functionality of ECM to build a process management system that ensures accuracy in business processes, effectively controlling all our documents and quality-related records," says Mitsubishi's Assistant General Manager of Quality and Environment Section, Department of Technical Administration.

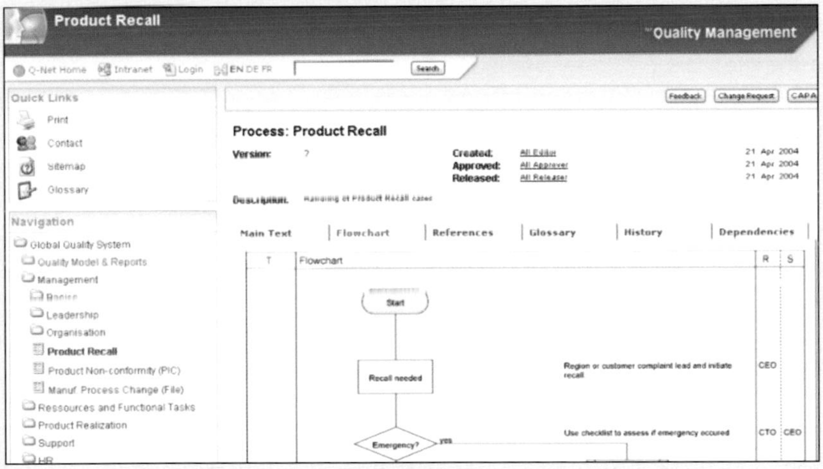

Figure 3.8: An Example of ECM for Quality Management

Web Content Management (WCM)

Web content management functionality allows organizations to effectively disseminate compliance or governance-related information to large numbers of employees. As part of an ECM solution, WCM reduces the cost of communicating standard operating procedures, quality control documentation and policies to a global audience. The ISO 9000 standard is an example of an international best practice that has been widely adopted by manufacturing organizations worldwide. The standard is so prevalent that certification has become a requirement for doing business in the manufacturing sector. ECM platforms have proven themselves essential to cost effective implementation of ISO 9000 quality documentation. Chapter 8 covers WCM in greater detail.

Search

Although the technologies outlined above help organizations to comply with standards and regulations, they do not prevent litigation or audits. Freedom of Information Act (FOIA) legislation can force organizations to produce information within very short periods of time. Search technology, as part of an integrated ECM solution, can help auditors or legal discovery staff locate all relevant or required information. A records management system can be used to group this information into a consolidated list, where "holds" can be applied to suspend the lifecycle of the information. Holds can be applied to entire categories of information using classifications and taxonomies. A workflow can be implemented to automate the review of all collected information. On completion of the review, export and packaging capabilities allow the information to be produced for delivery to the requesting party. For more information about Search technology, see Chapter 4.

Compliance Applications

Financial Services: Accreditation and Certification Management

In the financial industry, employees who deal in the sale of financial products (mutual funds, stocks and other investment products) must be registered with one or more regulatory authorities. Employees are registered with one or more of these authorities based on which geographical location the employee wishes to operate in and which products they wish to sell. These registrations are term-based (usually annual or multi-year) and are renewed based on criteria established by each authority.

In order to provide highly effective corporate management and training solutions for the financial services sector, ECM gives users the ability to provide corporate learning and training programs that will meet regulatory authority objectives.

ECM was designed from the beginning to address a number of needs: growth in regulatory reporting requirements; leveraging existing investments in training content and programs; maintaining detailed registration and licensing records for compliance management; and the need to manage all of the detailed records necessary to achieve regulatory compliance.

Financial Services: Anti-Money Laundering

In the wake of the September 11th terrorist attacks in the United States, the focus on money laundering prevention and detection has intensified. Governments around the world have enacted laws requiring banks and other financial institutions to take an active role in preventing and detecting money laundering. Money laundering is a risk that must be managed at the highest levels of an organization.

Financial institutions in particular are vulnerable to money laundering due to the range of customer relationships they manage and the array of products, services and transaction types they offer. Weaknesses in policies and procedures, regulatory and internal audit compliance functions, or transaction and information systems all compound the financial institution's exposure to money laundering risk.

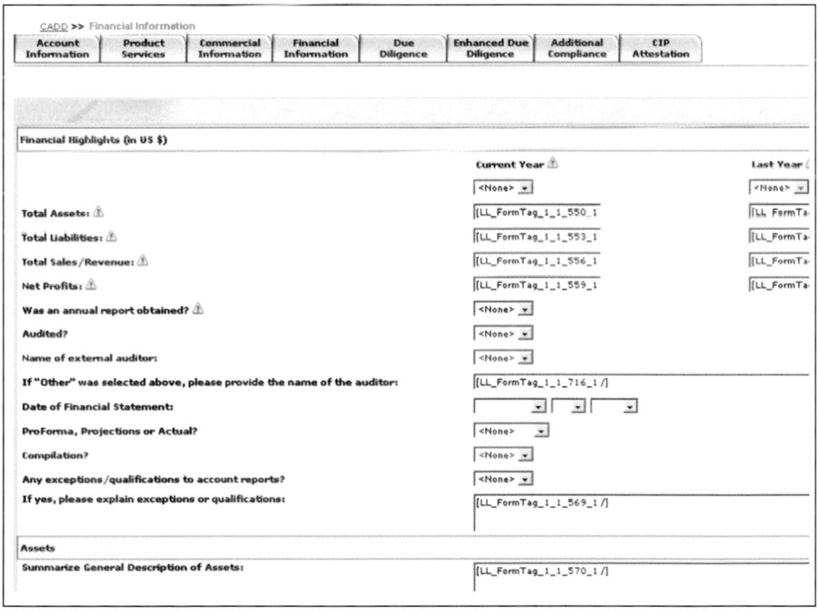

Figure 3.9: Anti-Money Laundering Application

ECM provides a secure environment for managing customer information, including multilingual forms and workflows used to capture, track and verify the information required to authenticate customers. As part of an integrated system, ECM provides a powerful and targeted tool for delivering information and training on anti-money laundering policies and procedures to all employees. The system ensures compliance with Sections 312 and 326 of the U.S. Patriot Act by automating the generation and escalation of notifications for account renewals, as well as enabling effective management of archived records when closing accounts. With this solution, ECM reduces the risk associated with non-compliance by making the control of the customer acquisition process more efficient and compliant.

Pharmaceutical: Clinical Trials

ECM provides the infrastructure, knowledge management and real-time collaborative workspaces that pharmaceutical employees need to share, manage and analyze clinical trial data throughout the entire clinical trial process. ECM's combined content management and collaboration functionality helps to reduce costs and improve quality by providing instant access to CRFs, SAEs, queries, patient diaries and inventory reports. ECM extends an organization's ability to manage and share clinical data across organizations and with partnering companies, such as Contract Research Organizations (CROs) and sponsor companies, by providing a secure extranet environment in which researchers can work together.

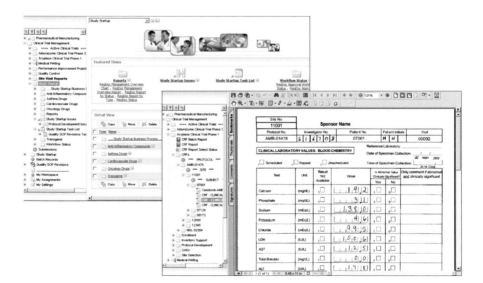

Figure 3.10: Clinical Trials Application

> Office of the Superintendent of Financial Institutions

The Office of the Superintendent of Financial Institutions (OSFI), the regulator of federally registered financial institutions operating in Canada, needed to implement a system to streamline, standardize and re-design internal processes and improve the management of information across the organization in response to a government legislation, which specifies that certain types of cases are automatically "deemed approved" if OSFI does not render a decision within 30 days.

OSFI deployed ECM technology to create a central repository for managing unstructured content, as well as process workflows and collaborative workspaces. Currently, OSFI's Case Management System makes it easy for case officers and other expert reviewers to find and share case information, ensuring everyone is spending more time focusing on higher-value areas that require their expertise and judgement.

In addition, OSFI's Business Systems Integration Initiative (BSII) provides a new level of automation, so that OSFI employees can quickly and efficiently manage regulatory processes, Improve risk management supervision and speed responses to key stakeholders.

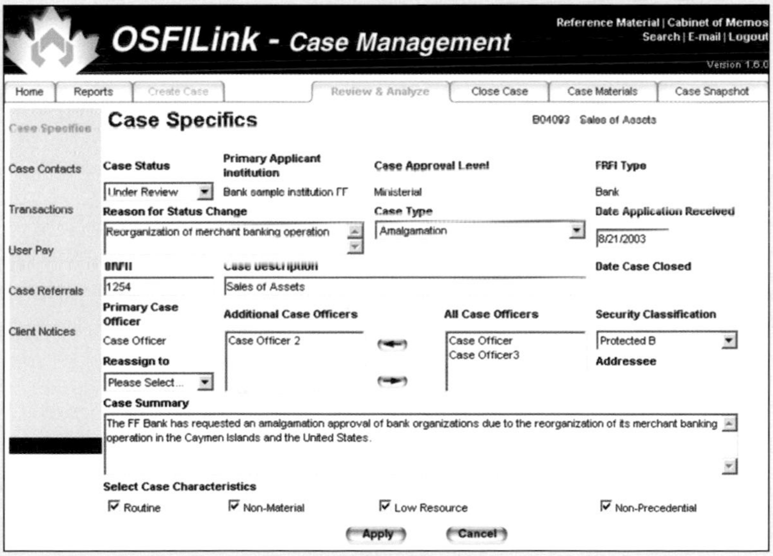

Figure 3.11: OSFI's Case Management

Government: Email Management

Email messages and attachments represent business records that must be retained and managed securely to support regulatory compliance, avoid legal fines or litigation costs and satisfy auditing requirements. Regulations, like SEC 17-a4, NASD 3010 or DoD 5015.2, define strict rules as to how and for how long emails must be retained. Indexes on emails and attachments allow for auditing and recovery of all content when requested. ECM solutions provide both the technical and logistical functionality to fulfill these requirements completely and efficiently.

ECM: Bringing it All Together

All companies today face the difficult challenge of maintaining performance while operating in an increasingly risky and regulated environment. The key to successful compliance with high corporate governance standards is to ensure that consistent processes are rapidly deployed throughout an organization, that all critical information is managed, and that people are fully trained and able to work together within the compliance framework.

ECM provides organizations with an enterprise-wide platform that delivers compliance and governance solutions. ECM solutions were designed to address a number of governance needs: growth in regulatory reporting requirements; leveraging existing investments in training content and programs; maintaining detailed registration and licensing records for compliance management; and the need to manage all detailed records necessary to achieve regulatory compliance.

With a proven history for implementing compliant records management solutions, including ISO 9000, the U.S. Patriot Act, SEC, DOE, and OSHA, ECM delivers the document and process management functionality required, for example, by the Sarbanes-Oxley Act in the U.S.A. ECM reduces the risks associated with non-compliance by making the control of information and processes more efficient and transparent.

In the chapters that follow, we'll take a closer look at all of the technologies inherent to effective Enterprise Content Management. The concluding section of the book brings all the technologies together and discusses the implementation of an ECM solution in more detail.

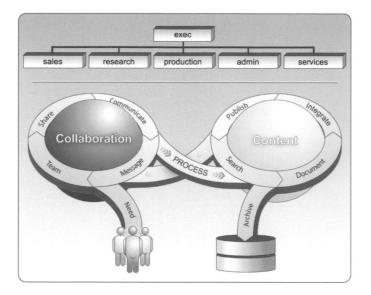

Figure 4.1: Search

Search is part of the Document Management component of the Content technology used in ECM suites.

This chapter introduces the reader to the development of search and retrieval technologies, including early online search services, the debut of enterprise search tools and the first search engine for the Internet. It also explains why Search is such an important element of ECM, especially as it relates to the information explosion within enterprises and on the World Wide Web. The user stories in this chapter focus on the challenges involved in creating, managing and providing access to considerable amounts of intellectual property within a large organization.

CHAPTER 4

SEARCH

Search and retrieval technologies enable us to manage the vast wealth of information available in the enterprise and on the Web; it is technology's answer to "finding a needle in a haystack."

Without search and retrieval tools, the enterprise and the Web are random collections or filing cabinets with no means to distinguish one from the other. According to the diagram below, research shows that more than half of business professionals spend more than two hours a day searching for the information they need to do their jobs.

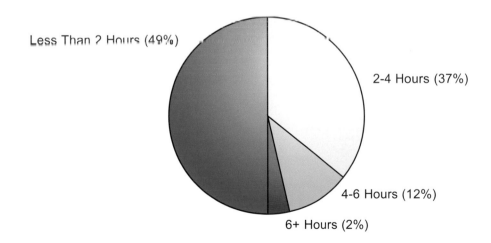

Less Than 2 Hours (49%)

2-4 Hours (37%)

4-6 Hours (12%)

6+ Hours (2%)

Figure 4.2: Time Spent Searching For Information

> National Economic Research Associates

NERA
Economic Consulting

A Marsh & McLennan Company, National Economic Research Associates (NERA) is a leading international firm of consulting economists. NERA's efforts and expertise provide objective analysis that is often applied to making complex legal decisions. The ability to collaborate and draw on relevant documentation can play a significant part in supporting litigation and other business-critical efforts.

NERA implemented a library management solution to consolidate the information holdings of nine geographically distributed NERA libraries, which contained physical resources, digital collections and commercial databases. The enterprise-wide solution addresses document control as well as traditional library management functions.

For the first time, NERA can offer its entire organization a single point of entry to access research document and print collections in the nine libraries. Automation of traditional library services enhances collaboration among locations and unifies control over information resources, improving consultant access to valuable research and optimizing NERA's investment in print collections.

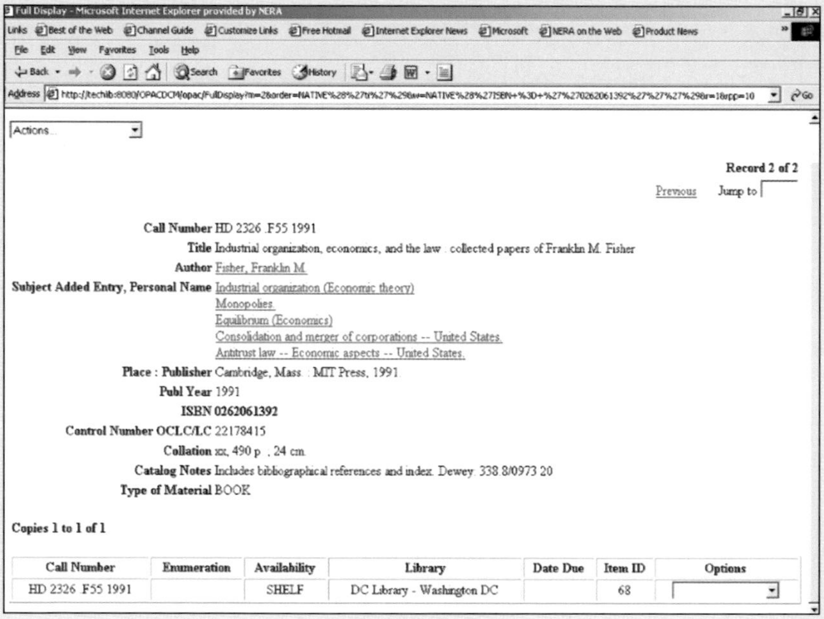

Figure 4.3: NERA's Library Management

Search software first became popular as a means of indexing books and libraries, and the technology was accordingly modeled after the indexes that writers used to organize their thoughts at the conclusion of a book.

One of the most decisive works describing the concept of search and retrieval was published in 1945, in Vannevar Bush's article entitled "As We May Think," featured in Atlantic Monthly. This seminal work envisioned a search and retrieval appliance named "memex." The article was a precursor to the confluence of computers, inexpensive data storage and computer networking that combined in late 1960s and early 1970s to bring about the beginning of the online information industry.

Early companies such as Dialog and SDC began to offer databases of information to librarians and other researchers. In 1976, a group of researchers left the New York State Education Department to start a company dedicated to educational and medical researchers. The search service ran on IBM mainframes using entire rooms of disk drives to provide private and public database services to thousands of customers, eventually becoming the third-largest online service in the world.

Software companies in the late 1970s and early 1980s created technology that could index and search millions of documents, primarily for online services and litigation support of large legal cases. In the late 1980s, as the popularity of the World Wide Web began to increase, this technology was re-purposed to include indexing the Web. Since then, search technology has rapidly evolved to adapt to the ever-changing needs of both business users and Web surfers alike. More and more companies began to create their own internal Web sites (called intranets) for sharing documents and to index the growing amount of information within their enterprises. As the volumes of content increased, so too did the requirements for search technology to help users locate content.

This chapter discusses the evolution of search technology and its symbiotic relationship with Enterprise Content Management solutions.

Search Fundamentals

Today most people use search services like Google™ and Excite® to locate information on the Web. Search tools are easy to use, but it can be frustrating when you search for a specific item and the search engine offers you 200,000 pages from which to choose. A little understanding can go a long way to making searches much more effective. Technology is moving toward understanding and categorizing information the way humans do.

A book index is only a few pages long and contains keywords and topics, but when search tools index documents, they index almost every word (most software programs are instructed to ignore commonly used words like *and*, *of*, *is* and *the*). Full text search basically means that when searching, you are searching the complete text in a document. This makes it important to enter queries that are not too broad in context. For this reason, most people start with just a few descriptive words and then refine the search by adding more words to the search terms already entered. The new query will return a smaller subset of the pages.

Adding information to the document in the form of meta-data tags makes search tools much more selective. Let's say that you are looking for this year's annual report and you know that it was written by Bob Cratchit in accounting. Being able to add these extra criteria (that is, specifying the the author's name) to your search would yield a better result. Search facilities in modern ECM suites provide this capability.

The key to building an index is extracting the essential keywords from the text and then noting at what location (that is, page number) in the text that the keyword is encountered. Whether a traditional book index or a search engine index, most function in this basic manner.

An electronic search engine scans the content of a document or Web page and extracts key words based on any number of specified criteria (such as placement, frequency, proximity and so on). An index of these words is compiled into a file that links each entry to the location in the document or Web page where that word is used. When you search the World Wide Web, you are not searching through all pages on the Internet; you are actually searching through a previously compiled index of those pages.

Computers can process information very quickly; while it might take a writer days to index a book, it takes a computer seconds. Nonetheless, the Web contains an unimaginable number of documents and pages that are changing constantly. To create an index that allows users to search the Internet requires serious computing power and some very sophisticated algorithms.

Making Sense of Search Results

Two key concepts are discussed most often in academic literature on search and information retrieval. *Recall* is defined as the ability to index and retrieve all information for which a user is looking, while *precision* is defined as the ability to retrieve only information relevant to the user's query. Both of these measurements can be represented by percentages. The goal is to retrieve information that is relevant while ignoring information that is not.

There are a number of features that search engines use to increase precision or recall. These include Boolean operators, wildcarding, proximity and parametric searches.

Most search tools include the ability to use Boolean operators to link search terms. For example: *dog OR beagle* will return documents that contain either term. You can also use AND to connect separate concepts. Using AND narrows your search, for example: *doctor AND surgeon* will return only documents that contain both of these terms. You can also use NOT to eliminate separate concepts, for example: *kennedy NOT politician* will eliminate documents about President John F. Kennedy.

Another search technique is called wildcarding or truncation. Wildcarding allows you to use an asterisk to replace one or more characters at the end of a search term, or multiple characters within a search term. For example: *drug** retrieves drug, drugs and druggist; and *m*donald* retrieves mcdonald and macdonald. Some engines also support what is known as left hand wildcarding, or truncation where the wildcard is placed at the beginning of a term, such as **optical* to retrieve all of the terms in the repository ending in *optical*.

Proximity searches allow users to specify search terms that are within some number of words from one another, or within the same sentence or paragraph. Typically, the operator for a sentence-proximity query is a term such as NEAR. In this example, *cow NEAR calf* might retrieve documents containing these terms within five words of each other, in any order. A typical paragraph-proximity operator might be SAME, where *genome SAME research* would find only documents containing these two terms in the same paragraph.

Parametric searches allow the searcher to restrict search terms to a particular field or paragraph. For example, *title CONTAINS genome* or *genome[title]* would retrieve only documents with the word genome in the title. Other examples might be *date > 2003-06-03* or *quantity < 100*. These searches are typically used with other search operators to increase precision while maintaining recall.

These and other techniques, such as thesauri, synonyms, and base word forms, are ways that search tools can improve search results through the balance of recall versus precision, providing what is termed improved search fidelity. It is important to keep recall high so that relevant documents are not missed, yet balanced with accuracy so that the result set is not too large for the searcher to reasonably tackle.

Search tools generate search results. These are usually presented as Web pages containing a list of documents or pages that satisfy a search query. The software attempts to order search results by placing the closest matches highest in the results list. This is often known as ranking results by relevance. Most Web-based search engines return results ordered in what that search engine determines is the most relevant order. Typically, the relevance score is calculated based on a statistical analysis of the search terms and the document results, to identify the documents most likely to be the ones the user was looking for.

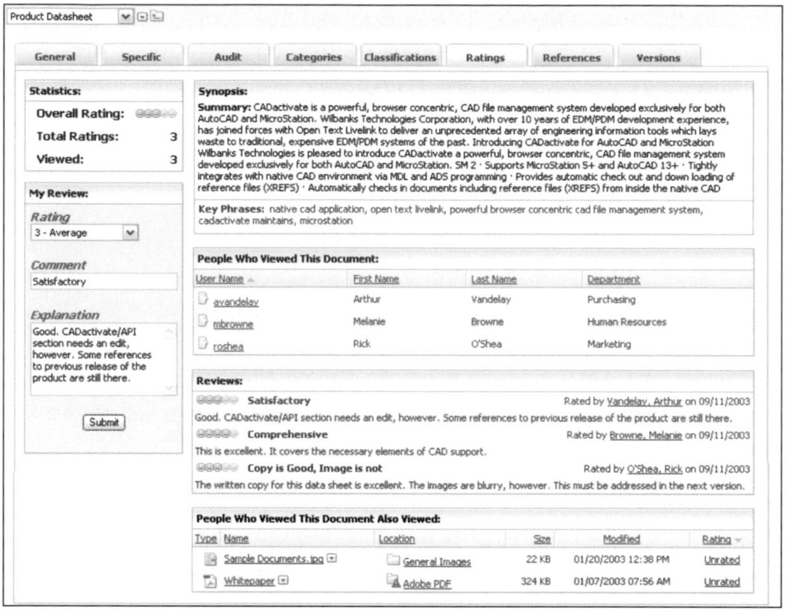

Figure 4.4: Search Ratings

Sophisticated search tools enable administrators to adjust and tune the mechanisms that determine relevance ranking. This adds a somewhat humanistic touch to the search results. The results themselves are typically represented as a long list of links to the actual Web pages and documents.

When we think about search results on the World Wide Web, it is important to consider that many of the documents are filled with hyperlinks that reference other documents—most of the Web is HTML documents, after all. The fact that there are references to other documents embedded within the main document provides a powerful means to determine relevance.

Google's renowned search engine exploits this method of relevance ranking for sorting search results. Each document retrieved by the search engine is assigned a relevance score, that is then modified according to the relevance scores of each document hyperlinked within that document. This method enables the search engine to base the value of a document on not just the document itself, but on the value of the documents within its context.

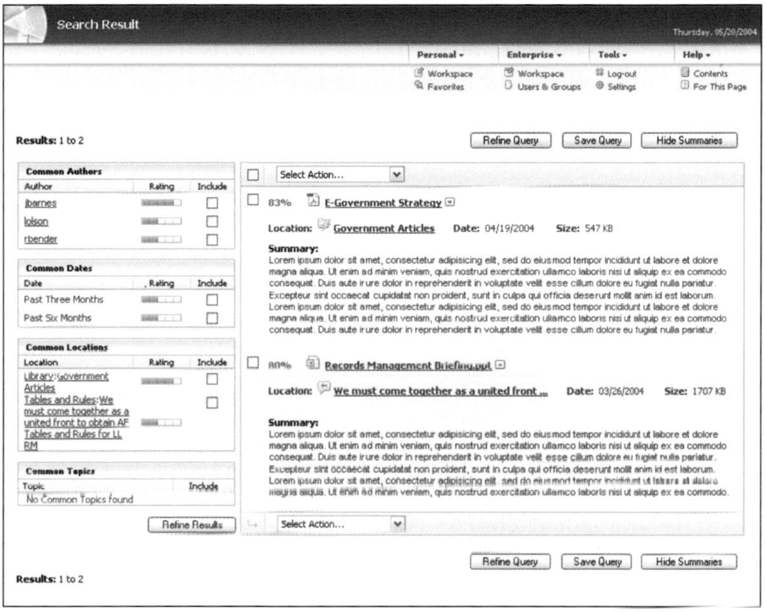

Figure 4.5: Search Results

Modern search tools provide you with a brief abstract from the document under each document title that helps to distinguish the relevant hits from the unwanted hits. They also might offer hit highlighting, a very useful facility that highlights and displays search terms in the document or on the Web page. This can be remarkably useful if the term that you are searching for is located on the last page of a 1,000-page thesis. Similarly, hit-to-hit navigation provides the capability to quickly move from a page containing one or more search terms to the next page in the document containing a relevant search term.

Another search facility is user-requested result ordering. Often, the user may be interested in seeing the most recently modified documents, or documents sorted by author or title. In some cases, users may want to specify several sort keys to aid the display of results.

Future search tools will learn about user behavior. They will know that when presented with a list of search results, you often click on documents authored by Tom and rarely those authored by Joe. They will learn that people from your department are interested in marketing documents rather than legal papers. Armed with this knowledge, future search tools will find the documents that you need. And that will make us all happier and more productive.

A survey conducted at defense contractor Northrop Grumman set out to discover how much time employees were spending during a typical working week searching for information needed to do their jobs. The results were alarming.

In a typical workweek, employees spent the following percentage of work time searching for information:

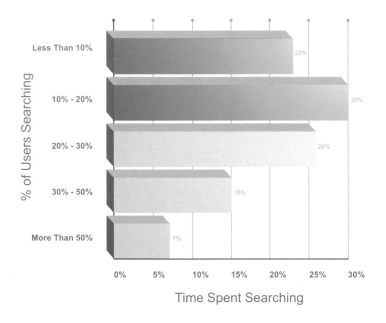

Figure 4.6: User Statistics for Search at Northrop Grumman

The graph indicates that over 50 percent of Northrop Grumman staff spent over 20 percent of their work week just searching for information. With some quick mental arithmetic we can deduce that this wasted time equates to over one billion dollars!

Total Number Of Employees	100,000
Annual Cost Per Employee	$100,000
Employees Searching	50%
Time Spent Searching	20%
Cost Of Searching	$1,000,000,000

Figure 4.7: The High Cost of Finding Information

Northrop Grumman shares the same goals as other organizations—to improve customer satisfaction, reduce the cost of delivering information and speed time-to-market. To reach these objectives, Northrop Grumman used ECM to develop a comprehensive solution for managing critical intellectual capital and sharing that information electronically with its customers, partners and suppliers.

Through ECM's shared technological infrastructure, Northrop Grumman Integrated Systems is creating networks that build trust among its employees. Using collaboration as the online medium for transforming business areas into product teams and communities of practice across geographical and cultural boundaries provides a documented process for innovation that is transferable and can be reprocessed for future initiatives to reduce reinvention and rework.

"The knowledge management techniques we developed enable Northrop Grumman to identify, capture, and share knowledge across many geographical and organizational boundaries. Furthermore, our solution provides new and secure ways to collaborate across the extended enterprise, reaching customers, suppliers and remote teams," says Northrop Grumman's Knowledge Management Program Manager, Integrated Systems Sector.

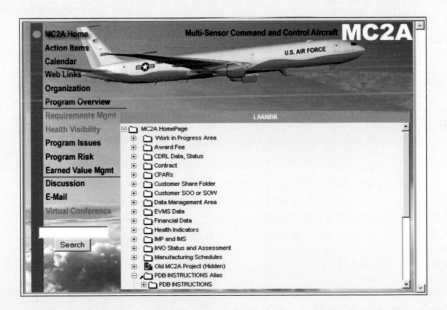

Figure 4.8: Northrop Grumman's Knowledge Management

One of the main benefits that organizations hope to realize from their investment in an ECM system is the cost savings that result from users being able to find information faster. Easier access to information means decisions can be made more quickly, and that those decisions are more knowledgeable and informed. Information retrieval tools are a critical component of document management and Web content management systems—they create a full text index of all the documents and other objects stored in an organization's content repository, updating the index on the fly as new documents are added or updated. For this reason, search technologies are a fundamental aspect of both KM and comprehensive ECM suites.

Today's search and retrieval systems provide a number of state-of-the-art capabilities to aid in the searching, filtering, organization and extraction of information. These include:

• natural language queries, where users type in a sentence or phrase or even cut and paste an entire paragraph into the query box;

• document summarization, where a statistical summary of the document is automatically generated;

• dynamic clustering of results, where similar results are placed into groups automatically;

• concept mining and extraction, where key names, phrases and concepts are automatically extracted from a set of results;

• federated search, which allows users to query and aggregate results from multiple search repositories and sources including public search engines;

• automatic categorization or classification of information based on pre-defined or user-created taxonomies, and

• taxonomy navigation, which allows users to explore the various nodes of a taxonomy while dynamically viewing the documents that fulfill that category.

These features deliver unprecedented capabilities to organize and analyze the unstructured information in any organization. When combined with document and records management functionality, new and enhanced search capabilities provide organizations with even better ways to find and leverage the information contained within ECM systems.

Improving Search

As the quantity of information grows exponentially both inside and outside global enterprises, the research and development of search and related technologies continues to increase. Technologies that work well for millions of documents need to be examined and made capable of supporting billions and trillions of documents.

Techniques such as concept and entity extraction will fuel automatic fact gathering and begin the process of automatically hypothesizing and creating structure from the nuggets of information found within today's textual documents. Creating and linking these nuggets together to answer questions or to deduce new facts will be a major area of research in coming years.

Personalization and user analysis is an ongoing area of research. Collecting information about a user's search preferences and needs based on query and document selection history will result in more targeted results and system "suggestion" of queries based on the collective history of the user's search sessions. As the technology develops, it will be more closely integrated with portal technology to provide personalized, filtered and relevant information. These targeted interfaces will enable users to leverage effective collaborative and process management capabilities contained within an ECM system. Portal technology and the integral role it plays when combined with search as part of an ECM solution is discussed in further detail in Chapter 11.

> United States Patent and Trademark Office

Faced with aging IT systems, a growing user base and a need to ease access to its patent and trademark resources, the U.S. Patent and Trademark Office (USPTO) needed to re-invent its massive repositories of intellectual property.

As part of USPTO's ECM strategy, their highly scalable information repository and search solutions have enabled the organization to reduce IT costs and streamline IT management efforts, while giving both USPTO examiners and the public a better way to seek out the information they need from more than 200 years worth of patent and trademark records.

- A dedicated search system allows examiners to search the USPTO text and image databases, while simultaneously exploring abstracts and full text of patents issued in Europe and Asia.

- Bringing over six million patents to the Web, USPTO has given the public access to the same U.S. patent information that patent examiners have, using Web browsers. The site receives tens of millions of hits per month.

- Enabling sophisticated technology, a trademark search system accommodates the escalating number of trademarks and the growing size of the 350-person team of examiners.

USPTO PATENT FULL-TEXT AND IMAGE DATABASE

| Home | Quick | Advanced | Pat Num | Help |

View Cart

Data current through 08/24/2004

Query [Help]

Examples:
ttl/(tennis and (racquet or racket))
isd/1/8/2002 and motorcycle
in/newmar-julie

Select Years [Help]

1976 to present [full-text]

Search
Reset

Patents from 1790 through 1975 are searchable only by Patent Number and Current US Classification!

Field Code	Field Name	Field Code	Field Name
PN	Patent Number	IN	Inventor Name
ISD	Issue Date	IC	Inventor City
TTL	Title	IS	Inventor State
ABST	Abstract	ICN	Inventor Country
ACLM	Claim(s)	LREP	Attorney or Agent
SPEC	Description/Specification	AN	Assignee Name
CCL	Current US Classification	AC	Assignee City
ICL	International Classification	AS	Assignee State
APN	Application Serial Number	ACN	Assignee Country

Figure 4.9: USPTO Patent Full-Text and Image Database

Other Chapters Related to Search

If a company is solving only part of its content management problem, it will only realize a portion of the benefits. Search technology is a fundamental requirement for any ECM solution because as a starting point, it allows people to locate relevant information.

The following technologies are related to search technology:

Chapter 5: **Knowledge Management**	Search is typically used to access a knowledge base of documents organized in a knowledge management (KM) system.
Chapter 6: **Document Management**	Locating information describes only a portion of ECM. A document management system provides secure access for documents in a repository.
Chapter 7: **Archiving & DLM**	Search is a key component for the discovery of documents in an archive system.
Chapter 8: **Web Content Management**	A search engine is critical to the navigation of a Web site created using a Web content management system.
Chapter 10: **Teams and Collaboration**	When a document is found, most organizations employ a collaboration system to discuss and modify the content of documents.
Chapter 11: **Portals**	Portals organize information found using search engines in more intuitive ways (by role or job title, for example). Portals categorize collected information into a logical table of contents for browsing.

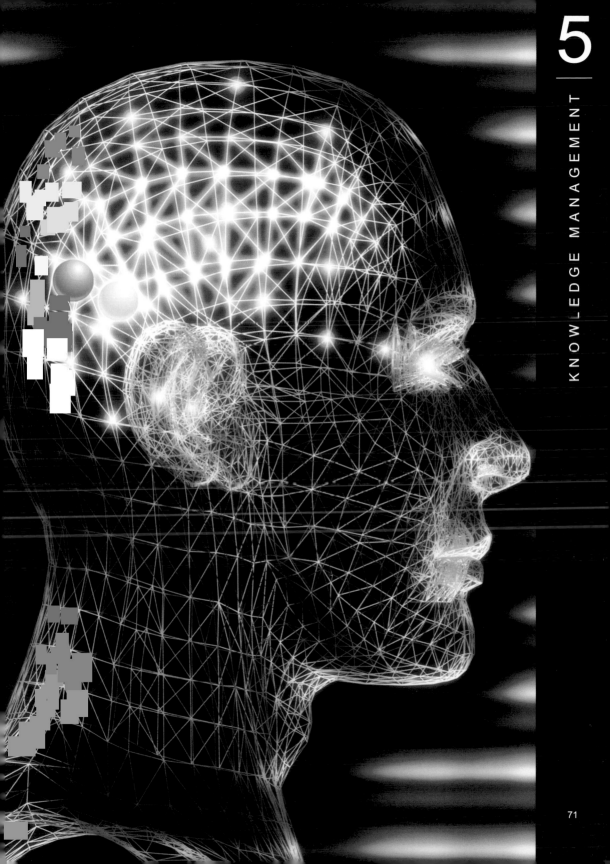

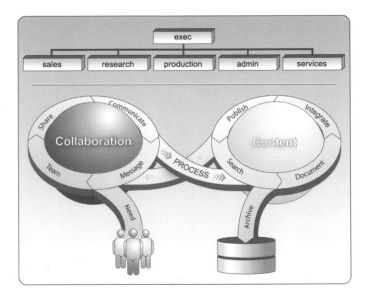

Figure 5.1: Knowledge Management

Knowledge Management is part of the Document Management component of the Content technology used in ECM suites.

ECM is really all about providing a single solution that supports combined collaboration and content management. In this chapter, we emphasize the content part of the equation and explain how Knowledge Management adds value to content within an organization. This concept is illustrated by the organizations profiled in this chapter that rely on ECM to share knowledge with customers, partners and suppliers to manage new programs and proposals and develop effective communities of practice.

KNOWLEDGE MANAGEMENT

International Data Corporation, a research firm that focuses on technology, esti-
mates that poorly managed knowledge costs the Fortune 500 about $12 billion a
year. Reasons for the lost money, by IDC's reckoning: substandard performance,
intellectual rework, and a lack of available knowledge management resources
(Business 2.0, February 2002).

By 1997, the Information Age was upon us. The factory automation that revolutionized life for the blue-collar worker in the 1970s and 1980s was replaced by computer technology that soon infiltrated every cubicle in every office in the nineties. A work force once domi nated by blue-collar workers was overtaken by white collar "knowledge workers" using Enterprise Resource Planning (ERP) systems, groupware, intranets, extranets and the Web to get their jobs done. At the same time, many industries experienced significant restructuring and downsizing. While knowledge was always sought, used and valued, it was only after a great deal of experience, expertise and knowledge had been dismissed that organizations began to appreciate its value. This revolution distinguished knowledge or intellectual capital as an organization's most critical asset. Since successful businesses were those that could capitalize on their collective knowledge—and use it to create competitive advantage—it became apparent that this knowledge needed to be managed.

With the Information Age, then, came the advent of knowledge management.

But what exactly is knowledge management, or KM?

Knowledge management does not define a particular technology. It is not a directive, or even a strategy. In fact, it does not even have a single definition; perhaps this is because the term knowledge itself, in the context of business, defies singular description.

Put simply, "knowledge management is the leveraging of collective wisdom—or intellectual capital—to increase responsiveness and innovation" (Carl Frappaolo, Knowledge Management, pg. 8). The value of KM lies in its ability to transform information into knowledge and innovation. Applying information to resolve a problem is the key to understanding what knowledge really is: without resolution, it is only information. Knowledge management really only exists in action (the application of knowledge). The application of knowledge management is just as elusive as its definition.

The effective application, practice or implementation of knowledge management within an organization is a tall order. The intranet has been useful in breaking down longstanding barriers to effectively implementing a KM system.

The first and most obvious barrier to KM adoption that organizations face is cultural. Knowledge management necessitates a culture that promotes the free exchange and sharing of knowledge. But how do you get an organization to maximize its use of internal information? Knowledge is power, after all. The first (and most obvious) way is to adopt an enterprise solution that allows people to share information and apply this knowledge in novel ways across geographic and organizational boundaries. If the solution chosen is easy-to-use and readily adopted, individuals and the company as a whole will commit to using it. Employees will accept the fact that they must share the knowledge they possess and the implementation will not fail as a "top down" directive. In order to ensure that KM becomes part of a corporate culture, the sharing of information should be directly related to individual success. In other words, employees need incentives to drive adoption and widespread use.

Leveraging the intellect of an enterprise requires a sustainable, well-organized and authenticated knowledge base with an effective system of information capture and dissemination. To overcome technological barriers to KM, companies must create an infrastructure that ensures that information is secure and accurate. Web-based intranets that encompass multiple knowledge repositories, document management, search technology and workflow offer an effective, trusted ECM solution. The system or infrastructure must leverage existing technologies (to prevent disruption in daily work activities) and provide a focal point for dispersed and virtual teams.

Finally, organizations are faced with operational challenges when they decide to adopt a company-wide KM strategy or solution. For KM to work, a system needs to effortlessly integrate with the daily activities of every department, project team and individual. An effective KM system should reduce the impact on established routines and extend existing enterprise applications. If employees are reticent to use the system, return on investment is negligible. Entrenching a Web-based intranet in each worker's daily routine is an effective way to sell KM across an organization.

> Turner Construction Company

Turner

Long recognized as a leading builder of commercial structures, Turner Construction Company saw a combination of knowledge management, collaboration and online learning as the strategy that would facilitate its projected growth and enable the organization to develop the most highly informed workers in the construction industry—a goal intended to provide a decisive competitive edge in bid scenarios.

Turner Construction uses ECM to provide its employees with online access to documentation and information that covers all aspects of any construction project. This extensive library helps project teams collectively achieve the highest possible levels of efficiency by enabling knowledge sharing across all business units.

"Our project team members all work from the same up-to-date knowledge base, enabling projects to run more smoothly and effectively. ECM has provided a solid and reliable foundation for our project teams to share information and access knowledge critical to the overall success of our goals," said the Senior Vice President of Turner Construction Company.

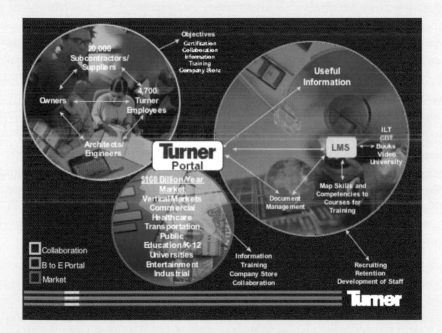

Figure 5.2: Turner's Knowledge Network

Information in Context

By the late nineties, the document management market had hit a ceiling. Microsoft was providing basic functionality at the low end and specialized functionality was becoming less and less affordable at the high end. With an opportunity identified and a market taking shape, knowledge management was well positioned to capitalize on the quantity of information available and the challenges organizations were facing to manage this information. Technology provides the infrastructure to facilitate human interaction with knowledge and with the processes that transform information into knowledge. The following outlines the basic advance of the discipline and the technology that supports it.

Information was first managed using traditional Management Information Systems (MIS) that captured, stored and retrieved raw data. Information would be delivered on request and returned without contextual details. Once the information was "consumed" it was usually discarded. Data warehousing fits into this category because it contains corporate data like documents, email, files and other forms of information. Raw data is not knowledge, because knowledge only results when information is transformed into action.

In order to become actionable as knowledge, information must be organized and filtered. Soon, technology put information into context by providing a layer of intelligence that gathered information about information—where it was stored, when it was stored, who stored it, who accessed it, what it pertained to, and more. In other words, information was gaining new intelligence in the form of attributes that were assigned with use.

Let's look at search to illustrate this new intelligence. Searching large content repositories can be an exercise in frustration. Many of us do not possess the analytic skills of a librarian; our ability to pose multi-word Boolean queries is limited. Often, a single word question or "query" results in tens of thousands of answers, or search results. An effective way to find more specific information is to provide search results with greater precision. Adding context to the content dramatically improves precision. The most important way to create context for content is to capture the objects related to the content at the time it is created. These objects, or collaboration elements, can be tracked and saved when content is created.

Examples of these elements are author, date and editors. The difference that context brings to content can be illustrated by comparing a still photograph to a movie of the same photograph as it is being taken. Both media objects consist of content, but the movie contains more information about the photograph. It contains the context surrounding the content of the photograph and provides greater opportunity for recall and comprehension.

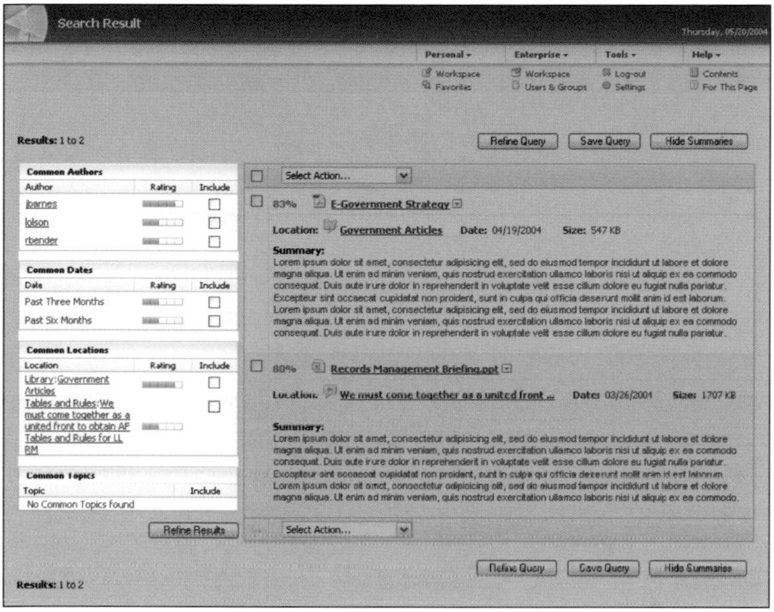

Figure 5.3: Search Results with Content In Context

The above screenshot provides an example of context assisting with results selection.

Search results display both the creators and users of the content. This form of editorial context assists users greatly in determining the relevance of the content in a results list. Context can also be provided by other documents created at the same time, or by the sequence of meetings and discussions surrounding the creation or modification of content. Content with collaboration is a powerful way to add value to information within an organization.

Categorization of Knowledge

Categorization was the next stage in the information technology evolution for KM. Systems were developed to intelligently "tag" every piece of information with relevant contextual information. Once systems were capable of gathering and retaining information about information, or meta-data, it became possible to use that context to categorize and organize the knowledge repository. The next generation of systems could benefit from applying principles of information science. Organizations realized the added value of being able to navigate or retrieve knowledge based on a familiar map of the enterprise or industry. Knowledge architects designed authoritative, hierarchical taxonomies and

Sinclair Knight Merz is one of Australia's leading global professional services consulting firms. Having been involved in several of the world's high profile infrastructure developments, the company faced the challenge of connecting dispersed employees with scattered sources of vital knowledge and harnessing specialist skills on a global scale.

By collating the firm's collective skills and cumulative experience into a globally accessible knowledge library, and providing tools to manage project-related information, such as 'virtual' teams areas, ECM can help reduce duplication, encourage reuse of existing proposals and project documents, promote consistency and streamline project management.

"ECM will provide us with a truly open, shared information environment that will meet our business objectives of encouraging a culture of learning and innovation, while delivering commercial and technical solutions that create value for our clients, producing measurable, tangible results. It will have a catalytic impact on our innovation as a company bringing teams together like never before," says the Information Systems Manager, Sinclair Knight Merz Group.

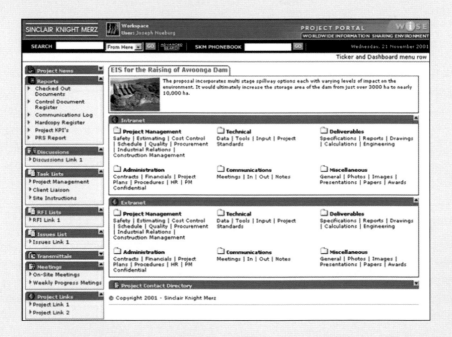

Figure 5.4: SKM's Project Workspace

thesauri that significantly improved access to information to support decision making and innovation. Similarly, centralized and well-organized collections of related content become destinations for subject matter experts.

Communities of Practice

A final stage in the evolution of KM technology is the support for building Communities of Practice. Knowledge management is ultimately about people, relationships, communities and defining new ways to work. Communities of practice combine technologies with advances in knowledge management into a single interface that is targeted toward a specific group of users or "experts" with similar goals and interests.

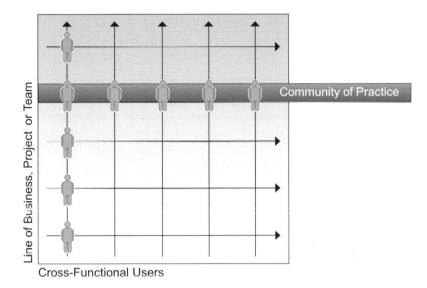

Figure 5.5: Exponential Value of Communities of Practice

Most knowledge workers are passionate about what they do and how they do it; it's what they want to talk about. Communities of practice encourage Web-based interaction and expertise location between organizations and their stakeholders, including employees, customers and partners. This interaction establishes relationships, improves productivity and fosters innovation on many levels.

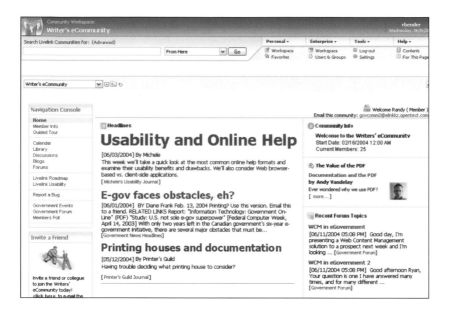

Figure 5.6: An Online Community of Practice

People and ideas lie at the heart of an online community. These communities enable people to make their ideas public and this knowledge exchange incites a process that raises awareness, encourages interaction, identifies experts and captures collective wisdom to establish best practices.

Collaborative Knowledge Management

With the advent of the Internet, people were using Web browsers to access legacy data, corporate knowledge bases, customer information and research data. The use of an intranet to facilitate communication was becoming more widespread. As a result, intranets were being developed at a furious pace.

Every organization has a wealth of intellectual capital. Although it is of the highest value, it is also the most under-utilized. Information is not knowledge until people add value to it, transforming raw data into business advantages. Accessing information is only the beginning of the knowledge-transformation process.

> Kerr-McGee

KERR-MCGEE CORPORATION

A leader in oil and gas exploration, Kerr-McGee places a large value on relevant technical information. "We cannot find oil without knowing exactly where that oil is," says Kerr-McGee's Web Principal. The need to leverage the company's intellectual capital as well as to ensure global communications consistency and verified knowledge delivery prompted Kerr-McGee to turn to ECM technology.

A Global Knowledge Management & Information Delivery Program provides timely, customer friendly access to accurate information and relevant documents at Kerr-McGee.

At the core of the solution are an interactive, self-service oriented, Web-based document management system; centralized tracking of document consumption; workflow-based human resources processes; and a rich media component.

Currently, Kerr-McGee can trust its vital technical documents to be always accessible and up-to-date. Global collaboration has seen a significant increase, resulting in improved project management, while knowledge tracking has enabled verifiable delivery. Kerr-McGee has experienced considerable resource and time savings, which directly translate to cost-savings.

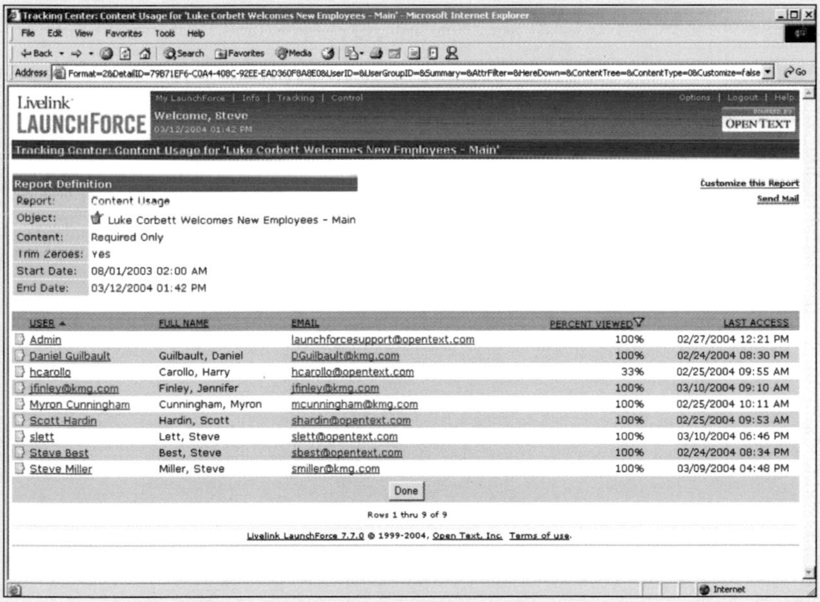

Figure 5.7: Kerr-McGee Tracking Center Report

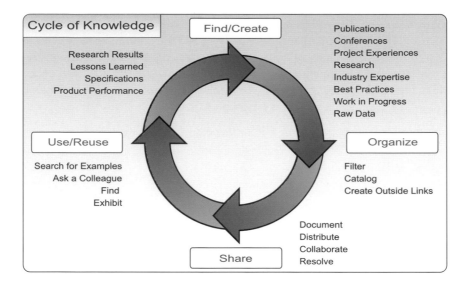

Figure 5.8: Cycle of Knowledge in Organizations

Capitalizing on collective knowledge and intellectual assets takes more than an intranet, a shared repository, some search and document management functionality.

It takes collaborative knowledge management—a complete knowledge management system that addresses all four elements of the cycle of knowledge:

1. **Knowledge Discovery and Initiation** refers to people searching for information to help them do their jobs to achieve business objectives. This stage ranges from the simple search and retrieval of a manufacturing bill of materials to the review and preparation of complex reports and executive briefings.

2. **Knowledge Organization** is the collection and management of information according to recognized principles that will ensure its enduring value and contribution to enterprise success.

3. **Knowledge Sharing** refers to taking advantage of centralized infrastructure to store information so that it can be distributed and shared across an organization.

4. **Knowledge Use/Reuse** summarizes collaborative knowledge development, where people take action and work together to create projects, form teams, develop project deliverables and manage projects and processes through various stages and cycles.

Intranets were the first solutions that supported the entire knowledge process by integrating knowledge management with collaboration on a Web-based platform.

KM includes the methodology and tools that enable e-learning. E-learning describes learning software and services that enable people to connect online in real time to work, learn and collaborate through interfaces for Web conferencing, Web events, Web seminars, online meetings and virtual classes. By delivering online training in a format that imitates classroom interaction, e-learning enables organizations to train employees to improve productivity and ensure that procedures are followed.

Real time Web collaboration and knowledge management solutions enable organizations to get employees, partners, and suppliers rapidly up to speed and focused on organizational business goals.

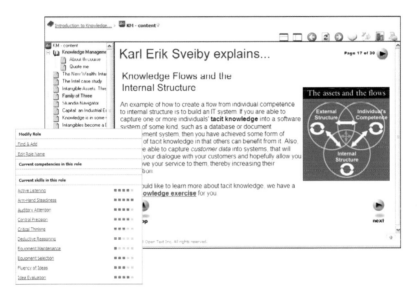

Figure 5.9: Learning and Skills Management

In today's business climate, organizations must remain competitive and innovative, but with fewer resources. Corporate training through e-learning is one way for organizations to efficiently and effectively instruct employees across globally dispersed locations, without incurring the high cost of travel and related expenses.

ECM and KM: The Hyperlinked Organization

Integrated collaboration and content management extends the connective power of the Web to support collaborative efforts and deliver knowledge across continents and diverse computing platforms, without any dependency on proprietary client software. Organizations all over the world have relied on these solutions to turn their networked organization into a hyperlinked organization—transforming knowledge into business advantage in the process.

ECM typically delivers knowledge library management services that enable organizations to capture, organize, classify and share explicit and tacit knowledge in a single, secure Web-based repository. These services are tightly integrated with collaboration capabilities. This means that people's "work" is intrinsically connected to the knowledge generated and this knowledge is intrinsically connected to work. Such knowledge repositories allow people to manage knowledge within context to create real business value. Workflow and electronic forms place valuable information in the context of critical business processes, enabling organizations to become more productive and efficient.

The value of most corporations today resides largely in their knowledge assets. Success depends on the ability to manage, preserve and leverage these assets. It is inefficient to depend on uncontrolled email systems and shared network drives as a repository for corporate knowledge. Doing so can put an organization at risk of litigation or non-compliance with government regulations. ECM enables organizations to foster a knowledge sharing culture that facilitates the flow of information throughout an organization.

German car manufacturing giant Audi is acutely aware that knowledge can be a key factor in creating competitive advantage. The company originally adopted ECM as a fundamental part of its knowledge management projects at Audi headquarters in Ingolstadt, Germany, and in 2002, the solution was extended enterprise-wide.

Audi's initial application of ECM was to develop a complex market research information system specifically designed to store and track all information about competitors' vehicles. The availability of this content to the customers of the unit supports planning and greatly improves decision-making reliability. Today, Audi's ECM solution serves as the organization's information retrieval system for expert knowledge, as well as a platform for group-wide communities.

"Our market research information system based on ECM has enabled us to make our research activities transparent enterprise wide and ensure that all people involved in these activities are fully informed with access to the most current knowledge of the market in general and of our competitors in particular," says Audi's Project Manager.

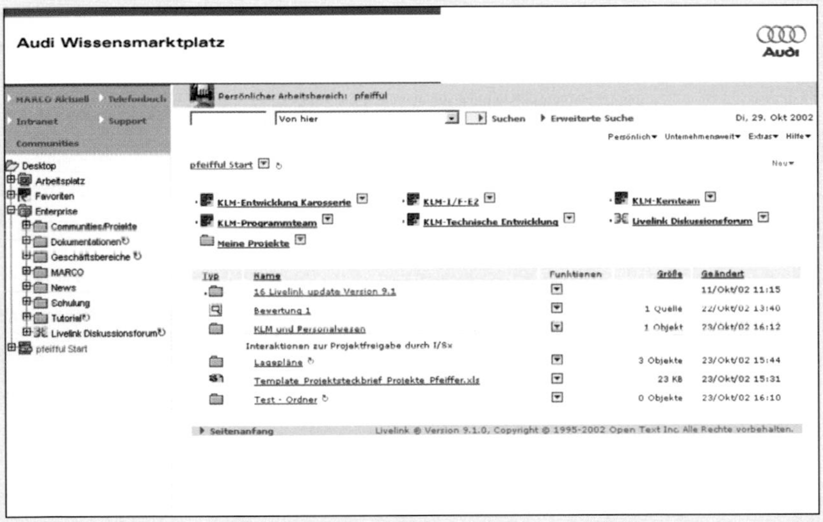

Figure 5.10: Audi's Knowledge Management

Other Chapters Related to Knowledge Management

KM is critical to the leveraging an ECM solution since it extends the usefulness of content across the enterprise.

Chapter 4: **Search**	Search is typically used to access a knowledge base of documents organized in a knowledge management system.
Chapter 6: **Document Management**	KM can only be applied effectively if content or documents are collected and managed in a document management system. Through a secure repository and features like version control, a DM system provides improved access to accurate content.
Chapter 7: **Archiving & DLM**	The value of KM systems can be extended by providing access to archived information.
Chapter 10: **Teams and Collaboration**	When a document is found within a KM system, most organizations use collaboration applications to form teams to discuss and modify content or documentation as a group.
Chapter 11: **Portals**	Portals organize information typically found using search technology. Portals categorize relevant information into a logical table of contents for browsing.
Chapter 14: **BPM**	Once a document has been located, the process associated with the document provides a critical context for understanding the document and how it is used.

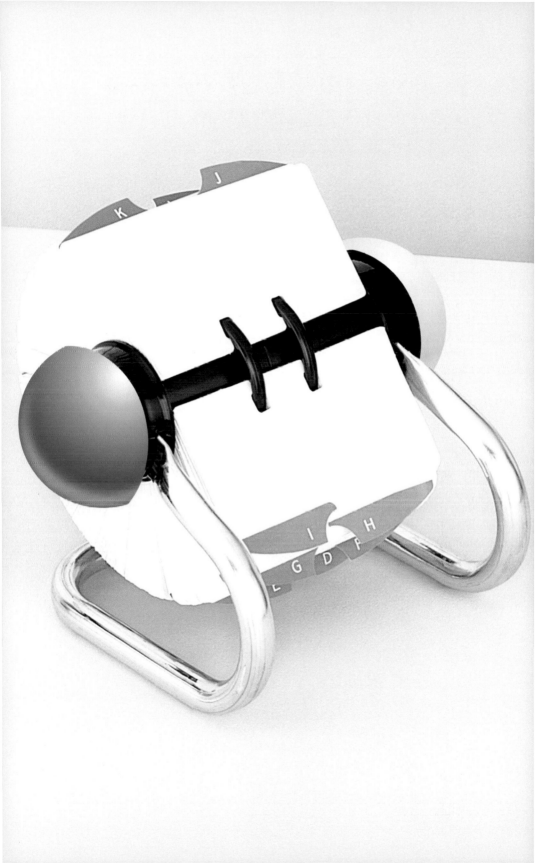

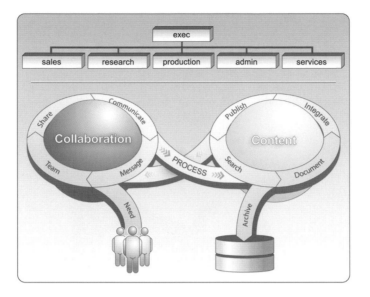

Figure 6.1: Document Management

Document Management is part of the Content technology used in ECM suites.

Welcome to the world of Document Management (DM). This chapter traces DM's origins as a solution to the proliferation of information, and its evolving role in managing structured and unstructured data. We also elaborate on DM's ability to support collaborative environments when integrated with automated business processes. This chapter includes profiles on how leading organizations maximize document management capabilities within an ECM solution to save time and money, and improve overall productivity.

DOCUMENT MANAGEMENT

Document management tools first emerged in the 1980s to help airline, pharmaceutical and financial industries more efficiently handle the paper-based processes that drive their business. Drug companies, for example, regularly produce thousands of pages of research and rely on these to develop and manufacture medication. Aircraft maintenance manuals are similarly monstrous tomes containing hundreds of technical illustrations and related text. And financial institutions process tens of thousands of insurance claims, stock trades and new account inquiries each day.

One common denominator links all companies in these fast-paced industries—their dependency on documents to support their business. Companies that cannot efficiently manage their documents not only risk losing new business, they may also fail to adequately support existing business operations. It is fair to say, then, that without their documents, most businesses could not function. Effectively managing documents empowers companies to succeed by increasing efficiencies and productivity and reducing expenses.

Companies within these industries also share another common bond—a requirement to comply with stringent government regulations. Documents represent the only means organizations have to achieve compliance. To illustrate this, we can once again turn to pharmaceutical companies in America. The U.S. Food and Drug Administration (FDA) regulates and oversees nearly every aspect of drug manufacturing and requires that multiple departments submit ongoing documentation providing details on the research, development, sales and distribution of a new drug.

The FDA protects public health by helping safe and effective pharmaceutical products reach the market in a timely way, and monitoring products for continued safety after they are in use. Any delay in the process to submit an application for a new drug to the U.S. FDA costs pharmaceutical companies millions of dollars and may even directly affect the lives of patients waiting for treatment.

Similarly, airlines must abide by Federal Aviation Administration (FAA) laws, which will prohibit passenger aircraft from flying if they cannot produce supporting maintenance documents.

Financial services companies can also suffer catastrophic losses if they do not comply with regulations, which require that they securely manage documents and implement disaster recovery measures. For example, a United Kingdom-based insurance company fell into bankruptcy just weeks after an IRA bomb destroyed their office and scattered customer documentation across the city like tickertape. Documents and the processes that control their creation, authorization, publication, compliance and storage are as vital to many industries as core business processes like sales, accounting and development.

Doing business in these worlds requires adhering to best practice rules designed to prevent mistakes from happening. As described in Chapter 3 on Regulatory Compliance, without an effective ECM solution, many of these businesses would simply collapse under the weight of paper documents and the growing need to control them.

Document Creation

Document management systems fall into two camps: those that deal with documents created on a computer using desktop tools such as word processors and spreadsheets, and those that deal with paper documents that are converted to raster images using scanning equipment (commonly referred to as Image Management or Document Imaging). Let's examine each of these concepts and the technologies behind them.

Electronic Document Management (EDM)

Before the arrival of the Internet, client-server applications were beginning to integrate electronic documents and processes. Word processing technology evolved quickly and documents once impossible to create electronically could be easily produced with little or no computer skills. The next big challenge revolved around what to do with these new documents, where to store them and how to control access to them. Companies realized that people throughout the organization needed to share documents, with only a select few able to modify content.

> U.S. Air Force

The frustrations involved with sending large attachments via email led the U.S. Air Force logistics team to try ECM collaborative technology. "We needed some way to get rid of the huge attachments and centralize them so people could simply get a short email message notifying them that a document was available for them to review," says the Integrated Data Manager for the F-15 Program's Systems Integration Division at Robins Air Force Base.

The Air Force's Electronic Systems Center at Hansom Air Force Base Massachusetts, is using ECM to connect online collaboration tools with a document management solution for air traffic and surveillance targeting programs. ECM provides version control and automatic notification of changes for analytical briefings detailing various military options.

"The briefings go up through the staff chain to get approval. Checking documents into a particular folder through the Web…avails the knowledge of where they stand in the chain of events for the final version." Knowledge Management Program Manager, Electronic Systems Center, Hansom Air Force Base.

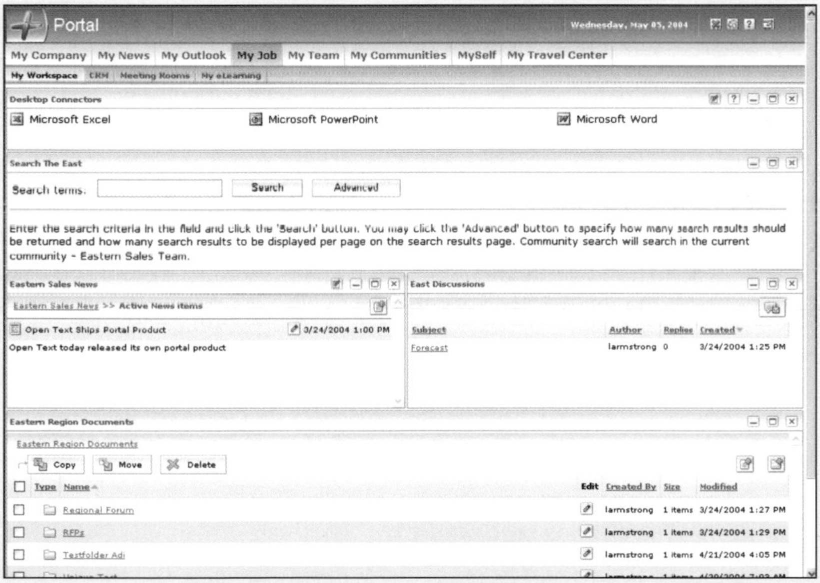

Figure 6.2: U.S. Air Force's Knowledge Center

Shared Drives

The surge in networking helped meet part of this challenge as networks enabled computers to talk to one another and share common resources such as printers and backup facilities. Shared drives also addressed initial storage requirements as they allowed personal computers to share disk storage on a network. Using shared drives, companies could share electronic documents, creating a hierarchy of folders to categorize different types of content. Many companies have used shared drives to establish a communal space for electronic documents to live, but they face other document-related challenges.

Version Control

Understanding the limitations of shared drives and the need for more sophisticated document facilities, several forward-thinking companies designed and built the first Electronic Document Management (EDM) systems.

EDM systems addressed the need to control document access without restricting information from those who needed it. These early document management systems became well-suited for collaborative environments as they fostered teamwork, allowing multiple users to access, share and modify documents while effectively managing each version.

For example, library management facilities required that documents be "checked-out" of the file store before they could be modified. When a document was checked out it was locked in a read-only state to prevent multiple users from simultaneously accessing and changing it. When an author finished making changes he or she would "check-in" the modified document and the system would mark the changes as a new document version. Version control allowed reviewers to see changes made in different document releases. EDM tools also provided auditing capabilities that allowed people to examine the document's history, when it was checked-out, for how long, by whom, and so on.

Having addressed the need to manage document versions, emerging document management vendors had to face the next challenge: integrating document management with key business processes. Meanwhile, the document's role in each process had to be tracked and any changes made to the document had to be controlled and mapped according to the sequence they followed.

Linking Documents, Processes and Search

Document management can also be understood by examining how it is applied in different environments.

Documents of all types and origin play an essential role in business processes and workflows, from routine approval processes to complex accounting operations. They are accessed by multiple people and integrated into multiple processes. Often this integration occurs manually as employees enter data from the accessed document into an enterprise application, such as an enterprise resource planning (ERP) or customer relationship management (CRM) system. ECM solutions can eliminate this error-prone manual step by integrating document management functionality directly with the enterprise application. We cover this more specifically in Chapter 9, Enterprise Application Extensions.

Integrating ECM with enterprise applications incorporates unstructured documents relevant to specific business processes with structured digital information. ECM enables people to attach a document record, such as a signed contract, to a customer file in a CRM system, placing the information people need at their fingertips.

Workflow Integration

Not only does ECM effectively extend into enterprise applications; it also enables organizations to automate business processes. Consider the development of a technical manual. Like other business processes, developing a manual consists of numerous document reviews typically carried out by several subject matter experts. Different individuals review different documents types often using a workflow to route a document through an approval cycle with tools that automate internal business processes. We discuss workflow in more detail in Chapter 14, Workflows and Business Process Management. For now, you simply need to know that a workflow can replace a paper-based process by electronically routing documents from one person to the next, bringing efficiency and manageability to cumbersome manual processes.

Let's look at a very simple workflow used to manage the review and approval of a purchase order (PO). The process is initiated by a staff member completing a purchase order form. Next, the form is routed to a peer group for first level approval. If it receives approval, it proceeds to the next step. Otherwise it is returned to the originator with comments. Let's assume that the PO passed the first level of inspection and is allowed to proceed to the next step. If the PO exceeds the sign-off limit of the department head, it is routed to the next highest sign-off authority for authorization, and so on. This kind of business logic can be built into a workflow model using electronic signatures to automate the process, saving time and eliminating error. When all the correct approvals have been granted, the PO form is routed to the finance and accounting department and a PO number is added to the purchase ledger. The originator is granted approval to proceed and a form is sent to the vendor.

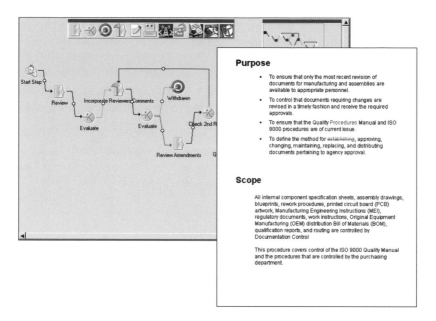

Figure 6.3: Document Review Process

Workflow tools were integrated with document management tools to automate similar review and approval processes for technical documents, replacing traditional paper-shuffling practices.

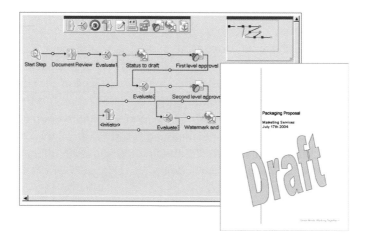

Figure 6.4: Document Approval Process

Of course, after creating an electronic library of thousands of technical documents, organizations needed document management systems with integrated search tools so documents could be easily located. This combination of document management, workflow and search technology was known at the time as Integrated Document Management (IDM). These IDM tools proved to be ideal for process-based environments that required collaborative efforts from multiple, distributed people. IDM systems could also support process-intensive departments by linking documents to related documents, as well as integrating them into the business process.

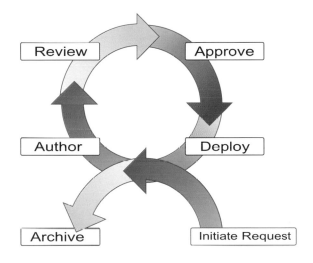

Figure 6.5: Document Lifecycle Management

Traditionally, employees created multiple copies of key documents, filed them in multiple locations and distributed them to several individuals, following a business process. Companies desired a document management system that could support multiple uses of single documents and automatically link the documents to the corresponding processes. No longer isolated objects in a network, IDM optimized document content by placing it in the context of business processes.

The Web Brings IDM to the Masses

IDM tools gained limited market acceptance throughout the 1980s. They were complex, expensive to deploy and difficult to use, but the function they served was critically important. IDM systems used client-server technology to share documents in a central-ized library governed by a relational database. Because they were client-server based,

IDM systems were cumbersome and difficult to use. The advent of the Web changed this, making IDM technology widely available to all users within an organization. Whereas client-server systems could connect only a small number of users, Internet technology could connect thousands. The universal compatibility of the Web facilitated the collaborative aspects of IDM, eliminating the problems inherent to client-server technology. Client software no longer needed to be installed on each user's personal workstation; all users needed to join an online IDM community was access to the Internet, a username and password.

Portable Document Format (PDF)

Another significant milestone in the IDM story was Adobe's development of Acrobat® and Portable Document Format or PDF.

PDF started off as part of an internal project involving the creation of a file format that allowed documents produced on different systems to be displayed on any computer in the company. It was to become one of the most important and significant developments for IDM. PDF provided a way for documents to be reviewed online without access to the originating application. As well, PDF documents could be write-protected, enabling them to be shared but not manipulated. Adobe® Acrobat® Reader is free software that allows you to view and print PDF files. It works within Web browsers providing a host of rich facilities to work with high fidelity electronic documents online.

Many ECM systems make use of PDF technology to automate document approval processes. A document is first passed around a peer group for editing and review. When the content is ready for release it is passed on by workflow for approval. The document is converted into PDF format in the process, preventing it from being changed while pending approval. When approval is granted, the authorizing signature is added to the PDF document automatically by the workflow tools.

The combination of PDF, workflow and IDM technology has helped companies comply with regulations concerning document security and integrity, such as the FDA's 21 CFR Part 11, and Sarbanes-Oxley Section 302.

Security and Permissions

As the infrastructure for accessing and editing information throughout distributed environments evolved within every global enterprise, the methods for managing and securing information followed suit. This remained easier said than done, as the colloquialism "to have true electronic security, you must also have true physical security" has remained a thorn in Information Technology's side. Firewalls and password protection do little good for the laptop left in the trunk of a taxi cab or stolen from an airport baggage claim!

> # National Institute on Drug Abuse

Expanding research and increasing competition have prompted the National Institute on Drug Abuse (NIDA) to scale up existing clinical and informatics programs by leveraging personnel and technology to design, launch and manage what would become a six-fold increase in clinical studies over a five-year period.

NIDA relies on ECM to host a repository of structured and unstructured information, including clinical project plans, standard operating procedures, clinical study protocols and study operational documents. In addition, document management gives user groups of any size or expertise control over content within the context of enterprise-wide security requirements.

"The strategic decision to establish document management as a core service was critical to NIDA's ability to leverage ECM to support the expanded clinical trial program. It is unlikely that the number of clinical studies could have been designed and initiated in such short time without a solution for managing both documents and collaboration," says NIDA's Chief of Informatics.

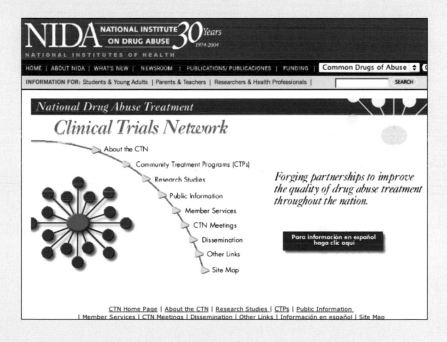

Figure 6.6: NIDA's Clinical Trials Network Web Site

Networks and ECM have improved security by removing the inherent vulnerability of storing digital assets on employee laptops. By centralizing and securing a server farm from power failure, physical security breaches and other variables, the global enterprise can deliver near indefinite application availability to its workforce. Methods for logically securing files and digital assets are evolving at a similar pace.

An Enterprise Content Management suite can serve as a secure, auditable platform as long as each user, object and container has its own set of security permissions. Take for instance the writing of this book, which involved various contributors. Allowing users to simultaneously make changes to each draft creates a nightmare for the editor trying to consolidate all the edits. Long documents are inherently complex and what is needed is individual control of portions of the document to prevent users from changing or accessing portions of the text. Couple this with a process that must allow rights to make changes on one day, but prevent changes the next as dictated by a regulated process—the complexity of permissions and security required by an effective DM system becomes apparent.

The flexibility of the granular permission structures present in today's Enterprise Content Management suites allows users and administrators to closely emulate their desired physical security. Every object, be it a document, folder, workflow or image must have a unique set of permissions for every user and group in the system. In some cases, where the volume of users exceeds 100,000, the number of permissions models managed by the system expands quickly into the billions and beyond. Complex as it may seem, without the ability to apply unique permissions structures at the most granular level of the system, an ECM system is not truly secure.

Image Management

Remember the paperless office? It was going to happen in the 1980s, then the 1990s, then by the end of the millennium. Thanks to laser printers and copiers, today's businesses create even more paper than ever. Far from disappearing, the problem of managing paper documents is still around.

Scanning technology has been present for many years. A scanner is a device that can convert paper documents into raster images. Scanners use a collection of tiny light sensitive diodes to convert light into electrical charges—the brighter the light, the greater the electrical charge. The image of a document is created by sweeping a bright lamp across a document. Light is then bounced off mirrors through a lens and onto the diode array. The electrical signals from the diodes are converted into data that is passed onto your computer and turned into pictures.

Most scanners speak to computers via a common language, TWAIN. TWAIN is an acronym for Technology Without An Interesting Name.

Many scanning systems include OCR (Optical Character Recognition) software. OCR allows you to scan the words on a paper document and convert them into computer-based text, using an averaging process to determine the shape of a character and then match it to the correct letter or number.

Imaging technology has been widely deployed by insurance, health management and managed care organizations that process tens of thousands of documents every week, such as claims, enrollment forms, referrals and reports. Managing and processing these documents involves tedious filing, copying, data entry and storage. Scanning the original paper documents creates an electronic copy that can then be more effectively managed.

IDM vendors integrate scanning technology and workflow. Using workflow, companies can automate the complex paper processes for sharing and tracking documents, such as those required for insurance underwriting, claims processing and customer service. A perfect solution? Frankly, no. Scanned documents are not as easy to work with as electronic originals. They are harder to search because they contain patterns of dots rather than text that can be selected. They take up much more space on a computer, are harder to read online and cannot be edited.

Scanning and Meta-Data

Image management vendors have tried to compensate for scanning limitations by allowing users to add meta-data to images, such as annotations to instruct readers about the document's content. Meta-data serves as value-added information used to categorize different documents and often includes the document author, title, creation date, size and so on. Additional meta-data might include information more specific to the application, for instance, policy number, underwriter or account name.

Scanning represents a critical first step in tracking and managing paper documents by importing and consolidating huge volumes of paper documents into an electronic system. Scanning eliminates cumbersome paper files but remains an incomplete and ineffective solution unless integrated with technology that can "file" each document in the proper context, and archiving technology that can efficiently store it for designated periods while making it easily accessible upon demand.

As part of an ECM solution, imaging and archiving capabilities can help companies reduce administrative costs and increase accuracy by eliminating manual processes. As well, productivity and satisfaction levels improve as employees are freed from completing tedious tasks.

Document Capture and Dissemination

Imaging management has evolved to support a wide variety of data formats and can interface with several different applications to import unstructured and structured data and link this data to corresponding processes.

Integrated imaging capabilities enable an ECM system to quickly capture scanned documents, eliminating the need to maintain large paper files. The document management system deposits the scanned information into a secure repository. By centralizing information in one repository, the system can provide a single point of access throughout the organization. Users can access information using a Web browser or report viewer.

An integrated document and image management system can also classify information upon receipt and index documents to facilitate quick search and retrieval. Content in archived documents often supports multiple business processes and users. For example, content generated by a sales department is often used in accounting reports. Requiring accounting clerks to read through sales reports to find this information is inefficient at best. ECM helps users retrieve the information they need by separating archived reports into segments and indexing each segment. Report segments from multiple documents can then be consolidated into a bundle and used to populate a specific report. Report bundles can be converted to PDF, viewed using a report viewer, emailed to users or printed out. For future use, they can also be archived as a bundle and retrieved from the system on demand.

COLD and Data Archiving

COLD (Computer Output to Laser Disk) is a system for archiving business reports and documents from IDM systems in a compressed but easily retrieved format. COLD systems can store more than one million paper pages on a single-inch optical disk. COLD systems consist of software and hardware. The software allows users to archive documents to the COLD system and organizes them for access and retrieval. The hardware consists of optical disk drives, typically mounted on a unit called a jukebox. COLD systems often perform automatic archiving at scheduled times of the day.

COLD systems are used to archive accounting reports, credit reports, loan records, inventories, shipping and receiving documents, customer bills, lab reports and many other kinds of reports and records. They are often used together with imaging systems.

Prior to the deployment of an ECM system, Samsonite, a manufacturing company, faced challenges that were creating roadblocks to information. The company needed more efficient distribution, storage and archiving of documents and reports. Samsonite also wanted to increase the cost effectiveness and productivity of its customer service, accounting and engineering departments.

The solution included the integration of an ECM system with Samsonite's existing ERP application, which enables the company's employees to access invoices, engineering drawings and supporting documentation through an intuitive interface.

Currently, users can retrieve all documents relating to a single account or transaction quickly and easily. In addition, Samsonite's employees frequently resolve issues in a single call and always have the most up-to-date information available to them. Cost-savings and efficiency gains were immediate as the process of retrieving, verifying and sending information decreased significantly.

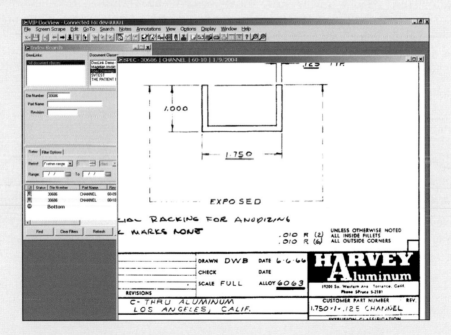

Figure 6.7: An Example of Engineering Document Management

ECM and Document Management

Documents drive business and for this reason they are integral to an effective ECM system. As part of a fully integrated ECM suite, DM delivers a single authoritative repository for storing and organizing electronic documents together with a set of sophisticated tools for managing and controlling documents. Search becomes critical for accessing the information contained in corporate documents, adding extensive indexing and search capabilities and support for many different file types.

Users need to do more than access documents; they also need to incorporate document content into business processes. In addition to archiving documents, an integrated ECM solution enables organizations to associate documents with related records. Workflow integration allows organizations to automate document change request, review and approval processes. Accounts Receivable (AR) employees, for example, need to be able to review information from multiple sources. Traditionally, these employees had to manually search for documents in both electronic and physical filing systems. A DM system can automatically link related structured and unstructured documents in virtual folders, allow users to attach notes to documents and provide audit trails. Integration with collaboration technologies enables multiple users to access information on demand to streamline processes, reduce project cycles and increase time-to-market.

As explained in Chapter 3, organizations must carefully track, manage and ensure that documents comply with a growing number of regulations. Imaging and archiving capabilities enable organizations to securely store and manage both paper-based documents and electronic records. When integrated with records management and archiving, DM can be used to manage the full lifecycle of documents to ensure that documents comply with regulations at every stage of development. We discuss records management and archiving in greater detail in Chapter 7, Archiving and Document Lifecycle Management.

Finally, approved content can be automatically published across various media, including corporate Web sites. In Chapter 8, Web Content Management, we examine how ECM can effectively incorporate DM and Web content management to maximize content re-use for greater returns on technology investment and significant improvements in productivity.

A major challenge for an organization like Oral-B Laboratories, with a vast sales staff in the field, is providing timely and accurate information to this critical team of personnel. Oral-B turned to an ECM solution for convenient and secure access to information from any location, while developing the expertise and resources to manage this process in-house.

The solution consists of two main components: a report management system running on the Oral-B server and the client program running on the laptop assigned to each manager or sales rep in the field. Oral-B sales staff in any location now has the ability to access timely report information with minimal IT staff support or intervention.

Significant cost savings are created as data extraction and distribution are handled in-house by Oral-B staff on the same hardware used to generate the original reports, rather than using third-party resources. The elimination of third-party vendors also means faster output of data and more flexibility for specific needs.

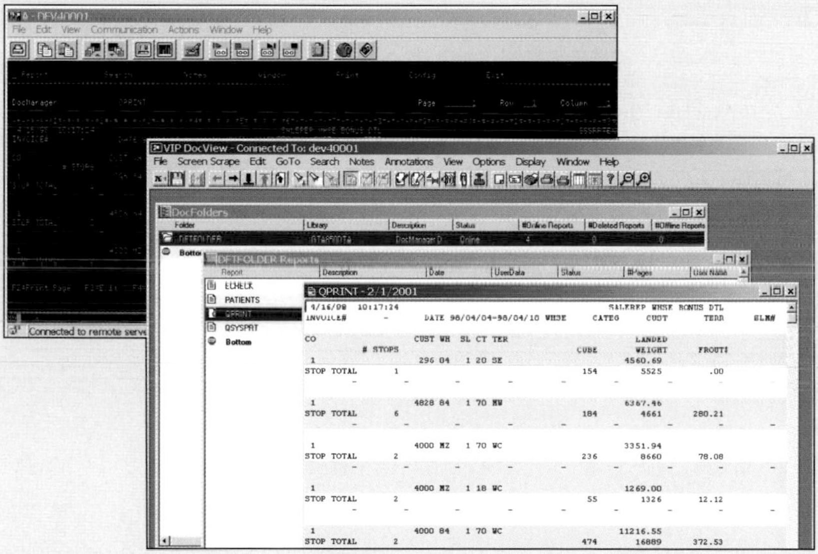

Figure 6.8: An Example of Report Management

Chapters Related to Document Management

Of all of the components in an ECM system, document management is the most important since it provides the core repository of all of the information. Virtually every ECM technology is related to document management in some way.

Chapter 4: **Search**	Search is typically used to access a knowledge base of documents organize in a document management (DM) system.
Chapter 5: **Knowledge Management**	KM is used to manage and access an organization's knowledge base or repository of information. Once a document management system exists, KM allows users to mine the information to make it more valuable.
Chapter 7: **DLM**	Many litigation, compliance and knowledge management systems require long-term storage of information in a secure electronic archive. A records management system provides a full audit trail and recall of documents to prove that critical information has not been tampered with or destroyed.
Chapter 8: **Web Content Management**	A WCM publishing system will use the documents stored in a repository as its source for text on a Web site.
Chapter 12: **Rich Media & DAM**	In addition to documents, rich media objects such as audio and video can be managed as secure objects in a document management system.
Chapter 13: **Messaging**	A messaging system will leverage a document repository to store attached documents, as well as the text found in messages, when necessary.
Chapter 14: **BPM**	Once a document has been accessed, it is typically edited and approved as part of a business process management system.

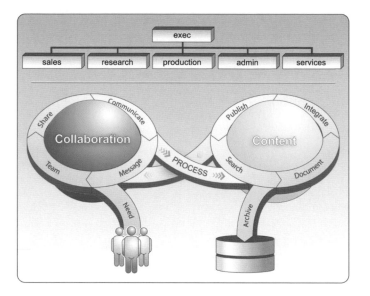

Figure 7.1: Document Lifecycle Management

Document Lifecycle Management (DLM) is part of the Content technology used in ECM suites.

This chapter traces the lifecycle of a document, from creation through to archiving and eventual deletion, positioned under the larger umbrella of ECM. In this chapter, you can read about how organizations use ECM as a records management solution to organize information across multiple repositories and achieve regulatory compliance.

ARCHIVING AND DOCUMENT LIFECYCLE

ECM is about enabling organizations to manage all types of business content—from initial creation to final archive—with the most comprehensive, end-to-end content lifecycle management solutions. By discussing document management technologies, we have set the stage to describe a larger picture: Document Lifecycle Management (DLM). Full document lifecycle management builds on core DM functionality but adds capabilities that recognize that every piece of information, both structured and unstructured, exists in a context that imparts different meaning to content as it changes over time. This chapter describes the stages of a document's lifecycle and the technologies, such as records management and archiving, used to manage content as it moves through these stages.

Document Lifecycle Management

An employee sends an email through the corporate email system; the accounts payable department scans and OCR's an invoice into PDF; a customer fills out an electronic order form on the Web—these are a few examples of how documents come to life within an organization. What happens after this point varies from document to document, but the lifecycle of each one typically includes the following phases:

1. Creation

2. Active processing

3. Retention and archiving

4. Destruction

Active Processing

Just as the creation of a document may vary according to the type of document, so do the lifecycle phases of a document. For example, the active phase of an email message is relatively short and involves reading, responding and then classifying the message as a business-relevant record to be retained or deleted. On the other hand, the active processing phase of an invoice can be a much more involved process, consisting of automatic field identification and data extraction, automatic business rules processing, manual approval, exception triggering, marking up and final approval using an electronic signature.

The technologies that come into play during the active processing phase of a document's lifecycle are:

• Redaction, review and markup

• Electronic and digital signing

• Classification and taxonomies

• Compound document assembly

• Publication

Redaction, Review and Markup

These three technologies facilitate the document review process, whether for the purposes of improving the quality of a CAD diagram during the design process, supporting customer billing inquiries in a call center or approving a purchase order.

Redaction technologies allow an ECM application to provide differentiated and selective access to portions of a single electronic document. The technology allows portions of PDF files, for example, to be blocked for some users but accessible to approved users. Redaction capabilities are generally integrated into ECM viewers, PDF viewers or document authoring tools.

Review and markup technologies enable many different stakeholders and constituents to review and mark up a document. This capability is generally supported by workflow technology, which guides the document through all the steps required in the approval process and allows markups to be stored separately with distinct permissions. Once a review phase is completed, the document author or owner can consolidate the comments, revise the document and repeat the process until no more changes are required.

A good ECM platform allows multiple reviewers to mark up a document in parallel and supports the markup of many different document formats, from CAD files, Word and PDF documents to images and more. Tightly integrated workflow and document management functionality is required to manage multiple iterations of a document and maintain an audit trail of all actions completed during the approval process. This has been covered in greater detail in Chapter 6, Document Management.

Electronic and Digital Signing

For critical documents, organizations or regulations may require additional authentication of a user at the time that approval is granted during a document review process. In this case, it is most effective for an ECM system to integrate electronic or digital signature capabilities with the redaction, review and markup functionality.

Electronic signature technology can be implemented in many different forms, but the underlying concept requires that the user authenticate themselves with the system using a password or one-time key at the time that their signature or approval is being granted. Electronic signatures do not require a significant supporting infrastructure to be deployed. Digital signatures are generally based on a public key infrastructure (PKI) and involve encryption technology. The user authenticates against the PKI and the user's private key is then used to create a "signature" of the document that can be validated against the user's public key. This digital signing protocol is integrated into the approval process in much the same way as that of the electronic signature.

Classification and Taxonomies

Most regulations and corporate policies stipulate that a document's lifecycle is dependent on what type of document it is, how relevant this type of document is to the business or the regulators, events that happen in the business itself, and the jurisdictions under which the document falls. For example, if the documents in question are Human Resources (HR) records for an employee working in the United States, then regulations in the United States stipulate that these records must be kept for a certain period of time after the employment relationship terminates. In order to be able to describe various document types, an organization needs to be able to apply various classifications according to predefined taxonomies.

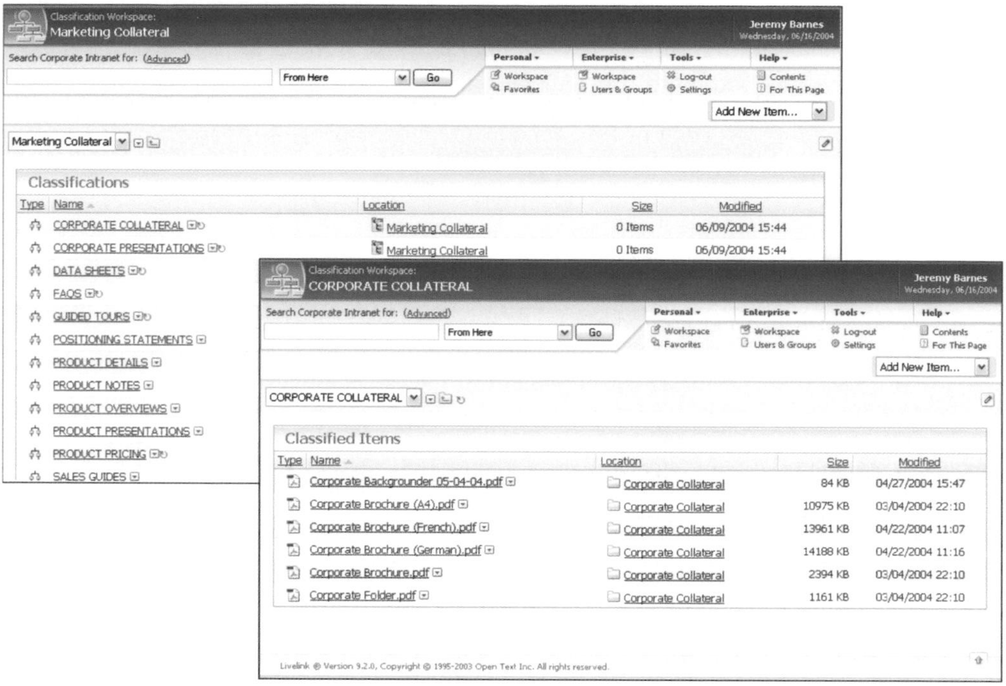

Figure 7.2: Classifications Taxonomy

Classification systems provide a representation of the organization's business functions, activities and transactions. Later in this chapter we discuss records management and retention schedules. When classifications are linked to a retention schedule, the full life-cycle of a document can be automatically and securely managed. To put this in simple terms: you can build a classification scheme that identifies all human resources records in the company and attach the document retention policies to those documents to ensure that they are kept safe for a number of years before being moved to a physical archive and, after sufficient time has elapsed, legally deleted.

Compound Document Assembly

Large, complex documents are often authored in chapters or sections, with different organizations, departments or individuals responsible for each component. This is especially true of technical publications and regulatory submissions. To streamline processes and allow for effective publication, compound documents can be created from multiple files in different formats. Sophisticated document management functionality allows people to place access rights on each component and ultimately assemble the

> U.S. Army Reserve

Before the deployment of a records management solution, The United States Army Reserve (USAR) was unable to locate vital records and to provide documents requested under the Freedom of Information Act (FOIA). A system was needed to manage documents critical to relief efforts and to improve search and retrieval of records.

Eliminating the confusion caused by individual control of data, records management (RM) provides a fully integrated, Web-based ECM solution for organizing information across multiple repositories throughout an enterprise. Ensuring file control, consistency and collaboration, records management considerably streamlines workflows and increases efficiency.

"ECM helps the U.S. Army Reserve fulfill its objective—to ensure that the Army Reserve soldiers are well trained and ready to be mobilized whenever they are needed. One of the highest forms of military praise is to say that something 'increases the readiness' of the USAR—RM does just that," says the Chief of the Records Management Branch of the USAR Office of the Chief Information Officer (CIO) and Project Manager for the Reserve Information Management System Electronic Documents Warehouse.

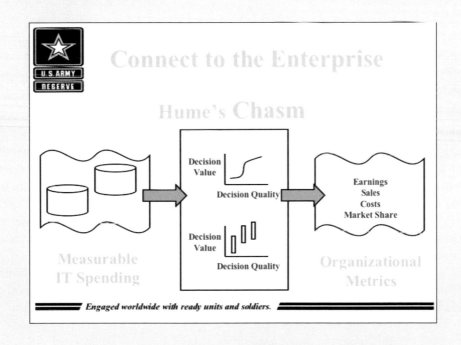

Figure 7.3: U.S. Army Reserve's Records Management

components into a single document for review, publication or submission. A regulatory submission is usually a compound document made up of Word components for internally authored sections, Excel spreadsheets for data collected from laboratory or field testing, PDF form data from the regulator's Web site, technical drawings and more.

Publication

Once a document is approved, it is ready for publication and distribution. ECM facilitates this by transforming and rendering documents into many formats. By integrating with a Web content management system, ECM enables organizations to publish authorized content to PDF for distribution at trade shows or HTML for presentation on internal and external Web sites. Search technology makes this content readily accessible, and therefore, more valuable. When search is combined with portal technology, the relevance of this information is improved as it is filtered to target user groups through a portal's personalization capabilities. We discuss this in more detail in Chapter 11 on Portals.

Archiving, Retention and Destruction

Once a document's active processing phase is complete, its classification determines the rest of its lifecycle. At this point, the technologies that automate storage management, document archiving, and records retention and destruction come into play. These technologies allow organizations to achieve the appropriate balance between cost and performance while remaining in compliance with appropriate regulations and governance guidelines.

Storage Management

Regulations or the threat of litigation often force organizations to maintain information for longer than their business would otherwise require. The extra storage space alone, whether virtual or physical, creates costly business overhead that could be minimized. ECM's storage management capabilities enable organizations to minimize their costs by migrating content from high-cost storage to lower-cost storage over the lifecycle of content. This allows two-year-old emails, which have outlived their business use, to be stored on low-cost disk, optical storage or tape. While this content is securely stored, it remains fully accessible from within the system, where it can be searched, retrieved and viewed. A financial services organization could use an ECM system to preserve correspondence documents that could not be modified, while simultaneously storing their marketing materials to be easily accessed and modified. An effective ECM system supports a breadth of storage management capabilities, lowering total cost of ownership by providing a platform for storage, archiving and managing records.

The globalization of financial markets has introduced a new dimension of competition in the banking industry, requiring banks to differentiate themselves and build long-term customer relationships through quality of customer service and unique service offerings. The mobility of UBS' clients demand immediate and site independent access to transaction-related documents. In the past, basic customer data and contractual agreements were available only to the branch that administered the account, potentially causing delays in authorizing a customer's transaction.

With over 110 million archived pages, UBS has one of the largest electronic archiving systems in the world. The archive consists of customer data and transaction files, many of which are updated daily.

UBS AG's Customer Service Department enables over 30,000 UBS employees to access information from an enormous archive in just seconds. This unprecedented access to information has resulted in such improvements in the quality of customer service that UBS can now concentrate on enhancing its service portfolio to further its competitive advantage.

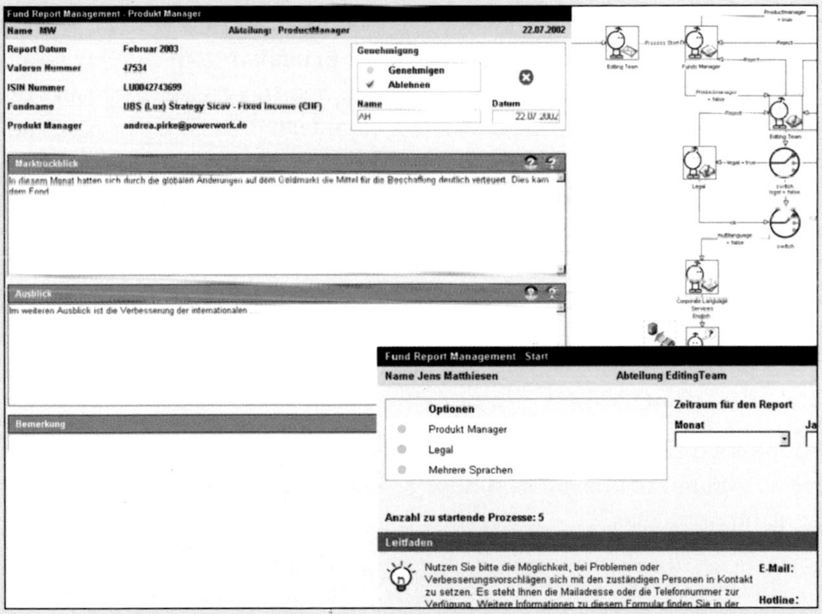

Figure 7.4: UBS Global Asset Management

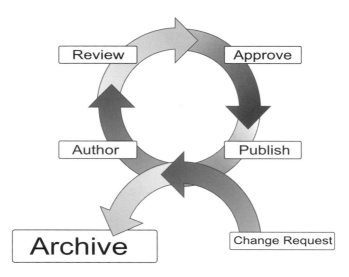

Figure 7.5: Document Lifecycle Management

Archiving

While some regulations and governance guidelines require content to be stored in an indexed, readily accessible manner (SEC 17a 4, for example), some simply require that their information be secured and easily restored upon request. Data archiving provides organizations with the ability to achieve this. Documents and content can be selected for archiving from the system, optionally converted to a long-term format such as PDF, then removed from the originating system. In some cases, the information may still be accessible from the originating systems (for example email archiving or ERP system archiving). Chapter 9 discusses how ECM can be extended to support many different enterprise applications, as well as many different accessibility options.

Records Management

The need to manage corporate records both for recall (say, to address a legal wrangle in the future) as well as their destruction (that is, when a record can legally be destroyed) is critical for all organizations.

Headquartered in Johannesburg, South Africa, Sasol is engaged in the commercial production and marketing of chemicals and liquid fuels. Sasol was established in 1950 by the South African government to manufacture fuels and chemicals from indigenous raw materials.

The company employed a document lifecycle management solution to aid with the archiving of data from its ERP system and a separate ECM system to manage capital projects, support ISO certification and processes and collaborate on research.

"What we see as the major benefit of the union [of ECM and data archiving technologies] is the potential to reduce total cost of ownership. Sasol can optimize its storage solutions and further consolidate systems to reduce costs and overhead," says Sasol's Information Manager.

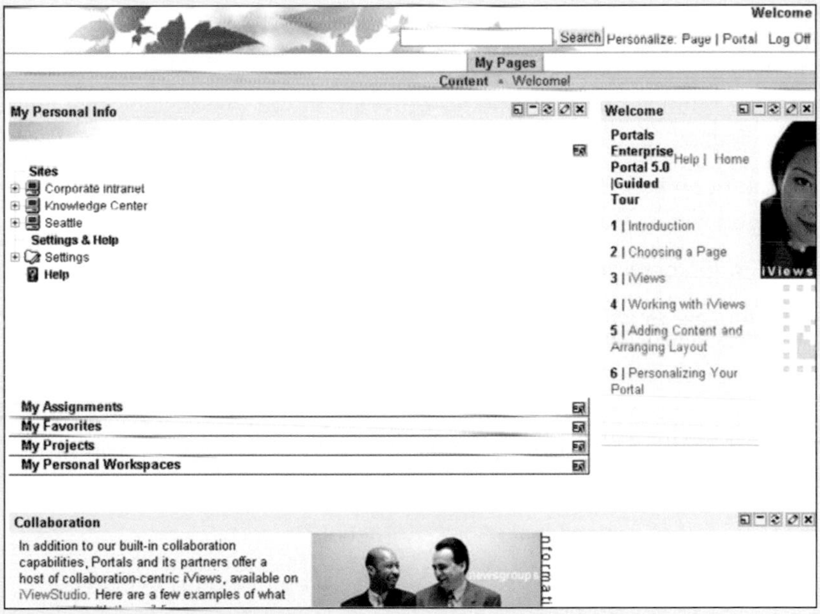

Figure 7.6: Sasol's ERP Interface

Professionals grapple with the unwieldy job of managing the constantly growing number of electronic records that their organizations amass every day. Email has become the number one means of communication in the business world, with U.S. workers sending over 2.8 billion emails messages every day. Do emails count as records? According to government legislation (the Interpretation Act, the Document Disposal Act, and the Freedom of Information and Protection of Privacy Act), the definition of "record" covers all recorded information, including information stored electronically. Email meets this requirement.

These government policies and many others like them are concerned with the need for organizations to practice effective records retention and destruction. Records retention and destruction are together known as records management. Records management technology allows an organization to ensure that all information is retained for as long as it must be, that audits can be performed in an efficient and cost effective manner and that information is destroyed on a consistent basis.

In order to achieve all of the above, a records management system must provide organizations with the ability to:

- define corporate retention policies and schedules and the underlying legal and/or corporate justification for these;

- apply these retention schedules to all relevant physical and electronic objects within their organization, without impacting business users;

- create "holds" in the case of an existing or impending legal action or audit;

- suspend the lifecycle of objects that are subject to a hold;

- prepare all relevant materials for delivery to the requesting party (for example, an auditor);

- find all objects that should and may be destroyed and facilitate their approval and destruction;

- keep an audit trail of all actions including destruction;

- support tracking the transfer of physical objects as they move from location to location;

- support the management of physical storage space such as warehouses.

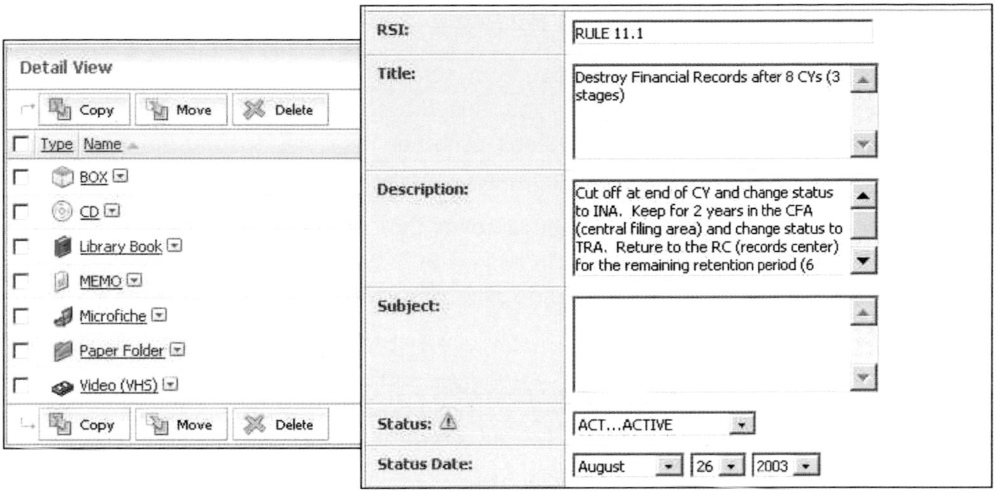

Figure 7.7: Records Management Rules

Document Retention Policies

How long should the records be saved and when can they be safely destroyed? It is common for companies to have written policies on document retention. Organizations should define and document policies for records management and should ensure that the policies are implemented and maintained at all levels in the organization.

One would think that, since almost all documents are now electronic, control and access would be a snap. Of course, this is not the case. Electronic records exist in many different locations, both on-site and remotely. Employees are accessing and storing records electronically at home and even on handheld computers.

Document retention policies are difficult to create and even more difficult to enforce. When Microsoft was fighting its anti-trust case with the U.S. Department of Justice, the prosecution was able to bring forth emails that had been circulated between Microsoft employees as evidence of anti-competitive business methods. Had Microsoft been more diligent in enforcing its records retention policies, those emails might have been legally destroyed.

ECM and Records Management

When integrated as a core component to a comprehensive ECM solution, records management enables organizations to manage the complete lifecycle of all types of corporate records and information holdings, whether they are documents in paper or electronic format, or physical objects such as CD-ROMs or video-cassettes.

ECM delivers an automated system that removes the complexities of records management. Integrating search and portal technology with ECM presents users with a common interface to access all forms of information and makes records management processes transparent to the end user.

U.S. Department of Defense (DOD) 5015.2 certification is an internationally recognized standard mandatory for all Electronic Document Management solution providers to the Department of Defense and other U.S. Government Departments. This standard is becoming mandatory for records management applications in the global market place; The Public Records Office for the U.K. Government has a similar certification to 5015.2, ISO has published its own standard for electronic records management (ISO 15489), and the pharmaceutical industry has CFR 21 Part 11. Effective ECM systems deliver support for certification with integrated records management technology.

ECM extends records management to other information management applications by offering solutions that are tightly integrated with email and document and records management systems to ensure content integrity and to minimize risk and litigation. The benefits of ECM move beyond minimizing risk and ensuring compliance. Records management allows for the migration of content from high-cost disk storage to low-cost storage devices when it reaches a certain point in its lifecycle, reducing operational costs. Because it can be extended to support full DLM, ECM improves total cost of ownership, eliminating the need to invest in new hardware to address content growth and lifecycle issues.

> TransLink

TransLink, the Regional Transportation Network for Greater Vancouver, British Columbia, Canada, provides public services and is thus subject to the rules and regulations governing the sector, which include keeping impeccable records. Every piece of communication and final work—electronic or paper—must be stored and managed throughout each object's entire lifecycle.

With ECM as a platform, TransLink's Automated Records and Document Management System offers a central and increasingly automated management of a vast store of corporate information. The user-friendly solution reduces business risks and enables the company to protect its intellectual capital.

"From the user perspective, the procedure has proved not to be an imposition, and the increased efficiency with which everyone can find information is a major benefit. From the corporate perspective, however, we are gaining a wealth of corporate knowledge, intelligence and data points, which we can use not only for risk management, but also for doing business better in the future," says TransLink's Corporate Records Manager.

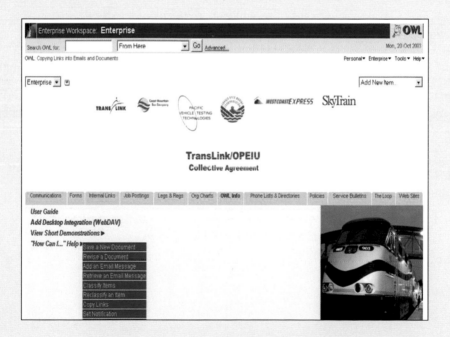

Figure 7.8: TransLink's Records Management Solution

Chapters Related to Document Lifecycle Management

A key aspect of ECM is the management of documents through their entire lifecycle—from creation through to final deletion. Once created, a document must be stored and managed in a DM system, located using search technology, modified with collaboration and workflow functionality and archived using records management capabilities.

Chapter 5: **Knowledge Management**	Search is typically used to access a knowledge base consisting of documents organized in a DLM system.
Chapter 6: **Document Management**	A process is only as good as the documents that are part of a sequence of events. A DM system ensures that documents are stored in a comprehensive and secure information repository.
Chapter 8: **Web Content Management**	A WCM publishing system will generate key documents that can be archived in a DLM system to help organizations achieve compliance.
Chapter 9: **Transactions & EAE**	Enterprise application extensions extend DLM to all departments in an organization by incorporating the numerical data and tables contained in ERP systems into an ECM system to manage compliance, for example.
Chapter 12: **Rich Media & DAM**	As Web sites become more sophisticated, DLM will evolve to include objects such as audio and video clips accessed and managed in a Digital Asset Management (DAM) system.
Chapter 13: **Messaging**	A messaging system can use DLM to manage the archiving of all message components.
Chapter 14: **BPM**	Workflow processes are objects that are recorded and archived in a DLM system.

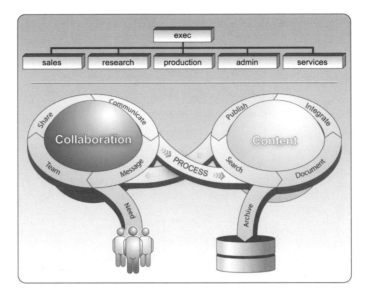

Figure 8.1: Web Content Management

Web Content Management is part of the Content technology used in ECM suites.

Today, Web sites play a key role in the way organizations do business. For this reason, Web Content Management is a critical corporate requirement and a key technology in an ECM suite. The benefits of implementing WCM within an ECM solution are explored and illustrated by the organizations profiled in this chapter.

CHAPTER 8

WEB CONTENT MANAGEMENT

Web sites are an integral part of any organization's operations. No longer simply relegated to the role of electronic billboards, Web sites today actively promote companies and products, deliver services and information, manage transactions and facilitate communication. To keep information current, changes must occur quickly—daily, hourly, even minute-by-minute.

This need for rapid turn-around, the "ripple effect" that changes can have throughout a site, combined with the sheer size of today's dynamic business sites, make it impossible for content revisions to flow through one or two people. Complexity and speed have created the demand for automated ways to effectively manage Web content.

When new information does not get posted quickly, what does it cost your organization? If you are a publicly traded company, incorrect financial postings can have serious consequences. Providing only accurate, timely product information can prevent misunderstandings that lead to customer dissatisfaction. Giving distributors and suppliers incorrect, out-of-date or partial information can hurt your bottom line.

The World Wide Web, intranets and extranets have developed from a collection of HTML pages into a central tool for the distribution and shared use of information. While the rapid distribution of information yields distinct competitive advantages, it simultaneously increases the risks associated with releasing this information—including the potential to misplace critical information or publish inaccurate information. Web content management, or WCM, provides the basis for the management, structuring and linking of corporate information for publication across various Web media or Web sites.

BMW was one of the first companies in the automotive industry to embrace e-business technology to enhance corporate communications. It was then no surprise when BMW turned to a Web content management solution to make content available on its intranet as quickly as possible, while minimizing costs and complying with the highest quality standards.

The implementation of a WCM solution allows for the separation of content and layout, and for the provision of uniform templates, enabling BMW to achieve a consistent appearance for its intranet. In addition, the allocation of authors to groups simplifies work processes, assigning clear responsibilities and improving quality control.

The capabilities of the WCM solution significantly boost the efficiency of workflows from content authoring to publication, ensuring that content is delivered to the intranet in a timely manner, while considerably improving administrative tasks. Consequently, the intranet reflects the qualities that set the BMW Group apart: flexibility, speed and state-of-the-art technology.

Figure 8.2: BMW's Web Site

Web Publishing

Internets, intranets or extranets can be subdivided into logical units commonly called Web sites, or sites for short. The content of Web sites is contained within HTML pages. These pages are developed using other Web objects such as graphics, other pages, or dynamic components such as Web applications (CGI programs or Java applets, for example). Web content management systems are concerned with managing Web sites and all the Web objects that they contain.

On closer inspection, it becomes clear that WCM tools have to manage more than just HTML pages: they have to manage content. The content of a Web site is either static or dynamic and can be structured or unstructured.

The term static content is used not only to refer to static HTML pages (that is, those whose content is the same each time you look at them), but also for other objects such as images, Microsoft® Office documents, PDF files, and so on.

If an HTML page is either wholly or partially created at the time of access, it is said to be dynamic. Such pages are used in a variety of scenarios. If information from a database is to be displayed on a page, it can be inserted in the HTML page at the time of display. An example might be a Web page that includes the company's current stock price or a page for a car dealership that provides a list of vehicles for sale at any given time. Another example of dynamic content is a personalized HTML page. There are HTML pages that are generated dynamically, based on some information that is known about the user at the time of access such as their preferred language or industry. Portals typically allow this time of customized access. We discuss portal technology in the context of ECM in Chapter 11.

As a Web site continues to develop, dynamic content plays an increasingly important part, and the integration capabilities of the WCM system acquire central importance. The more dynamic a Web site becomes, the more flexible the WCM system must be in order to support external applications, products or interfaces. While WCM systems do not manage content stored in external databases or ERP systems, they can integrate with these systems to push information to the Web. This is explained in more detail in Chapter 9, Enterprise Application Extensions.

For Web editors, it is crucial that their content has a degree of structure suitable for all areas in which they work. If many similar documents such as test reports, press releases and product data sheets are to be stored, it is important to first define a fixed structure for such documents. Compliance with this structure can be guaranteed by providing content contributors with a form-based tool or an editor used to add new content—for example, a form can be created for each type of content, whether it be a memo on the next company outing, a product announcement, or an upcoming merger. These pages are provided with a basic layout preserving the corporate brand, but the text itself is independent and freely designable.

WCM System Functionality

Independent of structuring level, file format and source, a WCM system must provide a way to edit content and integrate it into the Web site in an easy-to-use, consistent manner. Moreover, editors should not have to concern themselves with whether the content is delivered statically or dynamically, but should simply need to develop and link the content.

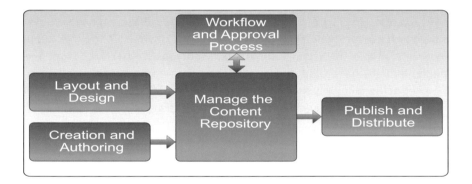

Figure 8.3: Simplified Content Management Lifecycle

With a WCM system, the editor creates new content or integrates existing content using a decentralized, tailored user interface. The new content is then automatically published to the Internet, intranet or extranet by the WCM system.

By separating content from layout, WCM systems support content authors in various ways. Using (cascaded) templates makes it possible to integrate less structured content created by means of an editor in a layout. Moreover, personalized layouts can be defined for highly structured content using style sheets. These layouts are integrated in the cascaded templates.

> British Council

One of the most culturally diverse and geographically dispersed organizations in the world, British Council faced a chaotic collection of 240 Web sites scattered across 110 countries. At least 200 HTML authors provided content from around the world, resulting in a considerable amount of duplication. British Council's online identity was also compromised by lack of agreement on format and layout.

The organization turned to Web content management technology to aid in content authoring and the creation of a standard template to support the development of a single, strong brand identity that would allow authors to work in multiple languages. Web content management software has now allowed 800 British Council communicators and marketers around the world to easily produce and update content on a Web site.

Calculating its return on investment based on efficiency savings, British Council estimates that by 2005, the Web content management solution will have created savings of over £1.3 million by consolidating their disparate Web sites and 80 Internet Service Providers onto one Web hosting location and a single Internet Service Provider.

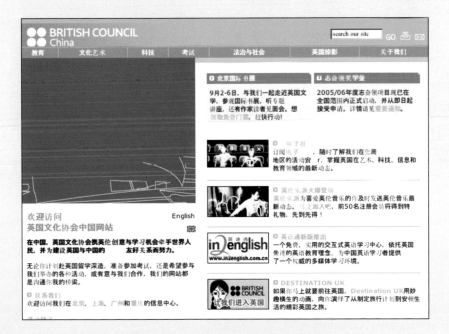

Figure 8.4: British Council's Web Site

Some WCM systems also allow users to dynamically define both the layout and the displayed content of a page. This means, for example, that you can determine that a user with a preference for sports is always provided with the five latest sports headlines on the overview page of the Web site.

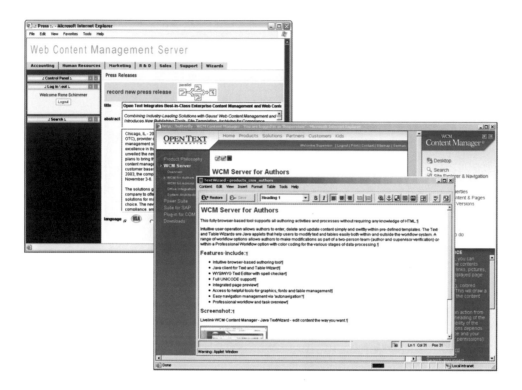

Figure 8.5: Web Content Management Application

The need for effective Web content management comes with the proliferation of content in all formats and the rise of the Web browser as a universal means of providing access to information from anywhere. Information published on a corporate Web site is duplicated across a number of subsequent media, from press releases, to intranets, to customer newsletters. All of this redundant content does more than create extra work; in regulated industries it can incite significant risk because it increases the potential for publishing outdated or inaccurate information.

Due to the sophisticated nature of modern Internet, extranet and intranet sites, WCM systems have to meet high standards of performance and usability. In this section, we'll describe some of the functionality required by modern WCM systems.

> Sultex Limited

Weaving manufacturer, Sultex Limited required a Web Content Management system (WCM) to complement and display WCM Server functionalities from within its enterprise portal. Seamless integration between the systems provides Sultex customers with rapid access to personalized data and allows Web authors to manage content flexibly and easily.

The new mySultex.com customer portal allows Sultex customers direct access to important information and news about Sulzer Textil weaving machines including internal and third-party catalogs of spare parts, availability check, price query and direct ordering from catalogs. Almost half of Sultex's entire sales of spare parts are generated via the customer portal. Since all content management functionalities can be used in the mySultex.com customer portal, unstructured Web content can be managed dynamically and securely.

"The solution has removed a huge burden from our IT department," says Sultex's Head of E-Business. "Support and content management tasks have been reduced dramatically and our team can now concentrate on its core tasks."

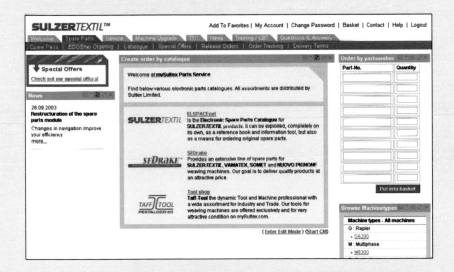

Figure 8.6: Sultex's Customer Portal

Distributed Team-Based Collaboration

A WCM system must be capable of serving a large number of editors at the same time. Moreover, the editors must be able to access the WCM system from wherever they work. Whether in the office, on the move or at home, the WCM system should make it possible to carry out editorial work at any time.

An integral feature of many WCM systems is that they allow any number of objects and files to be worked on by different people. All the editor needs is a browser with Web access. Once an object has been checked out for editing, other users cannot change it. When editing is complete, the object is checked back in and the changes become visible to other system users. This mechanism enforces orderly handling of all the content of a Web site and ensures data consistency.

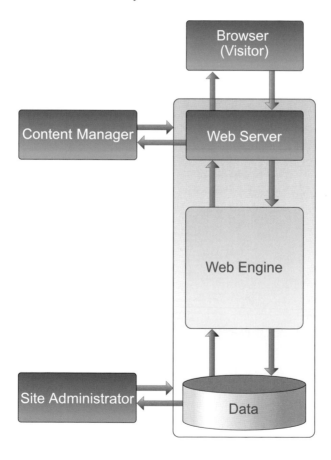

Figure 8.7: WCM Architecture

Editors working remotely using different "Web authoring" tools can edit objects managed using a WCM system. For this purpose, many WCM systems enable connections with desktop applications, which allow content on the Web to be edited in a familiar environment on the desktop of a user's workstation.

The user interface of a WCM system must support internationalization because often editors are from different countries and in many global organizations the content for a Web site exists in more than one language. A WCM system must offer a multilingual user interface that can handle the different character sets associated with diverse countries (such as Japan or Korea). WCM systems must also manage the generation of multilingual and unicode content in a Web-viewable format. This is an especially challenging task, considering that the output provided by Web servers is interpreted by a large variety of different client-side Web browsers which render content according to their own specifications.

WCM systems use sophisticated access control systems for Web objects. In addition to defining groups, users and roles, it is possible to very accurately assign access rights to specific object trees or individual objects. In addition to the basic capabilities of reading and writing, it should also be possible to impose restrictions on the ability to change object attributes. The right to rename, move or copy Web objects may be individually assigned.

One major problem with Web sites is checking consistency of references and links. Nearly every Internet user is familiar with the message 404: Object not found. In large Web sites, it is simply not possible to verify the consistency of all links and references manually. WCM systems can automatically ensure that there are no inconsistent links in the Web sites they publish.

To safeguard the corporate design of a company and ensure professional integration of other company-wide standards in an organization's Web sites, WCM systems offer various ways to separate layout and content. Each page in a Web site can be defined by a template. Templates contain the layout information for each page. Changing a page template results in automatic changes to the layout of all pages based on that template. The ability to change information is centralized within the template. This not only makes it easier to implement a style change, such as a new corporate brand, it also ensures content integrity. In many cases, content already exists in the form of documents in various formats. WCM systems offer facilities for managing documents in the system together with their HTML renditions (that is, a version of the document that can be looked at through a Web browser). The source document and its HTML representation (which may be several HTML pages and graphics) are treated as a single object, or a compound object by the WCM system.

Compound objects can also be used to create Web-viewable content from high-resolution vector graphics (such as CAD drawings) and images. The WCM system converts these formats automatically into a low-resolution graphic format for the Web (such as, JPEG, GIF or PNG), but when authors need to change the content they can easily edit the file in its original format.

Most professional Web sites include a search function that allows users to find specific data within that Web site. Many WCM systems include tools to add search capabilities to a site. The search tools need to effectively manage content changes. Any release, deletion or alteration of content needs to automatically trigger a message to the search engine to initiate a re-indexing of the updated objects.

ECM and WCM

A WCM system offers organizations many benefits. Web content management helps global organizations meet increasing demands placed on both internal and external Web sites to deliver business-critical information to various stakeholder groups in a timely manner. The technology provides the organizational framework to curb Web site content proliferation while enhancing communication, improving productivity and minimizing corporate risk.

Placing control of the process in the hands of business users reduces operational costs and improves productivity. The ease with which content authors can create, deploy, modify and manage content empowers them to build and manage Web sites with little or no dependence on valuable IT resources.

When integrated with an ECM system, WCM enables organizations to automate the complete Web content lifecycle. As soon as new content is developed, the system ensures that it goes live the moment it is intended to—not a minute earlier. By specifying timed releases and expiration dates, content is published to and removed from the Web according to recommendations, requirements and even regulations.

As part of an ECM system, Web content management enables organizations to effectively manage Web site content from conception through to publication—enabling tight controls that dovetail nicely into a comprehensive ECM system.

The International Organization for Standardization Central Secretariat (ISO) is a worldwide federation of national standards bodies from 120 countries. As more customers turned to the ISO Web store to purchase the requisite standards, the organization found that the interface needed to be more user friendly, while the lengthy delivery system and the non-integration with the back-end ERP financial system needed to be addressed.

ECM is already the foundation for ISO's document and Web content management. It was simply a matter of expanding on the existing platform to create a solution that featured an improved user interface, a personalized user area and online delivery. In addition, the solution is integrated with ISO's ERP system.

The new ISO Web store has eliminated the need for human intervention in the online ordering process. Customers can now place, track and retrieve orders, update personal details and find answers to queries online at their convenience, resulting in increased customer satisfaction. For ISO, the new Web store has meant lower costs and more time to focus on its core business.

Figure 8.8: ISO's Web Store

Other Chapters Related to Web Content Management

If a company is solving only part of its content management problem, it will only realize a portion of the benefits. A WCM system as part of a comprehensive ECM solution extends the management of content across the enterprise to improve efficiency and reduce costs.

Chapter 6: **Document Management**	In order to improve efficiency, organizations can implement a document management system inside the firewall to manage content for reuse on future Web sites, creating great efficiency and productivity gains.
Chapter 7: **Archiving & DLM**	Many litigation, compliance and knowledge management systems require the long-term storage of information in an electronic archive that saves all Web pages securely with recall over decades of time. A records management system provides a full audit trail and recall of important documents on Web sites to prove that critical information has not been tampered with or destroyed.
Chapter 9: **Transactions & EAE**	Numerical tables can be embedded into Web sites by integrating various ERP/CRM/SCM systems to provide real time updates to information.
Chapter 10: **Teams and Collaboration**	A WCM system can be extended to connect contributors in an internal corporate intranet to increase productivity and improve scaling across the enterprise.
Chapter 12: **Rich Media & DAM**	As Web sites become more sophisticated, sites will evolve from their newspaper-style presentation to a television-style presentation. This requires online creation and publishing of rich media objects, including audio and video clips. The most efficient way to manage and deliver rich media is using a Digital Asset Management (DAM) system.
Chapter 14: **BPM**	As Web sites grow in complexity, the generation of information adopts a production-style process and the best implementation for a high volume site employs business process management (BPM). BPM delivers an advanced workflow with extensive integration into other applications within an organization. A BPM system is highly structured and designed to be inflexible, but is able to perform many processes in a short period of time.

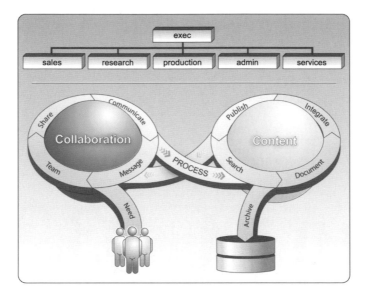

Figure 9.1: Enterprise Application Extensions

Enterprise Application Extensions or EAE describes a key component to the Content technology used in ECM suites. EAE combines business content (for example, docu-ments) with business context (transactional data in ERP and CRM systems), enabling organizations to extract the maximum value from content stored in Enterprise Applications. This chapter explains the business benefits experienced when EAE integrates ERP-based numerical information with a comprehensive ECM system. Sample applications and user stories are used to illustrate these benefits.

CHAPTER 9

TRANSACTIONS AND ENTERPRISE APPLICATION EXTENSIONS

The software industry has developed numerous applications that deal with transactional data in an attempt to efficiently handle the bits and bytes of electronic commerce. From basic spreadsheets to powerful enterprise applications such as Enterprise Resource Planning (ERP), Customer Relationship Management (CRM) and Supply Chain Management (SCM), these applications primarily deal with numerical data and incorporate it into core business operations such as Human Resources, Inventory Management, Accounting and Customer Relations. Although ECM is about the management of words, people work with numerical data as well. For this reason, simple and easy access to numerical data is critical to the effectiveness of ECM.

Traditionally, enterprise applications managed structured content; ECM takes on unstructured content, such as paper documents, contracts, proposals, invoices and even email, and incorporates it into the core enterprise application. Integrating ECM into enterprise applications satisfies a great need in managing enterprise content because it enhances numerical data-crunching applications with unstructured content relevant to each specific business process. For example, ECM enables companies to attach a document record, such as a signed contract, to a customer file. The focus is shifting rapidly toward integrated ECM systems as organizations have begun to realize that after spending millions of dollars on expensive back-end systems such as ERP, SCM and CRM, they still face an even bigger problem: managing documents.

The table below illustrates the connections between ECM and ERP:

Structured Data	Application Area	Unstructured Data ECM Solution
ERP	HR	DM—Policies and Procedures
ERP	Legal	DM—Contracts Management
ERP	Accounting	Image Management— Invoice Tracking
CRM	Customer Support	Collaboration—Call Center Tech Manuals
SCM	Component Tracking	DM—Contracts Management

In this chapter, we discuss how integrated ECM improves efficiencies by making the critical link between inherent record-oriented data found in enterprise applications and unstructured data in paper or electronic documents. ECM enables organizations to make use of all available information to maximize efficiency and effectiveness, while minimizing costs and risks associated with implementing diverse technologies and enterprise applications.

Enterprise applications like ERP or CRM systems presented organizations with a vision of high process transparency, lower costs and excellent customer service. However, for most companies, this vision remains unfulfilled due to the inability to seamlessly integrate disparate hardware and software environments and business processes with corporate content. On a departmental level, failing to integrate content into core business procedures, such as accounts payable or purchasing, translates into labor-intensive processes, higher costs and reduced levels of customer service.

Enterprise application extensions link document content to the business context of enterprise applications, eliminating information silos, as well as the need for resource-intensive regular mail, express delivery services and paper archives. An integrated solution allows organizations to jointly create, access, manage and securely archive all enterprise application content addressing stringent requirements for risk reduction, operational efficiency and IT cost savings.

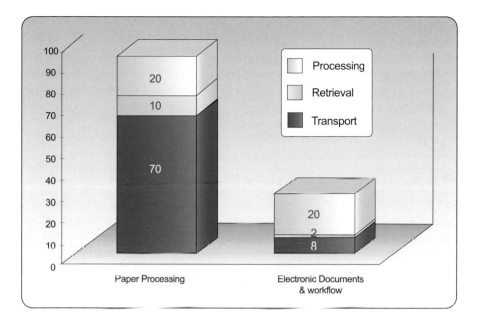

Figure 9.2: Typical Savings Incurred When an Integrated ECM Solution Enhances Processes

Unlocking Business Content

Content drives every domain of an organization's success. It assimilates the combined knowledge and efforts of an entire employee base. But content is only as effective as an organization's ability to leverage it. As we have discussed, collaboration and knowledge management tools play an essential role in developing and distributing mission-critical content and enabling colleagues to effectively work together, despite geographical locations.

Enterprise application extension bridges the gap between disparate sources of information, delivering the right information to the right people without requiring additional resources. Integrating related business content from multiple sources with the applications used to conduct business operations leverages content by putting it in the proper context and increasing its value.

Integrating Documents into Standard Enterprise Applications

To maximize its effectiveness, organizations need to connect content to the appropriate business processes—and make it automatically accessible to anyone involved in the process. Enterprise applications provide the underlying business structure that supports business processes. Allocating unstructured content to the corresponding business process places information at people's fingertips, without requiring them to search for individual documents. This means, for example, that accounting personnel will automatically see an original invoice, purchase order, custom request, receipt date and more when they open an account to prepare payment. From here, they could quickly submit payment for any early payment discounts. If the invoice and delivery receipts were not easily accessible in a centralized system, accounting clerks would have to search through multiple paper files to find the documents they need.

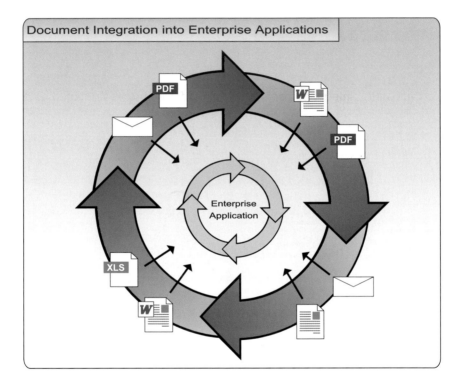

Figure 9.3: EAE Links to Structured and Unstructured Information Flows

Integrating Documents Without Corresponding Enterprise Application Objects

Not all documents fit neatly into a specific business structure or can be associated with a particular business object. However, these documents still contain vital content and to be effective, they should be integrated into the appropriate enterprise application. A special enterprise application extension capability links these documents to related business processes.

Securing Content

Obviously, content should be instantly accessible to some but not to everyone. Integrated enterprise application content is no exception and often involves stringent security requirements. Employee-related content, including resumes and salary histories, for example, is saved to a core Human Resource (HR) Management System as unstructured information. In this form, it must be protected from unauthorized access to protect employees, support company policies and fulfill legal requirements.

For this reason, an enterprise application should be configured to deliver the same security provisions for integrated content as it does for inherent, structured data.

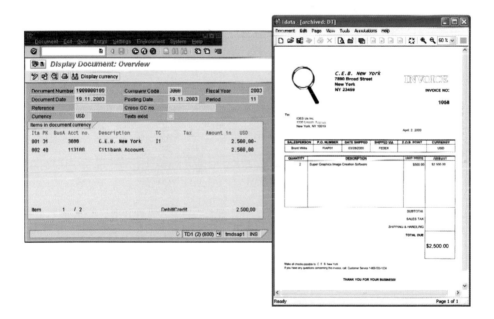

Figure 9.4: Accounts Payable—One Unified View to Business Information

From Transactions to Processes

To get the most out of content, organizations need to move beyond merely linking documents to transactions. To maximize content value, documents should be structured to align with business processes, rather than specific transactions. Typically, work is organized around a process designed to accomplish a specific objective (such as process orders or dispute management) rather than around completing simple transactions. For this reason, people often need access to content that exists beyond the scope of technologies that support transactions. Content needs to be structured to support entire processes. To recognize the need for this, let's examine a customer order. Customer orders span multiple technologies, including those that support:

• sales and distribution to process the initial order;

• production to create a requested product;

• materials management to initiate delivery; and

• a financial application to process the invoice.

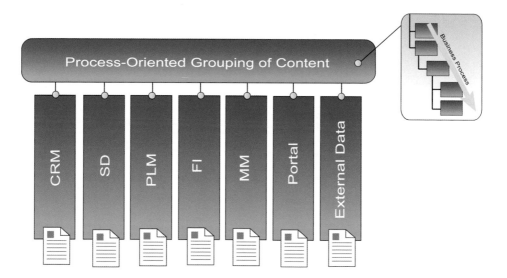

Figure 9.5: Moving From Transaction-based to Process-based Document Management

An integrated ECM system links documents and allows them to be associated with different business processes. In the case of a customer order, a folder can be created that displays all information related to the customer across various applications. Dynamically grouping real-time information effectively supports many daily operations. In such an example, an entry clerk accesses an account folder and sees all relevant documents, invoices, emails and receipts, regardless of where this content was created or which transactions were supported.

Leveraging Documents Across Disparate Applications

The days of one-shop enterprises have long passed as organizations today rely on best-of-breed implementations. This approach involves deploying various enterprise applications from different vendors. The same business content is often used across multiple applications and parts of documents are often isolated within specific applications or functions. These best-of-breed applications rarely integrate with each other, forcing organizations to develop custom interfaces to filter and feed relevant information. Document integration into enterprise applications provides a means to share business content across applications without extensive application development or customization. An underlying ECM system provides a central storage facility for all business content and grants access capabilities to various enterprise applications.

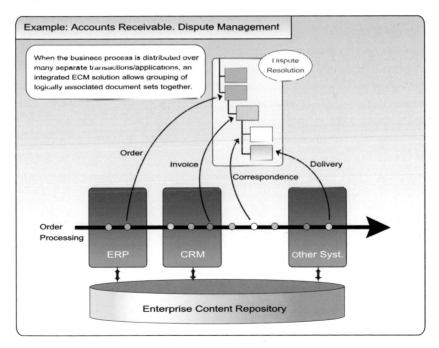

Figure 9.6: Process-Oriented Grouping of Related Documents
Spread Over Several Enterprise Applications

The Business Value of Enterprise Application Extensions

Now that we have explored how enterprise application extensions function, let's explore the business value delivered by EAE and examine some sample applications in accounts receivable, human resources and more.

Extending applications across an integrated ECM system improves operational efficiency and productivity, lowers technology and IT maintenance costs, and ensures compliance and reduced risk.

Improving Operational Efficiency and Productivity

In most accounting departments, core business operations revolve around optimizing working capital by efficiently handling receivables and managing payables, which encompasses dealing with volumes of paperwork. Across many organizations, accounting departments rely on counterproductive, resource-intensive and error-prone manual processes that increase costs, facilitate employee mistakes and decrease overall efficiency.

Accounts Payable: Taking Advantage of Cash Discounts

Most organizations find it increasingly difficult to manage the accounts payable process, since it involves numerous transactions and associated paper documents. Every invoice passes through several people for review, content edits and final sign-off before payment is made. Initially designed to ensure accurate appropriation and accounting, this lengthy process can cause missed due dates, incur late fees, and missed eligibility for cash discounts on invoices; not to mention the possibility for error each time an invoice is altered.

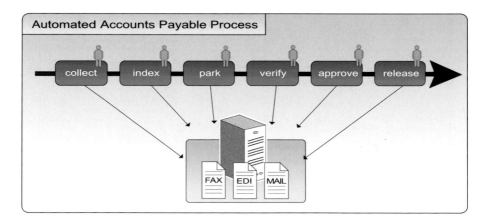

Figure 9.7: Central Electronic Document Storage Eliminates Manual Paper Handling

Global manufacturer Owens Corning required a solution to streamline its accounts payable process and automate the processing of 30,000 plus invoices per month, which entailed circumventing manual procedures, integrating disparate systems and eliminating underlying causes for errors.

Using an integrated ECM solution, employees open, sort and scan invoices into the system, which creates workflow items in both ERP and non-ERP systems that then route them to processors. "Prior to implementing the ECM solution, we had to depend on mail and faxes to route problem invoices to purchasing, which were much slower processes. Now, the purchasing agents can instantly pull up invoices. They can quickly call vendors, correct purchase orders and send them back to the Shared Services Center for processing so we can meet our discount terms," explains Owens Corning Senior Project Manager.

The ECM solution enabled Owens Corning a 40 percent boost of its output rate of invoices per day by eliminating manual procedures. Automatic processing and routing of EDI transactions to the purchaser saves about $2 per invoice and about $72,000 per year. Productivity gains also enhanced employee satisfaction, as they accomplish more with less time and frustration.

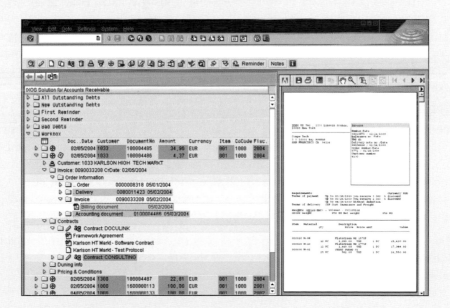

Figure 9.8: An Example of a Dispute Management Solution

An integrated ECM solution streamlines standard invoice verification, enabling paper documents to be scanned into the system in original format upon receipt, linking invoices to related documents in an ERP system and triggering the initiation of a workflow.

This workflow informs each appropriate agent of the invoice status, tracks the agent's activity and, when resolved, automatically sends it to the next agent until the process is complete and the final agent sends out payment. In minutes, an agent can validate the invoice electronically against order documents, since all relevant documents are scanned into the ECM repository. Robust document and records management capabilities enable the ECM system to maintain an audit trail of related activity for each invoice, so that agents can immediately review their status and perform invoice verification on an exceptional basis.

Accounts Receivable: Increasing Profitability by Reducing DSOs

The accounts receivable world revolves around collecting payment. The longer a payment remains outstanding (known as Daily Sales Outstanding or DSO), the less likely it will paid in full. An inefficient collection process prolongs collection time, increases bad debt and erodes bottom line revenue.

Employees in accounts receivable departments need supporting information from multiple sources to reconcile differences between customers and invoices. They must review account information generated throughout the organization before they can effectively field customer questions, troubleshoot problems and facilitate timely collection. Traditional processes have forced accounts receivable agents to manually pull relevant documents from multiple departments and filing systems, query colleagues and wait for information to be faxed or sent to them.

An integrated ECM solution streamlines the accounts receivable process by integrating disparate accounting, sales and support information into a central repository and providing a single point of access to it. The ECM solution captures order information as soon as it is entered or scanned into the system, links it to corresponding customer information and then archives this information. Accounts receivable staff simply need to enter basic customer information to access related information, reducing the time spent manually looking for information scattered across various systems.

In addition, an integrated ECM solution can deploy monitoring and measurement tools to track user activity and deliver an overview of the status of each process. This audit history helps accounts receivable agents understand and monitor the progress of each step in the collection process to identify where or why issues arise.

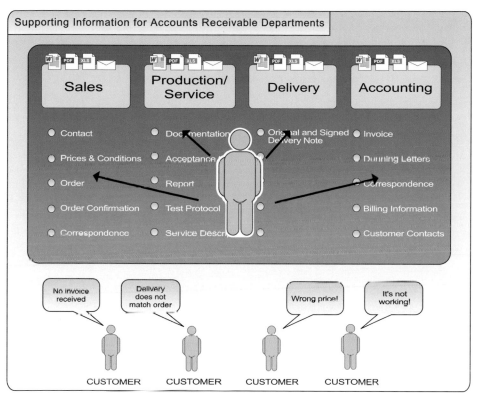

Employees in accounts receivable departments need supporting information from multiple sources to reconcile differences with customers.

Figure 9.9: Integrated ECM and EAF

By helping accounts receivable agents to identify issues that can delay payments, an integrated ECM solution helps to improve debt collection rates, increase free cash flow to lower the risk of bad debt write-off and reduce a company's credit line.

Reducing Operational Costs in Human Resource Departments

Human Resources (HR) professionals devote about 70 percent of their time performing routine administrative tasks such as changing address information, obtaining approval for travel or vacation and fielding employee questions regarding payment statements. These tasks generally require searching through stacks of paperwork, matching each document with the appropriate employee or candidate, populating forms and re-entering data into an HR system.

> Barclays Bank

BARCLAYS

Since its establishment over 300 years ago, Barclays Bank has earned a reputation as a leader in technological innovation. So, when mounds of accumulated HR paper documents started to threaten efficiency and the quality of service the organization offered to employees, Barclays Bank turned to technology for help.

Barclays implemented an ECM solution as their information hub that scans, stores, and links email and employee-related information and then, using a workflow, forwards it to the appropriate agent as an activity request. All 75,000 employee-related HR records are captured in a centralized repository and secure electronic access is provided to authorized users.

Records are now quickly retrieved and the need for many paper-based processes has been eliminated. As a result, response times to employee requests have significantly improved. In general, operational costs and resources have considerably decreased, while efficiency and productivity have increased.

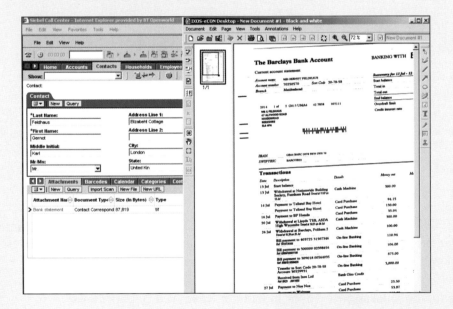

Figure 9.10: An Example of Document Access Within an ERP System

Integrating ECM with HR applications improves the overall performance of standard HR operations, while alleviating the demand these daily tasks place on HR staff. Traditionally, obtaining approval for sick leave might require HR staff to collect information from several people in multiple departments before submitting an approval request. An integrated solution provides instant access to the necessary information and associates it with corresponding policies, documents and colleagues.

Integrated solutions also increase HR employee productivity and reduce costs by streamlining employee administration, automating key business processes and offering employees self-service tools. The HR department is relieved from manually processing standard requests, enabling it to reassign staff to focus on more strategic tasks. Tight security controls enable organizations to comply with privacy regulations. All relevant information about an individual, whether applicant, employee or former employee, can be stored and maintained in a protected environment, reducing the risk of losing or misplacing confidential documents. ECM integrates this information with key business process applications to expedite the recruiting process, for example, and reduce the risk of losing good candidates due to a lengthy and complex hiring process.

Reduce IT Consolidation and Maintenance Costs

Managing Transactional Data

Every business process generates data and typically increases the volume of an enterprise application's database. The growing volume of data hampers system performance and slows down access to information. The prolonged backup and restoration of information adds to an administrator's workload and increases costs.

An integrated ECM solution offloads old data from an enterprise application, providing long-term access to archived information that is stored in a durable, tamper-proof format. This helps companies lower both the costs and risk associated with meeting data retention and disposal requirements. In addition, offloading data facilitates fast backup and recovery times, reduces administrative and hardware costs and decreases the time it takes to implement enterprise application upgrades.

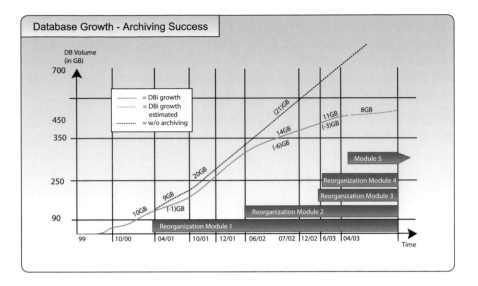

Figure 9.11: An Example of Data Archiving for Enterprise Applications

When an ECM solution offloads application data, it deletes it from a database, freeing up resources and space while allowing this information to be easily accessed. Users working within a transaction can access both online and offline data within seconds. Administrators can archive data when necessary and even schedule data archiving to enhance the application's performance.

Automating the Migration of Legacy Data

Organizations that rely on IT systems to support daily operations often need to access data that is generated long after some systems have become obsolete. Many primary business systems are relegated to legacy systems when organizations overhaul their IT infrastructure. This forces IT departments to integrate new applications and systems, while still maintaining a fragmented array of legacy systems once integral to the organization's operating efficiency. Consequently, many organizations decide to maintain legacy systems rather than decommission them, believing they can leverage their initial investment and maintain a more cost-effective solution. Maintaining these legacy systems often proves expensive, and can hamper future returns on technology investment and introduce operational inefficiencies.

General Motors (GM) India did not want excessive data slowing down its ERP system when it ramps up capacity or adds to its range of products. With a database that was growing at about 8 GB a month, the automotive giant decided that it made sense to maintain a ceiling on the database size, archive some data and yet have it within easy reach, rather than wait until the database was overloaded and resulted in a deterioration in performance.

The Opel division of GM India managed to achieve this objective—and more—by using an integrated ECM solution. Archived data comes from GM India's finance and materials management functions, which together generate most of the ERP data. In addition, local law requires that businesses retain financial data for a certain number of years, and the archiving system ensures that for GM India, such data is not just retained but readily available as well.

The result: a trimmer database, better ERP performance, improved business processes, and more—all without compromising usability and transparency. The integrated ECM solution has already begun to pay for itself with substantial initial direct savings, not to mention the cost of additional hard disks that GM India would have had to buy had it not decided to archive its ERP data. Besides these, the slimmer and more manageable database and better performance from its ERP system, other benefits GM India is deriving include faster management reporting and more timely input for financial analysis.

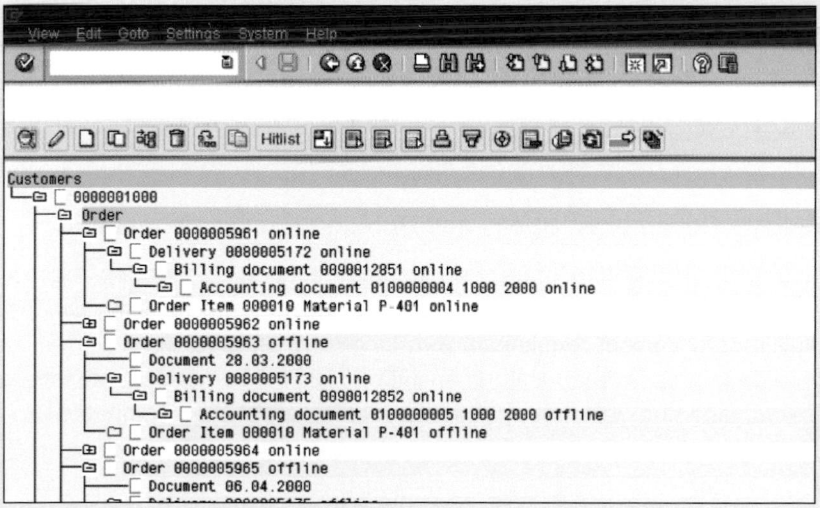

Figure 9.12: An Example of ERP Data Access

Capturing data and transforming it into usable information remains a critical objective in any organization, regardless of legacy programs, operating systems, hardware platforms and networks. Organizations that have a requirement to store data from inherited or outdated IT systems for reference or to comply with regulatory requirements should consider the following options:

1. Migrate data to more current systems: Large-scale legacy data migration can yield complexity, huge costs and significant risk to a project start-up.

2. Maintain existing legacy systems: Continuing to run and support old systems reduces legacy data migration costs but is not necessarily cost effective since maintaining access to old data can be expensive. This strategy also fails to address ongoing product and hardware support, as well as integration issues.

3. Legacy system data archiving: Adopting this strategy makes information and data readily available via various clients of the enterprise application. It avoids complex migration and associated costs, expedites the decommissioning process and ensures that regulatory requirements are fulfilled.

Ensuring Compliance and Reducing Risk

Although regulations vary from country to country, they consistently require that organizations track, manage and retain critical business information and present it upon request. Developing and implementing best practices for compliance requirements not only protects organizations from risk but helps them streamline operations, reduce administrative costs and proactively prepare to comply with emerging regulations. An integrated ECM solution plays an integral role in fulfilling evolving legal requirements by securely storing content for designated periods, linking related information, providing an audit history for each document and enabling organizations to access any document on demand.

Securely Retains Documents, Books and Booking Records/Vouchers

Financial records in accounting practices exemplify a core compliance requirement. Even though organizations generally store financial documents for extended periods, they fail to fulfill many current regulations with long-term storage alone. Organizations must also be able to present requested financial records on demand, demonstrate how each record was used and which other records contributed to the designated process.

Siemens was spending more and more money for the secure, long-term storage of its engineering drawings, invoices, reminder notices and other documents. The culprit responsible for the rising costs was their heterogeneous IT landscape which included nine different archiving systems.

A new, global archiving system with integrated document management functionality for the entire Siemens A&D group is solving this problem. All the technical documents created throughout the entire product lifecycle are archived; everything from engineering drawings to parts lists to customer service documents. The product data management system (PDMS) was also integrated directly with the document management solution.

Every location around the globe will benefit from the new solution, once it is linked. Authorized employees worldwide will be able to access the documents directly. The tedious photocopying, mailing and filing of duplicate copies at several locations will soon be a thing of the past. "The new document management solution greatly expedites our processes," reports Archiving Manager, Siemens A&D. "Siemens A&D has external partners manufacture various products for them. Soon, these partners will be able to retrieve the centrally archived engineering drawings themselves in just minutes—whereas mailing them used to take several days."

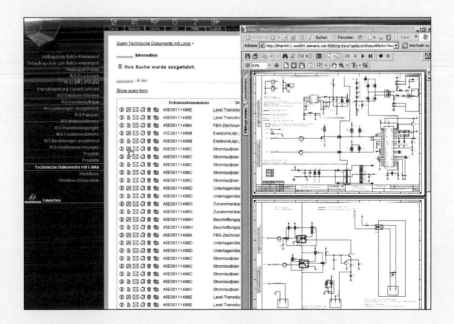

Figure 9.13: Siemens Automation & Drives' EAE Solution

An integrated ECM solution addresses these transaction-related requirements and satisfies fundamental storage requirements by archiving all documents in a central repository. The solution enables organizations to prove that financial records are accurate by linking these scanned records with related financial records. Employees can instantly retrieve purchase orders, customer requests, correspondence, supplier orders and amounts and distribution information to verify the accuracy of the amounts on the requested document.

An ECM solution also enables companies to link documents like invoices or lists to respective sections in an enterprise application. If an auditor requests a specific invoice, employees can quickly pull up all supporting documents to confirm the invoice's accuracy and justify its use. An audit trail will trace the activity path for each requested document. Administrators can prevent users from accessing confidential documents by encrypting data before the document is stored or transmitted. It also ensures secure, unalterable retention of documents in their original form, enabling organizations to benefit from aged ERP data that is maintained separately from the production environment and available on demand.

Jointly Managing Structured and Unstructured Content

A sales person who draws up a contract must collaborate with several departments and colleagues to complete the process: the legal department to ensure integrity; the technical department to check the project's feasibility and timeline; and corporate governance policies to make sure the contract follows guidelines. Only when the process is finished can the contract be linked to the sales process in the CRM or ERP system.

Enterprise Applications like ERP and CRM effectively perform transaction-oriented processing. However, data residing in enterprise applications is the result of work that has been performed and, in many cases, cannot effectively support other business processes. Many processes, like contract creation, still require collaborative efforts of employees across multiple departments.

Exception handling of invoices represents another process that requires employee collaboration. When an incoming vendor invoice does not fulfill the requirements in price, quality, quantity and more, it qualifies as an exception and requires special handling. For example, payment will be withheld if a product has a defective part. But payment has to be blocked in an ERP system before this can happen.

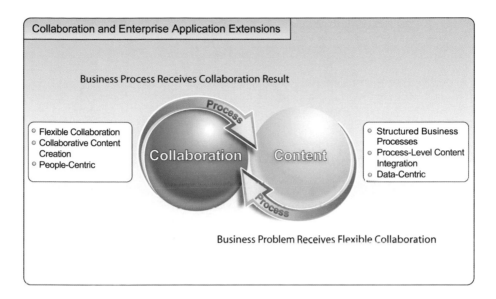

Figure 9.14: Collaboration and EAE

The accounting clerk has to contact the cost center that ordered the initial product. An employee then must personally resolve the conflict by writing letters, sending an email message or calling the vendor to rectify the problem. Resulting resolution efforts must be sent back to the ERP system, which will release or block the payment.

Integrating ECM with enterprise applications ensures that all content is available in multiple processes and instances, and that content availability does not depend on the originating enterprise application. Information is consolidated on a shared data model, permitting users to access structured information without having to work within a specific application. This improves productivity and efficiency by ensuring that everyone involved in key business processes can access related information, wherever it resides and at any time.

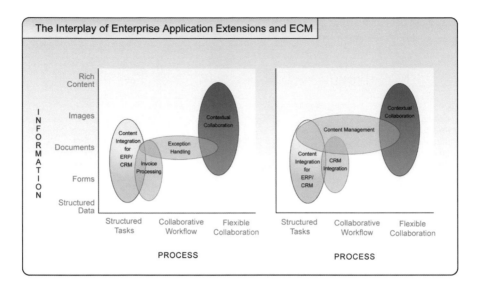

Figure 9.15: EAE in the Context of ECM

ECM and EAE

As part of an integrated platform, ECM promises to manage all business content—from paper documents, such as incoming vendor invoices and electronic records processed using an ERP system, to online documents, records, Web content and more. Enterprise application extensions enable employees to perform invoice verification and other routine procedures more effectively, using ECM to instantly access unstructured or structured content within enterprise applications. ECM gives organizations tight control over information in order to optimize business operations. By building a bridge to extend enterprise applications, ECM enables organizations to minimize the costs, risks and resources inherent in deploying disparate technologies and enterprise applications.

Chapters Related to Enterprise Application Extensions

Extending ERP into ECM further enables many components of ECM.

Chapter 4: **Search**	EAE enables users to search across numerical data using a basic word search, improving access to information in an organization's knowledge repository.
Chapter 6: **Document Management**	In order to improve efficiency, organizations can implement a document management system inside the firewall to manage all content, creating great efficiency and productivity gains.
Chapter 7: **Archiving & DLM**	Many litigation, compliance and knowledge management systems require the long-term storage of information in an electronic archive that saves content securely with recall over decades of time. A records management system provides a full audit trail and recall of important documents to prove that critical information has not been tampered with or destroyed.
Chapter 8: **WCM**	EAE extends ECM to all departments in an organization by incorporating the numerical data and tables contained in ERP systems into a secure knowledge repository. From here, content can be automatically published on Web sites to display accurate information in real time.
Chapter 14: **BPM**	BPM delivers an advanced workflow with extensive integration into other enterprise applications, incorporating transactions and numerical data into business processes as part of a comprehensive ECM solution.

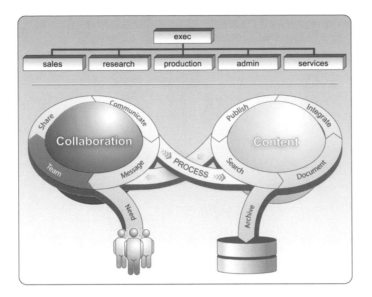

Figure 10.1: Collaboration

Teams are a component of Collaboration technology used in ECM suites.

Collaboration lies at the heart of teams and the way they work together. For this reason, it plays an important part in delivering comprehensive ECM solutions. In this chapter, we introduce the hyperlinked organization and discuss just how integral collaborative technologies are to ECM. User stories are included to illustrate key business benefits and demonstrate how ECM can streamline supply chain management and bid processing as an enterprise intranet and extranet solution.

TEAMS AND COLLABORATION

"The biggest, boldest, most stimulating and innovative projects often come from the most compelling need for a team or company to do something that will change the game: launch a sexy new product. Craft a breakthrough ad campaign. Change the logistics and the service rules in your niche." (Tom Peters, "The Wow Project," Fast Company, Issue 24).

In the new economy, change is the only constant. Exposed to a flood of new information daily, we continually filter and organize ideas, sources and content in order to make informed decisions. The pace of life has accelerated. We work in "Web time" to remain competitive in an increasingly complex environment. And we have to work hard to stay connected.

Sometimes we lose track of information. Good ideas get lost. We forget a link, erase a critical voicemail message, or lose an important attachment in our email inbox. But even if we could effectively capture new ideas, to execute them we need to gather people together, identify and work with experts and key contributors and find and distribute the right information. And we need to do it all in a heartbeat.

Collaboration in a business context links processes and individuals across different locations and time zones to create a combined work environment where people work together to share and circulate ideas, experiences and knowledge to meet project deadlines. These consolidated "work environments" are essentially virtual projects. Projects and project teams are central to the way we work today. According to Tom Peters, all white-collar work is project work, and therefore "all work of economic value is project work." For the office worker, project work is based on office automation using computer technology, groupware, intranets, extranets, the Web and e-commerce applications.

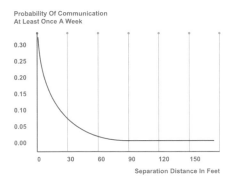

Office Location	Probability Of Research Collaboration
Same Corridor	10.3%
Same Floor	1.9%
Different Floor	0.3%
Different Buildings	0.4%

Figure 10.2: The Probability of Effective Collaboration Depends on Proximity

In this chapter, we will discuss three generations of collaborative offerings within global enterprises. The first generation focuses on tools as the actual means of facilitating collaborative exchanges: Team Collaborative Applications (TCAs), intranets, Web conferencing and virtual meeting rooms and instant messaging.

The second generation of enterprise collaboration acknowledges that these key capabilities have been provided and concentrates on the ability to connect them with one another and within the enterprise itself.

The third or future generation of enterprise collaboration describes the transformation from simple collaborative exchanges into rich collaborative experiences. This generation involves the full integration of collaborative tools with all applications within the ECM solution suite. And this integration will be transparent—an extension rather than a redefinition of the way that people work.

Team Collaborative Applications

TCAs are Web-based software programs that enable groups of users or project teams to work together using a variety of applications. These applications range from collaborative environments or shared "workspaces" to messaging and conferencing applications. According to this definition, email or the ability to electronically send messages from one computer to another through a telecommunications network could be considered a TCA.

Saving time was the critical driver behind the creation and development of team collaborative applications. By allowing people to collaborate according to individual schedules across different time zones, organizations could significantly shorten project cycles and release products and services to market faster, well before the competition. The benefit of "real-time" or synchronous collaboration becomes obvious when we consider that instant feedback allows teams to make immediate modifications, and allows everyone on the team to be more responsive. Synchronous collaborative software allows geographically distributed team members to work together in real time by transferring files, chatting, sharing a whiteboard and using voice or video technology. In comparison, asynchronous collaborative software allows teams to collaborate remotely, but requires each person to work separately, communicating with other members using file sharing applications or email messages.

Consider the following Lockheed Martin excerpt. Building the complex fighter planes requires the collaboration of hundreds of people across multiple organizations. Hardcopy documentation and email systems could not effectively support a project of this magnitude. Synchronous or real-time collaboration enables an organization to work with its partners and suppliers in a shared workspace, exchanging documents and following structured processes, without the typical constraints imposed by time and space.

Percentage of Global 2000 Knowledge Workers with Instant Messaging, Web Conferencing and Teamware Functionality

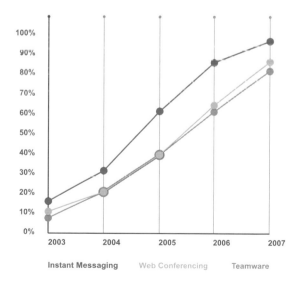

Figure 10.3: Predictions for Growth in Collaboration

Building complex combat airplanes requires collaboration among hundreds of people across multiple organizations and hundreds of requests for proposals from suppliers, all of which needs to be managed in a secure environment. For Lockheed Martin Tactical Aircraft Systems, using hardcopy documents for this purpose was no longer feasible.

Deployed for the Joint Strike Fighter (JSF) program, ECM is now the hub of Lockheed Martin's secure suppliers extranet, enabling the company to put its requirements online, allowing suppliers to access and bid on them, while managing the documents and workflow in the background. A collaboration engine provides team work support.

"ECM has the out-of-the-box functionality we needed for security and collaboration… and so far, its deployment for the JSF program has provided big paybacks in terms of time and cost savings," says Data Manager, Lockheed Martin Tactical Aircraft Systems.

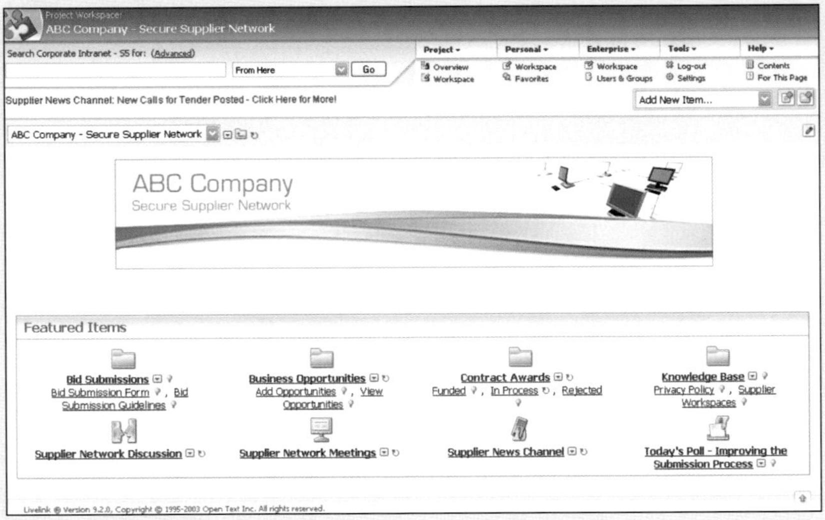

Figure 10.4: An Example of a Supplier Extranet

The trend to support synchronous collaboration has grown since 2001. Collaborative team software has evolved to incorporate third-party, real-time applications like instant messaging, file exchange, application sharing, whiteboarding and online meetings. Integrating these capabilities allows people to collaborate using one program without having to move among different applications to collaborate using different methods. This functionality has expanded beyond an online presence or project workspace to wireless access, as people can receive notification about project changes via a pager or cell phone.

With the development of TCAs and virtual project collaboration, the foundation for the Enterprise Content Management (ECM) market had been laid, driven by the need to provide workers with seamless access to combined collaboration and content.

Intranets as a Collaboration Platform

The development of intranets was a giant step forward in the evolution of collaborative applications and of the ECM market as a whole. Before Intranets there were main-frames, then mini-computers, then personal computers, then workstations and office networks. And then there were intranets. By 1996, most large corporations were busy building their first intranets.

Why the rush to build intranets? There were two reasons. First, large organizations had already invested heavily in placing a PC on every desktop and then building appropriate network infrastructures to connect all employees throughout far-flung enterprises. Secondly, the small incremental investment required to build intranets on top of existing networks made good business sense.

The initial excitement about intranets was tied to an internal publishing medium that enabled corporations to post internal policies and procedures, human resources forms and sales collateral. Electronic access to this new information-sharing medium eliminated the cost and time needed to physically reproduce lengthy documents and re-route them through inter-office mail or overnight delivery services. While this was important, it was just the beginning of the many benefits intranets would offer.

But intranets are about much more than publishing and sharing information. Intranets eliminate the barriers that keep people from collaborating on projects effectively. With an intranet, users plug in to project teams and workgroups via a Web browser, a phone jack and a password. Regardless of the number of team members and their locations, intranets erase time zones and geographic boundaries. Whether working in the office, on the road or at home, team members can be productive and contribute to their group's effort at any time by simply "logging on."

Unlike client-server environments, intranets provide a server-centric approach to project collaboration. Intranets create universally available, cross-platform networks that enable working groups to communicate, share tools and information, assign and track tasks, and manage complex projects. Consequently, companies find it cost effective to enhance their infrastructure using intranets because they can easily extend the reach of their business processes to remote users.

Intranets would eventually evolve into what we call "extranets" and extend the enterprise beyond project teams to include partners, suppliers, and customers in business projects and procedures.

Online Meetings

While intranets introduced a consolidated workplace that gives people a place to share information, they did not provide an effective means for users to collaborate on information in real time. The most effective collaborative applications incorporate a real-time meeting tool that lets users set up and attend meetings quickly and easily. Bringing together team members from multiple locations and times zones gives them a sense of proximity and ensures that projects stay on time and on course. By hosting meetings online, organizations can significantly reduce travel costs.

Figure 10.5: Online Meeting with Shared Chat Panel

The Miller Group, the UK's largest privately owned housebuilding, property development and construction company set out to diminish its project management costs and allow for increased collaboration and productivity within the company. This business strategy became an IT strategy, resulting in the implementation of a contact and document management solution.

The ECM-based system provides a basis for improved project management by allowing the company to set up a separate project work space for each customer. All necessary contact and production scheduling information can now be easily accessed within the system. The solution is also the foundation for an online accessible human resources system that holds all employee-related files, including payroll information.

Depending on the project's location, the Miller Group has to follow different planning and legal regulations. With the help of ECM, the company created a single repository to standardize processes and to accordingly simplify and ensure compliance. In brief, the increased accessibility, project and departmental collaboration have resulted in time, effort and cost savings.

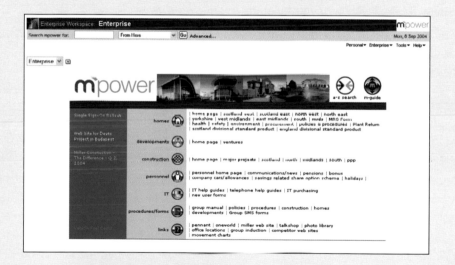

*Figure 10.6: The Miller Group's Enterprise Workspace for
Standardizing Business Processes*

When they are integrated with project workspaces, online meetings present teams with an effective structure for collaboration—before, during and after meetings. Coordinators can view personal and team calendars while scheduling a meeting. Real-time scheduling functionality ensures that people have an accurate view of everyone else's available time. During meetings, presenters can share their desktops with attendees for broadcasting and collaborative editing. Other collaboration tools such as whiteboards, Web polls, a shared chat panel and private instant messaging are also available. Once a meeting session is over, content from the meeting is automatically saved into a shared knowledge repository as a permanent, searchable knowledge asset.

Instant Messaging

While online meetings enable organizations to bring users together from across the globe, they do not facilitate immediate, one-time collaborative exchanges. Users have to set up a meeting, schedule attendees and formally gather in the virtual meeting space before any form of collaborative interaction can occur.

In the past, when users required a quick, one-time collaborative exchange with one another, they typically resorted to email. In recent years, organizations have become increasingly flooded with consumer instant messaging (IM) services.

There are two key benefits associated with enterprise instant messaging: real-time collaboration and compliance with regulations. The ability for users to initiate one-time collaborative exchanges with one another, or to host public conference rooms, delivers a new level of spontaneity to collaboration facilities. Enterprise instant messaging applications enable users to automatically save the contents of their collaborative exchanges into the information repository, building the corporate knowledge base as a by-product of collaboration. Furthermore, enterprise IM provides IT with better control over storing and indexing IM conversations.

In regulated industries such as financial services and healthcare, emerging SEC and HIPAA regulations are compelling organizations to archive the contents of instant messaging sessions in addition to the contents of emails. For example, a developer and project manager may have an important conversation about software architecture using IM. Two months later, when patent litigation demands that the company produces all records of interaction concerning this same architecture, the conversation can be easily accessed from a central repository, where it has been stored and indexed. To provide this degree of control over content, it is most effective to integrate IM with ECM.

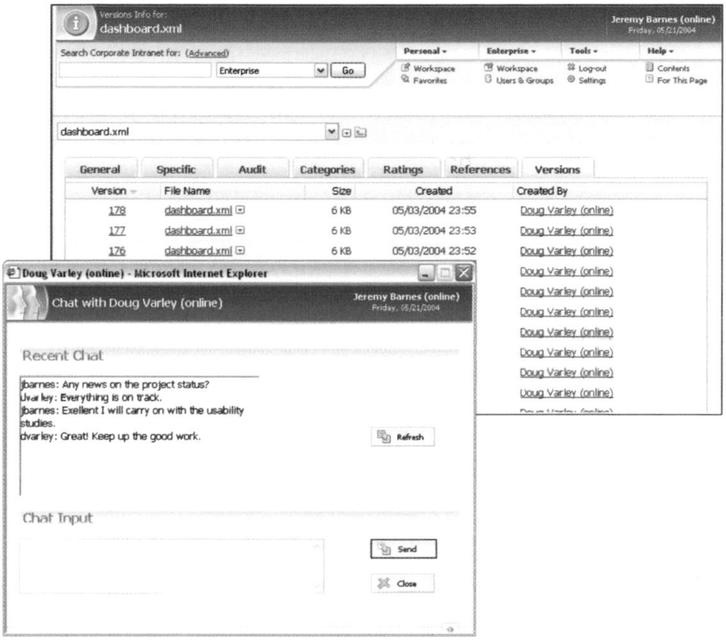

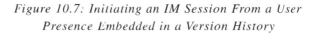

Figure 10.7: Initiating an IM Session From a User
Presence Embedded in a Version History

ECM and Application Integration

The first generation of enterprise collaborative tools emerged in response to the growth of the corporate email market, which in time would expose the challenges associated with asynchronous collaboration in an enterprise context. While these applications focused on enabling collaboration through specific feature sets, the second generation of collaborative tools evolved to integrate these features within an enterprise, extending the value of first generation collaborative tools. To illustrate this development, let's examine why email fails as an effective collaborative tool.

Repository-Based Collaboration; "Why Email is Not Enough"

Finding information in an ad hoc fashion over a computer network requires a search engine. Locating people on a network requires messaging technology. These two technologies are the primary tools adopted to support the business-to-consumer market on the Internet. Companies such as Google™ and Yahoo!® Messenger capitalized on this opportunity and have risen to the top in popularity.

Despite their popularity, these tools are not effective within a corporate intranet. This is because a corporation runs according to established procedures and processes. If a person within a company could search and locate any information, the company could risk exposing confidential or restricted information. To prevent this from happening, structured access to information is required. The technology that controls this access is known in broader terms as document management.

Furthermore, people working together in an ad hoc fashion are very inefficient. Email-based collaboration is an ineffectual way to work because it is fundamentally unordered or disorganized.

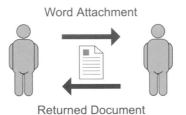

Figure 10.8: Email Collaboration Between Individuals

The most effective solution is repository-based collaboration.

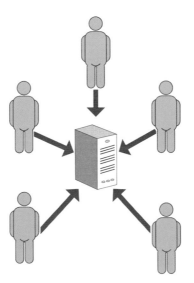

Figure 10.9: Document Collaboration Among Groups

Repository-based collaboration is different from email-based collaboration. For example, a knowledge worker is required to disseminate a document for approval to a group of colleagues. Using messaging-based collaboration entails a document being sent via email as an attachment. While it is possible to email a document to a group of people simultaneously, problems occur when modifications are made to the document, which is then emailed back to the author. Depending on the size of the group, the author could end up with many different versions of the same document and consolidating these would be a time consuming task.

By creating a library or repository that houses the document, group members can be given access to a single document in a single repository, and everyone shares in updating the document. This is called repository-based collaboration and it provides a global method for teams to work together and access knowledge. Confusion is eliminated because a definitive version of a document exists. People working on the document are much more productive because their work is organized according to a defined process. The flow of information can be outlined and mapped to a workflow. Chapter 14 describes in more detail using workflow to model processes.

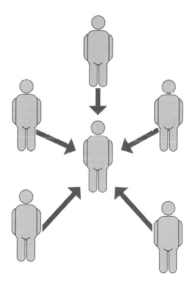

Figure 10.10: Support for Multiple Users

Repository-based collaboration enables organizations to become more agile because people can locate and collaborate on accurate information quickly and easily—making the appropriate decisions and leaving no lapse in time between opportunities and responses, or problems and resolutions. Effective ECM applications deliver integrated search, document management, workflow and project collaboration technologies, which can all be accessed via an industry standard browser. Such wide accessibility makes managing documents, projects and processes available to potentially thousands of users.

Online meeting and calendaring capabilities can be added to round out the offering and ensure that team meetings are prepared, scheduled and conducted effectively. Instant messaging applications can embed user presence directly into the enterprise application.

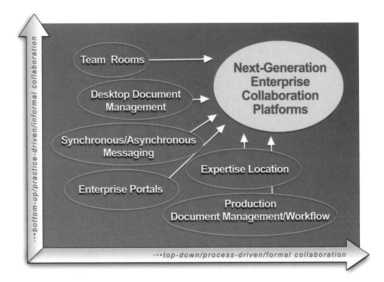

Figure 10.11: Next Generation Enterprise Collaboration Platforms
©Ovum Information Management Practice

Extranets and Online Communities

In order to streamline internal and external processes—and effectively manage business supply chains—Web-based extranets are emerging as a viable solution for many organizations' growing global collaboration needs.

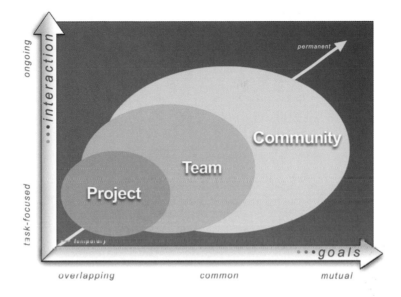

Figure 10.12: Collaborating Across Project Teams and Trading Communities

Collaboration with partners and suppliers poses an ongoing challenge as organizations work from remote locations and across time zones, often using disparate resources and pools of information. Just as intranets have enabled companies to share information and collaborate across the enterprise, Web-based extranets empower companies to strengthen external communications and increase efficiency by facilitating secure information exchange with partners and associates outside of the firewall.

Organizations were quick to understand the benefits of extending their intranet platform into the business operations of partners and suppliers. By involving external partners in their business processes, organizations can access external domain knowledge and expertise, implement best practices at every level with every process, enhance logistical processes, reduce product development cycles, create new services and improve competitive position.

From supply-chain management to regulatory compliance, manufacturing and engineering, an integrated extranet platform allows organizations to maximize their investment in diverse technologies and improve operational efficiency. Extranets enable organizations to create, sustain and manage e-communities or e-marketplaces—global trading communities where the borders and barriers between partners and suppliers are replaced by virtual teams. Essentially a collection of integrated extranets, an e-community lets organizations communicate across diverse computing environments, complete business-to-business transactions, improve logistics and share knowledge and expertise on a global scale to improve efficiencies and increase profits.

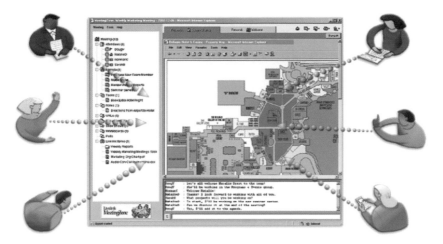

Figure 10.13: Global Collaboration

Global Reach With Wireless Access

While the wireless Web enables people to access the latest stock reports, weather, movie reviews and email conveniently from mobile devices, organizations still lack the business applications that enable their workers to obtain information and collaborate in real time. Wireless accessibility gives professionals access to information from mobile devices at any time, from anywhere, enabling them to react to new business opportunities more quickly to make better decisions. These devices allow users to continually collect information from multiple channels and distribute this information across the enterprise.

Contextual Collaboration

The success of projects, initiatives and innovations within organizations relies on performance. Successful businesses identify and manage key processes to drive performance. No matter how structured a process is, however, one component cannot be structured: people. The reality of businesses is that people run businesses—not technology. For this reason, ECM needs to effectively integrate people, processes and information.

Many organizations that have workflow, document management and collaborative applications in place are realizing the need for integration. Consider the value in combining an online review meeting with an approval workflow process. When the necessary stakeholders gather to review a document for approval, an integrated system allows approvals to occur at the conclusion of the meeting, without manually updating a workflow.

> CARE International

Having the right knowledge at the right time is critical when it comes to responding to humanitarian emergencies. With CARE's knowledge spread across 70 country offices and with federation members on every continent, it is imperative that CARE be able to capture, make accessible and leverage its knowledge resources.

Using collaboration technology, CARE International can streamline processes; manage, review and approve proposals for new projects, development and humanitarian efforts online; and securely share financial information, lengthy presentations and best practices around the world. Since 2001, CARE's ECM use has increased 600 percent.

For the past five years, ECM has been an essential part of CARE's strategy to develop a global e-community dedicated to relief efforts and the provision of humanitarian assistance. By adopting ECM globally, CARE International will be able to use ECM functionality to support approximately 800 projects in more than 70 countries.

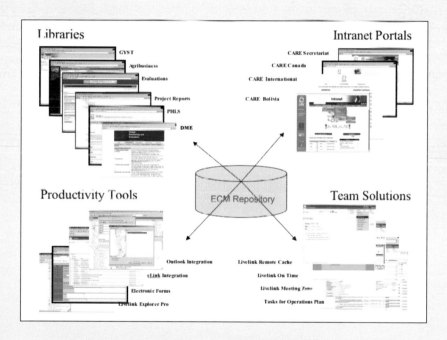

Figure 10.14: CARE's Global Team Solutions

The next generation of enterprise collaboration will introduce tighter integration of real-time collaboration with the full feature set of ECM applications like document management and workflow, Web content management (WCM), ERP, CRM and other applications within an ECM suite.

As technologies develop, we will see the graceful escalation from simple collaborative exchange to rich, interactive experiences. Collaborative capabilities will extend across the enterprise and touch all aspects of the ECM platform. The requirement to provide collaboration with context will cause organizations to create more targeted interfaces to leverage effective collaborative capabilities. Users will be able to initiate an IM session based on an email document stored inside an archiving or records management system. The document will be seamlessly accessed from a shared repository and the session could expand into a virtual meeting room to involve more participants. In this meeting, users could share applications to reach consensus about the document, and then automatically update content stored in the Web content management system. A persistent shared virtual workspace will allow users to collaborate simultaneously on content—for example, the screen will display two cursors and edits made in real time. What the future of collaborative applications promises is the ability to transparently connect content, people and processes between the back office and the front office of an enterprise, significantly improving productivity and cost-effectiveness.

> M+W Zander

As one of the world's leading companies in facility engineering and management, M+W Zander builds systems that often require the collaboration of several hundred engineers from all over the world. Engineering projects tend to last a year or longer, and the company incurs large costs trying to get all team members together in one place.

M+W Zander used an ECM solution to establish a single collaboration platform for all needs. The system is used to exchange vital documents and project information and it provides a virtual meeting place for the team members. The platform is also used to answer customer requests for information and pricing, and for communication with subcontractors and suppliers.

The collaboration platform has proven beneficial for all involved parties. Experts can now share their knowledge and expertise, team members save time and customers feel informed, giving M+W Zander a competitive edge by gaining more knowledge-able workers, saving costs and keeping customers happy.

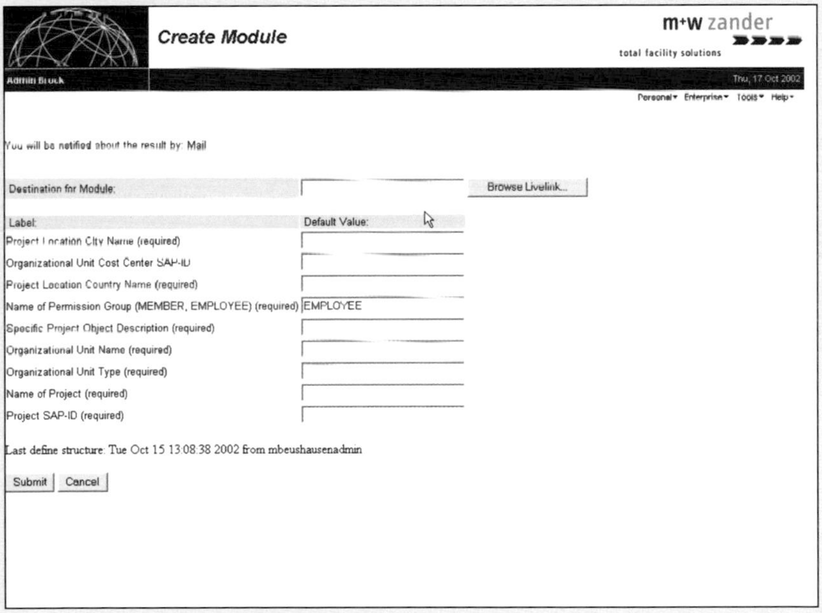

Figure 10.15: M+W Zander's Collaborative ECM Platform

Other Chapters Related to Teams and Collaboration

Collaboration is one of the key components of ECM. Many ECM technologies are related to collaboration.

Chapter 6: **Document Management**	To improve efficiency, organizations can implement a document management system inside the firewall to manage content in a secure repository, creating great efficiency and productivity gains.
Chapter 7: **Archiving & DLM**	Many litigation, compliance and knowledge management systems require the long-term storage of information in an electronic archive that saves content securely with recall over decades of time. A records management system provides a full audit trail and recall of important documents to prove that critical information has not been tampered with or destroyed.
Chapter 12: **Rich Media & DAM**	Rich media is the future of collaboration with online meetings, and support for integrated messaging technologies, including voice and video.
Chapter 14: **BPM**	BPM unites people, processes and information; collaboration plays a key role in many, if not all, business processes.

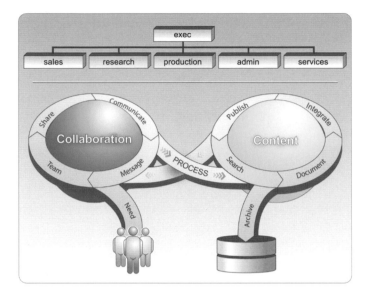

Figure 11.1: Portals

Portals are part of the Collaboration technology used in ECM suites. This chapter examines portal technology in detail in the larger context of ECM. The applications of ECM in this chapter include one company's transformation of a portal framework into an extranet application to manage quality control, inventory levels, employee training and sales and marketing programs.

PORTALS

Portal software provides access via a Web browser into all of an organization's information assets and applications. Under the portal umbrella, you will find all sorts of systems, including business Intelligence applications, content and document management, enterprise resource planning (ERP) systems, data warehouses, search and retrieval facilities, as well as any other application accessible through a Web interface.

Portals are often seen as the cure-all for integrating the various technological components of an Enterprise Content Management suite, but there is more to enabling software tools to work synergistically than simply providing a window into underlying applications. Nonetheless, portals have been widely adopted as a means of bringing knowledge-based applications to a mass audience.

Today, few "pure play" portal vendors remain In the market. That is not to say that the technology did not work or has gone away; conversely, most leading suppliers of portal software have been acquired by vendors of suite-based solutions to provide the infrastructure for integration of the suite components.

In order to respond to rapid growth, Krispy Kreme initially developed a business-to-business (B2B) extranet to streamline communications between its headquarters and retail outlets. The extranet, however, posed security risks by enabling any authorized user access to all of its content. With no means of segregating applications and data according to users' needs, Krispy Kreme's extranet precluded executives from sharing confidential financial data.

To gain the security and efficiency needed to support its growth, Krispy Kreme turned to a portal framework to develop MyKrispyKreme, a gateway to the company's operations. Using standard Web browsers, users access a unified, organized interface tailored to the content and applications they require for their responsibilities.

"The portal enables us to integrate our business processes across our store network into a complete, easy-to-use information framework. With MyKrispyKreme in place, we have elevated the time-honored business of making doughnuts, allowing us to operate more efficiently and gain competitive advantage," says Krispy Kreme's Chief Information Officer.

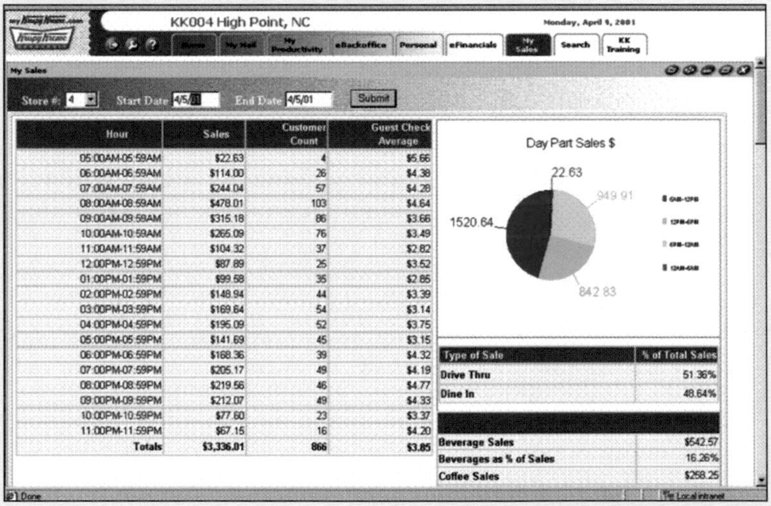

Figure 11.2: Krispy Kreme's Portal

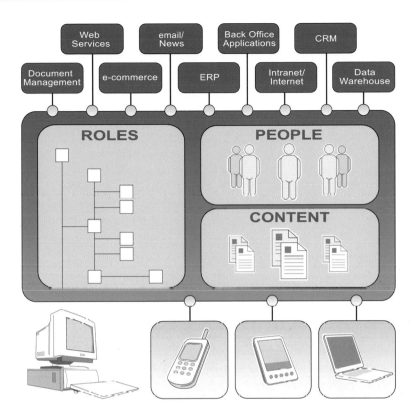

Figure 11.3: Systems Under the Portal Umbrella

Portal Components

Portals provide a secure, single point of interaction with diverse information, business processes and people, personalized to a user's specific needs and responsibilities. There is a good analogy between what portals add to Web applications and what window managers (like Microsoft® Windows) add to operating systems (like MS-DOS). Both provide a consistent and uniform way to interact with applications.

Portlets, widgets and gadgets are all names for the visible active components users see within portal pages. In simple terms, these are the connector programs that operate inside a portal to present information from another application or another information resource.

Portal servers provide common services such as application connectivity, integration, administration and presentation. Basically, a portal is the place where all the action takes place before you see a page appear in your Web browser window.

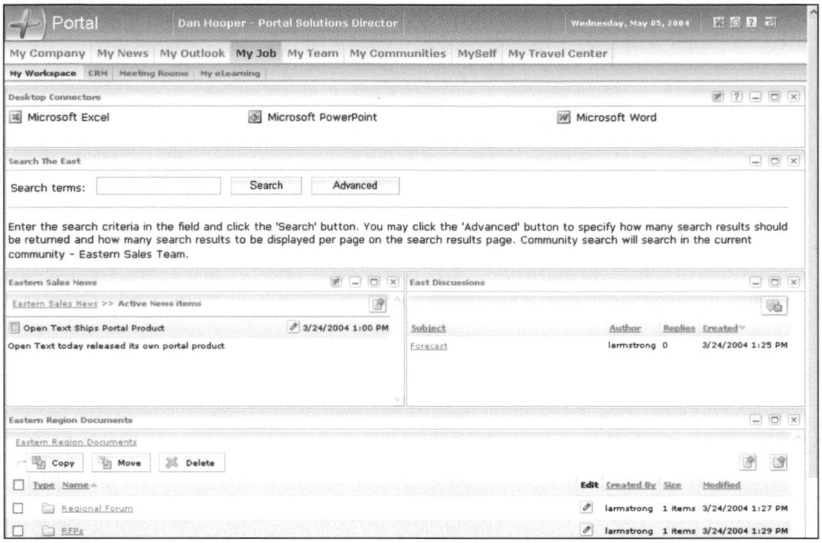

Figure 11.4: An Enterprise Portal

The beginnings of portal technology can be traced back to the late 1990s. The most frequently visited Internet sites were those that provided search tools to find information on the Web. In December, 1996, Yahoo!®, one of the most popular search sites, unveiled new personalization features that enabled its users to configure a personal page containing selected links and information resources, called My Yahoo!®. My Yahoo! went far beyond just being able to store links to your favorites Web pages; by pulling content from various Web applications, My Yahoo! allowed you to see stock quotations, weather reports, the latest news and movie releases all on a single (albeit busy) Web page. Other search sites including Infoseek, Lycos® and Excite® quickly followed suit and by the end of 1997, AOL®, Microsoft® and Netscape® sought to exploit their position as Web browser suppliers to jump on the personalization bandwagon.

The addition of portal technology would take business applications one step further by enabling users to automatically create a single, personalized interface to access internal corporate knowledge, along with external information. Portals brought new value by combining the type of personal information that was commonly available on consumer portals, such as My Yahoo!, with other external information, such as specialized subscription feeds, live news feeds and Web content pre-sorted into industry categories. Portals would provide customizable search, navigation and access to industry-specific categories of business content on the Web, as well as providing access to personalized views of content within various document repositories.

> Alte Leipziger Lebensversicherung

Today, more and more policies are sold by brokers and independent agents having a variety of product offerings from several companies in their portfolio. The Alte Leipziger Group already generates 80 percent of its revenue through this sales channel. The company's success therefore depends very much on the loyalty of these agents.

With its agent portal, the insurance company delivers a wealth of online information to its business partners. These include the policies sent, damage claims received, and any scanned correspondence. In addition, at the touch of a button, agents can view all printed material such as application forms or brochures. They can download them to their laptop, print them out or order hardcopies online.

Thanks to the quick availability of the latest information, agents are able to conduct more knowledgeable and effective sales presentations. The advantages to Alte Leipziger are obvious: the improved quality of services increases agent satisfaction and intensifies their loyalty to the company. The financial company benefits by attracting more agents, which in turn has the effect of winning more new customers. "Our agent portal strengthens the relationship with our brokers, reduces expenses and generates more revenue," says the Project Leader for Portal Development at Alte Leipziger.

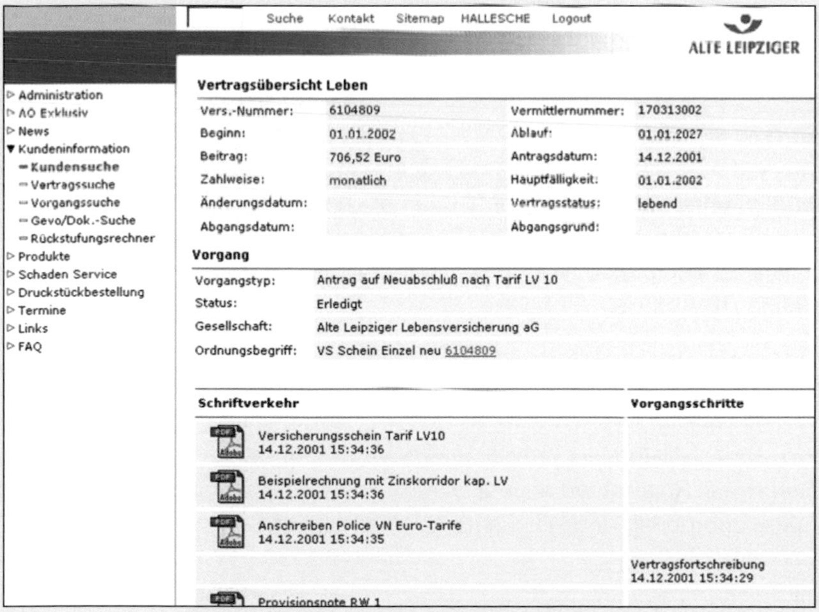

Figure 11.5: Alte Leipziger's Agent Portal

Aggregation

Effectively managing content and applications across the global enterprise becomes increasingly difficult as the user community expands and corporate responsibilities become more complex. Furthermore, constantly changing work environments complicate the delivery of information to users because the growing host of business applications cannot interact with one another. Portal technology enables organizations to effectively control the access and distribution of information with a unified point of access. A unique portal framework integrates and delivers all enterprise content and system resources.

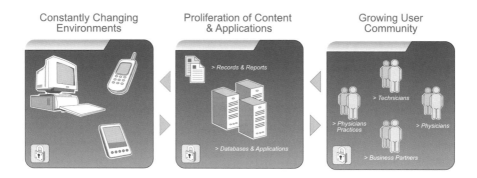

Figure 11.6: Creating Connections With Vital Assets

Enterprise portals allow for a seamless and transparent connection between collaborative environments and enterprise content. To refine and focus enterprise content, they provide a unified portal interface or "doorway" into other document or knowledge repositories and a wide range of enterprise applications. Connecting ECM applications and repositories offers organizations comprehensive content integration and greater return on investment from existing legacy systems.

Personalization

Portals allow administrators to provide users with content tailored to their assigned organizational roles. Role-based access control ensures that appropriate information is delivered to the appropriate individuals in the organization.

> St. John's Hospital

St. John's Hospital is a regional healthcare center serving central and southern Illinois. Over 600 physicians representing approximately 30 specialties and sub-specialties are on the medical staff. The healthcare industry is notorious for developing department-based solutions, so St John's challenge was to create a consistent environment that would support its close working relationship with another local healthcare institution, Memorial Medical Center.

In order to provide the physicians of both St. John's and Memorial with immediate access to the information and applications they need, St. John's implemented a physician's portal solution. SaintsNet, as it is called, delivers targeted, personalized content and applications to users based on their needs and preferences. Through a secure, single sign-on mechanism, the physician population has access to announcements, health sciences information and various other applications.

Prior to implementing the portal, approximately 600 doctors with privileges at both hospitals were required to learn different systems at each hospital and memorize several different sign-on sequences. A single point of access to all of the systems means that physicians can review critical information online from their homes, clinics and other locations. Since doctors can review images and confer online, an on-call radiologist, for example, who may be 15 to 20 miles from the hospital, can look at images online and make a decision immediately regarding a patient's status.

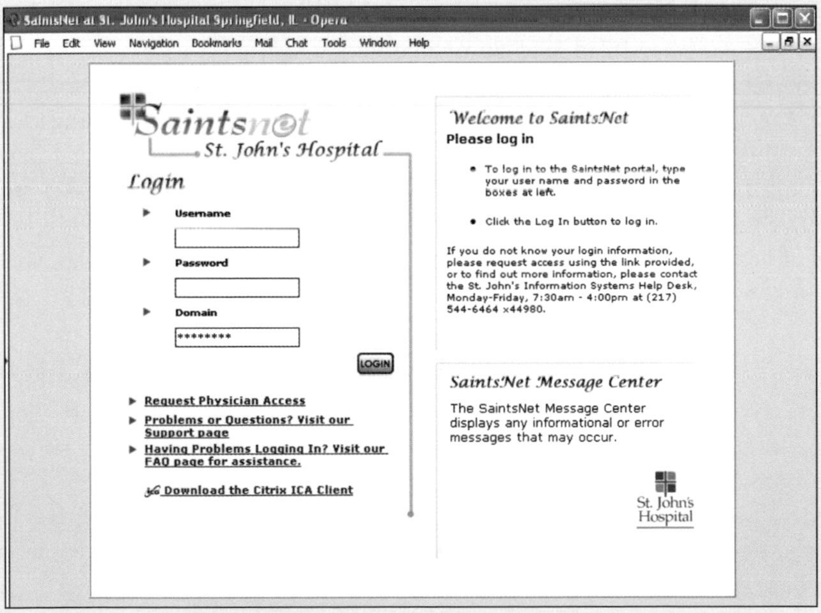

Figure 11.7: St. John's Intranet

To enhance productivity, portals provide a personalized environment that enables users to control information that is delivered to their workspaces. Used in combination with sophisticated search functionality, users can refine their access to information and further customize their work environments by choosing to view only a portion of the resources to which they have access. In addition to tailoring content and application access, users can easily customize many aspects of their portal interface. These attributes include colors, navigational orientation, frame size and position, tab order and general application and content organization.

Integration

Adding value to existing ECM systems, portals integrate with back-office and depart-mental applications, enabling users to view all the information relevant to their business needs. An integration framework allows organizations to unite their entire information infrastructure, including back-office, Microsoft® Office, ERP and CRM applications, as well as decision support tools. Chapter 9, Enterprise Application Extensions, describes how an ECM infrastructure can be extended to consolidate applications, increase productivity and improve return on investments in technology.

Hosting Services

Imagine the possibility of renting software on a "pay as you go" basis. Typically, we only use about one third of the full feature set of a software package and yet we pay for all the facilities that we do not use. Software is generally sold on a license-to-use basis—what customers actually pay for are the rights to use the software, not the physical disk that the software is shipped upon. Most licenses give the customer the rights to use the software in perpetuity. A good deal, but software develops at such a rapid rate that after a period of only two years, a product that was "ahead of its time" could become a dinosaur amid new products on the market. Therefore, in addition to purchasing a license to use a software product, there is typically an additional fee to maintain the software—that is, to automatically get all the new releases as the package is developed.

Application Service Providers (ASPs) saw the possibility of renting Web-based software products on a pay-per-use license. They would create powerful, secure computer warehouses to host software applications and allow customers to rent the software for an agreed period. The ASP would provide the back-office services such as regular backup and software maintenance as part of the deal, and customers could rent just the features they needed. Think of a hotel as a working analogy. You can rent a room, a suite or a whole floor; you can rent for a weekend, a week or a month.

To help improve the capabilities of the combat medic team, the U.S. Army had a goal of cross-training its entire field of medics. To achieve this goal, existing and future medical education documents, content, applications and services would need to be integrated through a worldwide training portal for 42,000 Army medics.

The portal is known as 91W, after the classification of medics who have advanced training in nursing and combat medicine. It provides medics, officers and other army personnel with secure and personalized role-based access to content, applications, services and productivity tools. By using the 91W portal, medics across the globe can review training materials, search medical cases and communicate with instructors and trainees. Medics and trainees also access the 91W portal through Army Knowledge Online (AKO), a Web site serving more than one million military personnel.

"This is a ground-breaking project for us. The 91W portal will help the U.S. Army achieve its goal of increasing medical readiness," says a Colonel in the U.S. Army Medical Service.

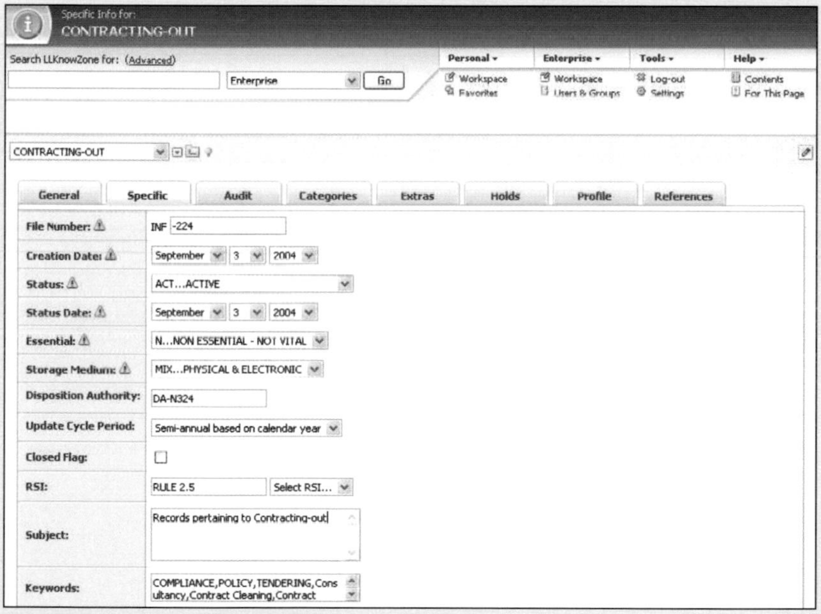

Figure 11.8: An Example of ECM for Records Management

ECM and Portals

Most organizations are struggling to manage the proliferation of content repositories that result from mergers and acquisitions, departmental solutions and customized applications. As their content stores grow, companies are realizing that this critical business asset needs to be supported by an integrated infrastructure that consolidates content repositories. When combined with ECM and search technology, portals provide doorways into multiple repositories and applications, improving access to information and productivity. Other returns on investment include reduced IT costs and accelerated decision making and time-to-market.

Other Chapters Related to Portals

Portal technology often provides valuable "doorways" into ECM, providing users with access to filtered, role-based, relevant information.

Chapter 4: **Search**	When combined with portal technology, search enables users to drill down into specific subject areas using direct queries. As critical components of an ECM system, portals present relevant information and search technology that allows users to refine access to pertinent information.
Chapter 5: **Knowledge Management**	Portal integration with a KM system increases the relevance of documents grouped together based on taxonomies such as subject and author
Chapter 6: **Document Management**	Portal and search technology enables users to locate accurate information. Once this information has been found, it is typically securely stored and managed using a document management system.
Chapter 9: **Transactions & EAE**	Portals can be used to aggregate information contained in enterprise applications such as ERP, CRM and SCM systems.

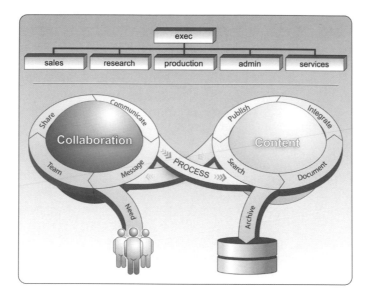

Figure 12.1: Rich Media

Rich media is part of the Collaboration technology used in ECM suites. As the collection of various forms of digital content, rich media is recognized as a corporate asset that needs to be managed. Digital Asset Management (DAM) delivers the sophisticated technical support required for the management of rich media content. In this chapter, we discuss the implementation of DAM as part of a larger ECM solution. You'll find out how organizations are using these solutions to unify messaging, train employees and improve communications across the enterprise.

RICH MEDIA AND DIGITAL ASSET MANAGEMENT

"What we're talking about is electronic real estate, a whole electronic reality. The problem we have is to organize the great continents of data that will soon become available. All the movies, all the TV, all libraries, all recordable knowl- edge... These are the vast natural crude oil reserves waiting to be tapped. In the fifteenth century we explored the planet, now we must prepare once more to chart, colonize and open up the whole new world of data. Software becomes the map and guides into that terrain." (Timothy Leary in an interview with David Gale in 1991, Understanding Hypermedia).

The Emergence of Rich Content

Art, film, television, telecommunications and the personal computer, or PC—these are the raw ingredients of rich media. In the late eighties and early nineties, these diverse types of media were brought together in a desktop environment, converging to form the digital domain that we call rich media (also called multimedia). Rich media is loosely defined as images, audio, video and any other visually oriented unstructured content such as animation and presentations. In recent years, rich media has exploded on the public Internet, as well as behind the firewall of the corporate enterprise. Rich media users are creators as well as consumers. Enabling technologies for rich media include broadband networks, digital video, digital cameras, MP3 players, personal video recorders, the Web, the audio compact disc, the digital video disc, high-definition television, three-dimensional modeling and advanced wireless devices.

Better performance and lower prices for personal computers and storage have made rich media increasingly commonplace. Today, rich media content serves a variety of audiences and needs in entertainment, marketing, training and intelligence, and comes from departments such as production, advertising, creative services and editorial. As broadband access expands and computing technology continues to advance, rich media will become pervasive and the critical need to manage this content will grow.

As the consumption of rich media becomes mainstream, organizations will become increasingly challenged to deliver products and messages to the market quickly and in more innovative ways. Organizations today realize the value of their digital content; they see rich media elements as true business assets that need to be managed and protected. As a result, the technology market has seen the development and standardization of technical solutions to bring efficiency and cost-savings to the production, management and distribution of rich digital media assets. This is a new category of content-centric computing called Digital Asset Management (DAM). Broadly defined, DAM combines the ability to re-express rich media content into new forms or products with the underlying organization and the supporting technologies that make this possible.

The Message is the Medium

"... it was not the machine, but what one did with the machine, that was its meaning or message." (Marshall McLuhan, Understanding Media)

Communications is a fundamental aspect of rich media, in both its past and present development. This is because rich media enables us to communicate ideas about complex situations with sophisticated simplicity. It employs many of our senses to assemble different elements to bring order and meaning to the world around us. Rich media content and technology supports the expression of creativity, whether it is a photograph, a hit single or a marketing campaign.

New technologies have changed the nature of "publishing" rich media. Historically, print and television dominated. Increasingly, however, new products and innovations have joined these traditional methods of delivery. Web sites, video games, mobile phones, electronic mail, desktop publishing, recordable CDs and even high-resolution digital displays on gas pumps, elevators and billboards have made global distribution of media files part of our everyday lives. These days, for instance, a single designer can sit at her desk and move seamlessly between graphical programs to create an advertisement—from storyboarding and illustration, to scanning, animation and editing. These diverse vehicles for content consumption require better management of rich media content.

Rich Media Content as Business Assets

In a business context, larger corporations are spending billions on the acquisition and protection of intellectual and creative property rights and the means to generate intellectual property that includes films, records, graphics and more. When we consider that the amount of unstructured data in large corporations makes up almost 90 percent of a company's information, it is fair to assume that rich media makes up a large portion of an organization's unstructured data.

An advertising agency, for example, needs to store, move and protect a great volume of content, including PDFs, image files, animations and more.

The design center in a large manufacturing company is required to store, protect and securely collaborate on rich media content, including PDF files, image and vector graphics and PowerPoint files.

A large consumer packaged goods company typically saves, reuses and collaborates on the rich media content employed in its advertising campaigns, including photographs, high-resolution Quark layouts and television commercials.

Finally, a global pharmaceutical company needs to assemble, store and distribute the rich media content used for its sales training, including PDF, PowerPoint, video and audio files.

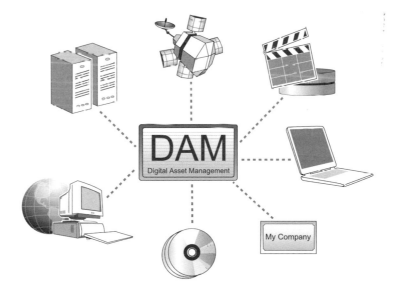

Figure 12.2: DAM as Hub

In each of the previous examples, rich media content constitutes a large portion of each company's business. In many cases, organizations invest millions of dollars into their unstructured data. And chances are good that this data contains a wealth of information that is potentially underused or undervalued because it is too difficult to access vast amounts of data to find relevant information.

Information is critical in creating competitive advantage. Information or raw data becomes knowledge when it prompts action and presents data that we can process and respond to intelligently. In today's business world, as the volume of information increases, decisions have to be made more quickly. The advantages of moving freely between different types of content become obvious. Once again, rich media helps us to manage complexity and gives us the speed required to transform information into advantage.

Digital Asset Management (DAM)

To exploit the value of their assets, organizations must develop a well thought-out strategy for managing their digital content. In developing this strategy, companies need to ask themselves:

- Do I have control over my production, creative and marketing content and processes?

- Am I spending money unnecessarily to re-create digital content instead of reusing assets that already exist?

- Can I quickly locate and identify the correct version of a digital asset?

- How can I reduce the cost to distribute digital media?

- Do I understand the distribution, licensing and other intellectual property rights associated with my digital content?

- Do I consistently represent our brand across all media types?

- How can I address bandwidth challenges in moving large digital media files?

- Am I missing revenue generating licensing opportunities?

- Can I efficiently support my distribution partners by supplying them with the latest marketing and production information?

Strategically, the owners of digital content assets are confronted with two overriding challenges—the desire to exploit this value as aggressively as possible, and the need to safeguard the material by vigorously enforcing the rights and licensing permissions associated with it.

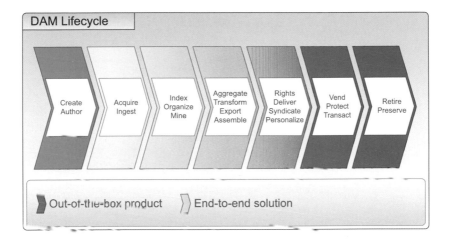

Figure 12.3: DAM Lifecycle

A digital asset management system delivers a secure platform that enables companies to manage digital media content. The typical functions of a DAM system include the ability to automatically import digital media content into a logically centralized repository where it can be easily searched, viewed and accessed. Along with this functionality, the system allows users to edit, package, transform and distribute the content. Since the ability to both protect and leverage an asset depends on knowing additional information about it, digital asset management as a methodology makes extensive use of "meta-data."

Meta-data is discussed in greater detail in Chapter 6 on Document Management. In the case of rich media, it is used to articulate the descriptive information gathered throughout an asset's lifecycle. For a media company, the ability to apply meta-data is essential. Usage information (for example, where the content element has been used) is critical to calculating the economic value of the content and evaluating the potential for future reuse. Likewise, rights information (for example, does an organization have the legal right to use a particular media element in a particular medium and/or within a geographic reach) is essential to the fundamental goal of content reuse and re-expression. This definition of a digital asset, as content plus meta-data, has driven other organizations outside of the media markets to take a closer and more strategic look at their content inventory.

A DAM infrastructure enables media companies to protect and enable rapid redeployment of their core business assets. Increasingly, more traditional corporations are learning that a well-planned DAM implementation can provide significant cost savings and competitive advantage.

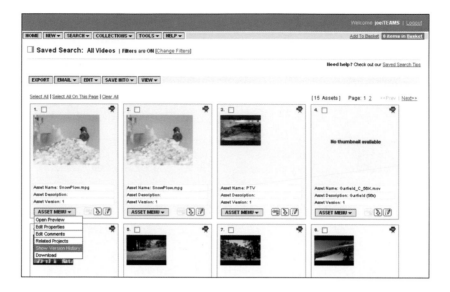

Figure 12.4: Meta-data and Digital Asset Management

With the advent of digital asset management technology, organizations are now able to streamline and simplify the management of digital content. If we examine DAM applied to production, branding and distribution, it becomes apparent that the centralization of an organization's digital assets, the systematic application of meta-data and Web-based search and access can dramatically improve a company's ability to affect these core business processes.

Production Asset Management

Digital technology affords the creative and production community unparalleled freedom in creating new products and messages. By its very nature, digital media production is a process that permits individuals to look at all of their assets at one time. Production asset management offers such digital content users as producers, editors, designers, and Web developers the ability to easily access a central repository of pre-approved digital assets, such as logos, photos, film, video and animation. This allows companies to dramatically reduce the time spent researching and searching for content while increasing time spent on actual creative production.

Digital asset management not only provides the ability to search and locate desired content, but also promotes content reuse, which lies at the heart of production asset management. The cost-savings can be enormous when we consider how much is spent

> Electronic Arts

As the leading interactive entertainment software company in the world, Electronic Arts (EA) understands the need to control its brand globally. The company insists on a consistent look, feel, and voice when distributing its products, even within the challenges of localization. Like many companies, EA's marketing content has traditionally been maintained in numerous systems across the enterprise, making it difficult to locate and distribute content.

With the introduction of a digital asset management system, EA established a centralized repository of their valuable digital marketing content, including broadcast commercials, print ads and Web content. The launch of a new title represents a significant investment that requires a highly coordinated, global team effort. Users across the company are able to securely access these assets via the Web as they develop new marketing campaigns. Once created, this marketing content can be securely distributed via the Web to regional offices and affiliates around the world.

Through this enhanced ability to reuse existing content, EA expects to realize ongoing cost savings, which include reduced production costs and the elimination of the expense of distributing of this material via a third party.

Figure 12.5: Electronic Arts' Digital Assets

to develop new media and the additional costs, both in dollars and human effort, to ready content for use in different media types across diverse platforms.

Figure 12.6: Production Asset Management

Brand Asset Management

Companies have spent millions of dollars developing, promoting and ensuring the integrity of their brand through tangible and non-tangible means, such as public perception and mind share. With so many media types and distribution channels, the challenges and opportunities exponentially increase from both a risk and cost perspective. By bringing a DAM system into an organization to address brand asset management, departments such as marketing, creative services and advertising can access and collaborate around a central database of approved digital brand assets. Types of assets may include logos, photographs, commercials, promotional videos, graphics, page layouts and completed campaigns.

> General Motors

General Motors exemplifies a company that sees its digital brand components as significant corporate assets. The development and evolution of the General Motors brand spans several decades and has created an historical archive of brand assets. Because General Motors is so brand conscious, early on they embraced the requirements and benefits of a Digital Asset Management (DAM) system. DAM is seen not only as a technical solution, but as a part of their overall brand strategy.

General Motors introduced a DAM brand marketing archive in its Global Marketing organization. That archive has grown to over half a million General Motors' brand assets, including vehicle photography, logos, television commercials, and other promotional materials. The system houses what is referred to as "the final version of the truth" in support of their internal marketing needs. In addition, external users can access the system to request and purchase use of licensed materials. Licensing content in this manner has generated significant revenue for General Motors.

According to the Manager of Media Services, "General Motors' media archiving process is constantly evolving to incorporate a number of technology-driven innovations. We believe it is critical to our long-term success that we have the ability to rapidly redeploy our existing brand content within all of these new delivery channels."

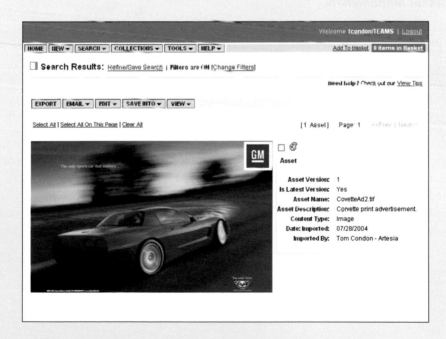

Figure 12.7: Media Archiving at General Motors

Distribution Asset Management

The evolution of digital technology and the Internet has changed the way we create and distribute all types of digital content including voice, pictures, films, videos, animations, graphic images, words, numbers, models and more. Probably the greatest impact on the distribution process is the ability to immediately get a product or messaging out into the market. The management of digital media grows more critical with each technological innovation as the competition to be first to market is tremendous.

Figure 12.8: Distribution Asset Management

Distribution asset management allows direct, field and channel marketing to automatically distribute finished brand and promotional media assets. As part of a DAM system, it provides a self-service model that allows authorized field personnel or affiliates to request or pull materials from a secure fulfillment system. Within the broadcast industry, for example, distribution asset management allows personnel to more specifically automate the schedule and delivery of finished digital programming materials.

Whirlpool is the world's leading manufacturer and marketer of major home appliances. A mega-brand like Whirlpool, with a corporate culture dedicated to identifying best-of-breed technology and continuous improvement, readily embraced Digital Asset Management Technology to manage and distribute valuable brand content.

Whirlpool has a complex retail distribution channel and many partners who require branded product and packaging information. Before the introduction of their DAM system, the process of disseminating such materials was highly manual. Every time new branding materials were developed or requested, a Whirlpool employee had to locate the media, re-format it to meet the requestor's specifications, burn it to a CD or copy it to a file, and mail it out at Whirlpool's expense.

With DAM in place at Whirlpool, locating a desired asset is as simple as searching on a Web-based screen. In a self-service manner, partners, distributors, or anyone with approved access can search and retrieve desired content, as well as the corresponding meta-data. The asset can then be transformed into the desired file format at export. And when new materials are available, the latest and approved marketing assets are quickly and easily imported into the DAM system.

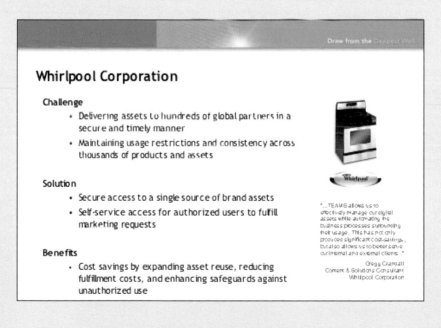

Figure 12.9: Whirlpool Manages Digital Assets

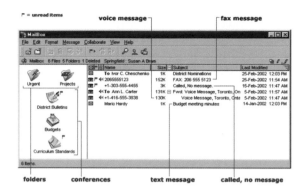

Figure 12.10: Integrated Messaging

Language is our main method of communication; conversation is our predominant method of exchanging ideas. But we are also using technology to host these conversations. Researchers of artificial intelligence are exploring the ability to converse with a computer system using the natural, spoken language. For example, speech recognition software can be trained to recognize spoken commands. Because rich media focuses on communicating complex ideas, it is pushing the limits in the development of both voice and video technologies.

The integration between voice and technology includes the use of recorded voice-overs for help, interactive videos for training and voice annotation, which involves people adding voice-over "notes" to existing information. The tools used to integrate voice and technology combine elements of audio, video and graphic files.

Video has been used in interactive programming for years and today, motion video can be integrated on most rich media platforms (like an Apple computer, for example). Researches are exploring the combination of linear (timed) video with the non-linear (ad hoc) structure of rich media. For example, online education, or e-learning, presents a combination of a structured environment (where people are guided through the subject matter or content) in an unstructured situation (where people can access and review content at their own convenience). Video integrates these two approaches into a seamless experience for the user. It transforms the passive student into an active participant, creating new ways of communicating and processing information.

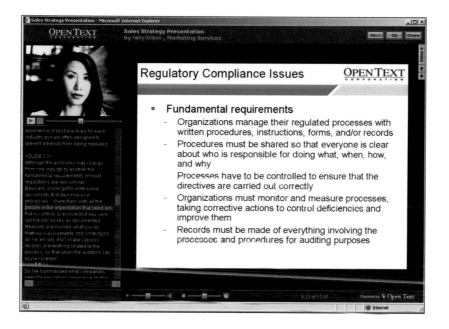

Figure 12.11: Rich Media Presentation

Rich media prompts us to explore information and interact in new ways. The Internet and hypertext have changed the way we consume and create digital media. Passages of text are linked together to provide explanations and present information in a tighter format. Their elements are tagged to create a context of information about the information to enrich content and make it more consumable. The Internet presents us with a vast body of information that can be explored interactively. The Internet is following the trend in which computing, rich media and telecommunications have merged to create an overarching information system that is personal, corporate and global in essence.

ECM and DAM

Advances in technology are providing organizations with the agility they need to process information more quickly. Almost every organization today is exchanging some form of digital content using messaging programs like email, instant messaging, voicemail and fax machines. These messaging systems are not designed for "mission critical" usage and pose a potential security risk. Most companies deploy systems that store critical information in emails in each employee's personal computer. If these computers break down, valuable information could be lost. Often, larger organizations need to move large amounts of data. What content or parts of content do they save? What do they destroy? In short, content as an organization's key asset is not protected.

As the Internet grows to support these formats and technologies, the business world will follow suit. Ubiquitous computing and real-time collaboration will characterize the next major frontier for ECM.

Companies with separate repositories for multiple types of unstructured content have identified the critical need to integrate or minimize their repositories into an ECM framework that can store and manage numerous content types, including rich media. As part of an integrated ECM system, DAM enables geographically dispersed groups to access and collaborate around a centralized repository. Advanced searching capabilities will enable people to find the information they need when they need it—whether they are searching for a specific email over the phone or using the PC to locate and listen to a voicemail recording. Selected assets can easily move through the workflow process expediting such steps as review and approval, while also capturing and storing information along with way. Those starting a new project can reap the benefits of the collected history of an asset or groups of assets. Relationships, versions and notations about leveraged content are now available throughout an enterprise.

When integrated with ECM's collaboration and document lifecycle management, DAM, organizations can fully automate the lifecycle of an asset and dramatically expand its use or value. Consider, for example, a company that buys and sells digital photographs. With an integrated ECM and DAM system in place, that company can significantly speed the time a photograph is brought in house and readied for purchase; thus speeding the time an asset can begin to show a return on investment for the company.

The long-term vision of Enterprise Content Management is the consolidation of all media into a seamless system, or infrastructure that offers new ways to communicate and process knowledge. ECM is moving toward the integration of real-time collaboration with a secure digital asset management system that manages rich media objects, such as video, images and voice data.

Moving beyond voice recognition, effective ECM tools will help to extract the information within voice data, analyze non-verbal sounds to identify defects in products and extract information from digital files. Consider, for example, security applications with the ability to analyze in real time the visual data from video footage recorded by close circuit television systems. These applications would "search" the rich media (or video footage) for anomalies in a parking lot, for instance, to alert security staff when suspicious behavior is recorded. The future of ECM will see voice and video communications integrate closely with the digital knowledge management world.

> Time Warner Book Group

With its rich history and vast holdings, Time Warner Book Group looked to digital asset management as a solution to support its publishing, marketing and new media activities. Time Warner Book Group required a solution to enhance its organizational efficiencies by enabling it to find and retrieve assets more quickly and easily, while also simplifying the packaging of promotional materials for distribution to its internal Web sites and external eTailers.

The company's approach was to break its books into their digital components and establish a common meta-data standard to allow asset sharing across the company. Time Warner Book Group was able to bring formally outsourced processes, such as eBook production, in house. Additionally, the asset management solution enables its sales force to create presentations in the field tailored to their specific customers.

For Time Warner Book Group, the benefits of establishing such a centralized repository include the elimination of redundancies and islands of information; the ability to repurpose core information; major efficiency gains in the distribution of content and marketing materials to online and brick and mortar trading partners; a vast reduction in hardcopy circulation, photocopying, large email attachments and scanning; and reduced time spent distributing and accessing online assets.

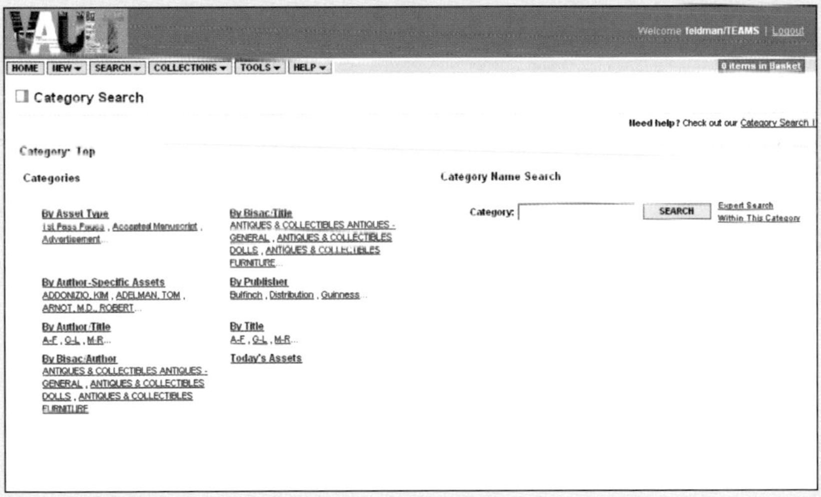

Figure 12.12: Time Warner Book Group's Digital Asset Vault

Other Chapters Related to Rich Media and DAM

To optimize content management across an organization, DAM can be deployed with other ECM technologies to manage content in many evolving and critical formats.

Chapter 4: **Search**	Search is typically used to access a knowledge base of images and rich media files contained in a DAM system as part of a larger KM system.
Chapter 6: **Document Management**	A DAM process normally manages images and rich media. Written documents are managed on a much larger scale in a document management system. DAM and DM should inter-operate within an organization to maximize content management.
Chapter 8: **WCM**	A DAM system makes WCM more effective by enabling the easy management of images and rich media for implementation on various Web sites.
Chapter 10: **Collaboration and Teams**	When a document or image is found, most organizations use collaborative applications to distribute, discuss and modify documents or rich media files.

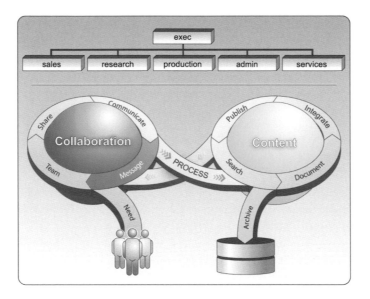

Figure 13.1: Messaging and Email Management

Messaging belongs to the Collaboration technology used in ECM suites.

Email has become an integral business tool used to maximize productivity. At the same time, email presents significant risk for organizations because it is not managed. In this chapter, we'll take a look at email as the prevalent form of messaging, the risks it presents and how organizations can integrate a Managed Messaging Environment (MME) with ECM to maximize information exchange and minimize risk.

CHAPTER 13

MESSAGING AND
EMAIL MANAGEMENT

Over the past 30 years, email systems have evolved from simple tools used to facilitate individual communication into a global network supporting hundreds of millions of users. At the same time, the content of email has changed, maturing from the exchange of simple text messages into the sharing of unstructured content, including documents and image files. Inside the organization, email has become one of the most pervasive and universal communication technologies, rivaled only by the telephone. Email systems operate outside of business applications and departments, cutting across traditional boundaries in an organization. Further to this, email has become the most popular method for sending and receiving unstructured electronic content outside the organization.

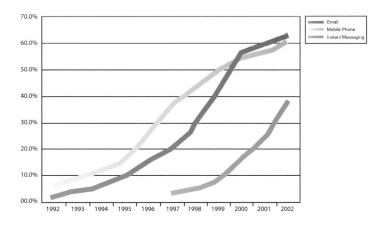

Figure 13.2: Percentage of People using Various Methods of Communication

Figure 13.2 illustrates the rise in popularity of email as a messaging system. When we consider that an average corporate employee sends and receives about 76 emails at 7 MB each day, we can see how email has become essential to doing business. Typically, the information contained within email is not available to a company as an accessible resource, whether it is a contract, employment offer or product information. Information contained in this format can become a potential liability in a legal situation, putting an organization at risk and expending IT resources to manage data backup, recovery and storage. Considering the metrics of usage alone, email management is a daunting task—one that requires careful training and a solution outside of a company's messaging system. In this chapter, we'll examine messaging and email management in the context of an extensive ECM solution.

The Components of Messaging

Messaging has also evolved over the years to encompass additional computer-based services. Examples of this include fax and voice messaging, now in widespread use throughout the world. The need for rapid, ad-hoc communication has fueled the rise of instant messaging (IM) services. Other messaging technologies such as video messaging and advanced virtual meeting services are emerging in the corporate world.

A critical difference between email and other communication technologies, such as the telephone, is that email is a persistent technology. That is, email messages are not just transmitted, they can also be retained. Since these retained messages contain not only the message content itself, but also unstructured attached content, email systems have become the repository for vast quantities of information and knowledge. In fact, in most organizations a messaging system is the single largest repository of content. And yet, in almost every organization, the management, security, archiving and retention of this content is entrusted to systems that were originally designed to do no more than transmit simple text messages from one user to another.

Because messaging systems serve as both the source of a large proportion of enterprise content and the destination (a repository) for this same content, an effective ECM system should include some form of content management for messaging systems. Left unmanaged, a messaging system represents substantial risk for an organization.

The Unmanaged Messaging Environment

When analyzed from a content management point of view, current messaging environments used in today's organizations present two shortcomings:

1. Quality of content: how content is managed, where content is stored, the fidelity of stored content and so on.

2. Scope of content management: how much content may be realistically retained, what media types are managed, which messaging systems are included in the management and so on.

Because existing messaging systems were created to send messages instead of retaining them, the load created by retaining gigabytes or even terabytes of data has lead to ungainly, unreliable, unscalable and unsecured corporate email systems. Since unmanaged messaging systems are typically stand-alone, any archiving and records management capabilities tend to be single-platform and proprietary. Finally, to break free of the scalability and data storage issues, many organizations make the decision to simply push the data out to user machines—the least-secure, least-managed and least-controlled environment of all. This approach represents substantial risk for the long-term success of an organization's content management strategy.

To determine if it is at risk, an organization needs to determine how its messages are stored, what the audit trail of messages is and what degree of control the organization has over messaging content.

Message Storage

The first step toward implementing effective messaging management is to determine where messages are stored. This includes sent and received messages, as well as confidential corporate contact and customer information. If the answer is, "on my laptop;" then corporate content is at risk. If a laptop is stolen or lost, stored messages can be accessed. Passwords can be breached in as little as 30 seconds. Every byte of data in a local message store can be made available to anyone who has possession of a computer. Furthermore, message content is not the only data available; contacts are also typically stored locally on a machine. How valuable would it be for a competitor to have a complete list of every customer, or for a headhunter to have a complete list of all employees in an organization?

Unscrupulous users can easily copy critical corporate data. Employees wishing to cover up signs of illegal activity can delete incriminating messages. A departing employee may take a copy of customer correspondence to a competitor. And even unintentional slipups can lead to lost laptops and the loss of confidential corporate data.

The Audit Trail of Messages

Organizations are learning that messaging data is as sensitive as accounting data and that the key to maintaining messaging system integrity is to maintain a clear audit trail.

Companies need to determine whether or not a user can delete a message without an audit trail, and if it can track the computer that was used to send a particular message. An effective messaging system also needs to be able to track messages sent using alternative messaging services, for example, instant messaging and voice mail. If the messaging system does not maintain an audit trail, an organization could be at risk if either external or internal needs require verification of messaging data.

Degrees of Control

The final risk factor in an unmanaged messaging environment is contingent upon the tools available to those responsible for enterprise content management. For example, could an individual responsible for the management of enterprise messaging content recover a copy of all messages belonging to a user, without the user's knowledge? Can users search all messages stored in a repository for specific content? Does the system enable the company to certify that messaging content storage is compliant with applicable regulations, such as HIPAA?

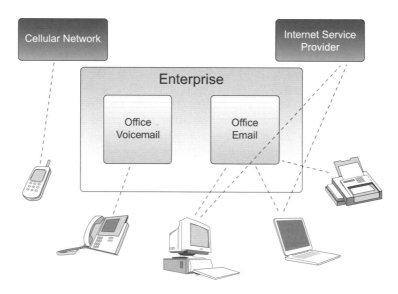

Figure 13.3: Unmanaged Messaging

The issues listed above are applicable to other messaging services besides an email system. In particular, organizations must be aware of existing unmanaged messaging services for voice mail, fax and instant messaging.

Controlling Existing Unmanaged Messaging Systems

Once an organization has determined that its messaging system is not managed, a good first step toward reducing risk, increasing data accuracy and improving productivity is the management of messaging content.

Improving Managed Messaging

Since so much organizational data is contained in its messaging system, a critical component of any Enterprise Content Management system is a Managed Messaging Environment (MME). The Managed Messaging Environment is distinguished from existing unmanaged messaging environments by the following key characteristics:

• a secure network-based solution;

• policy-based access;

• a comprehensive audit trail;

• integrated records management;

• immunity to content payloads;

• support for all messaging services.

For a deeper understanding of a Managed Message Environment, let's examine each of these characteristics in depth.

A Secure Network-Based Solution

The exponential growth of email data stores has become a corporate management issue. An MME requires that all content reside on a network as opposed to on an end-user device such as a laptop. This includes not only direct messaging content, but other messaging-oriented content such as contacts, mail lists and shared folders. A network- or server-based solution requires an organization's network services to be architected to accommodate an ever-growing MME content store. The MME should provide the flexibility and performance associated with a traditional unmanaged messaging systems without requiring storage on a local device. This is not to say that selected content may not be migrated from the network onto individual devices such as laptops, PDAs and cell phones; the critical factor for such migration is that it must be policy-based. This is because as soon as content is replicated onto individual computers and laptops, it becomes unmanaged. In this case, the choice to replicate data off the server should be made by the system administrator rather than the end user.

Even with the challenges of carrying more than 12 million customers per year across 40 cities and three countries, Alaska Airlines has developed a reputation for outstanding service. "Providing a reliable messaging system is a major problem for an organization such as ours," says the Senior Office Systems Analyst. "Not only do we face natural challenges such as distance and weather, but we also have to respect the demands of operating in a highly regulated environment." Further heightening these challenges, the airline business guarantees that users won't always be at their own computer.

To meet complex messaging requirements, Alaska Airlines installed a powerful network-based managed messaging system. The system has 11,000 users in over 50 locations. "Our messaging system is reliable and that's critical in an industry such as ours. We use our messaging system for company-wide and departmental communications, announcements and policy changes."

Choosing a secure, network-based managed messaging system has enabled Alaska Airlines to concentrate IT resources on supporting their core business instead of wrestling with email infrastructure. Messaging traffic at Alaska has soared since Alaska Airlines fully implemented their managed messaging system in 2000.

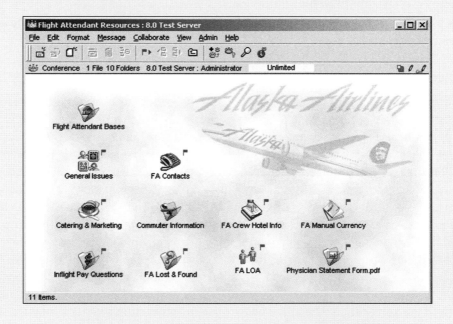

Figure 13.4: Alaska Airlines' Global Messaging System

Policy-Based Access to Messaging Content

An MME typically provides organizations with the ability to control a complete range of access levels to all messaging content. These levels include the ability to restrict access from certain types of information and may even include the ability to restrict the copying, saving or printing of sensitive data critical for certain compliance regulations, such as HIPAA. Because access is largely role-based, this facility should be tightly integrated with an organizational directory.

Comprehensive Audit Trail of Content Access

In order to provide transparency into corporate data, an MME can perform detailed real-time and historical audits of user and content activity. This makes it possible to determine who created a message, when it was sent, whom it was read by and when it was deleted. All of this data must be maintained on the network to prevent unauthorized tampering with the audit trail. In addition to the basic audit trail described above, an MME also provides additional audit data such as the tracking of IP addresses of all user connections and the logging of other user activities. This audit trail does not, however, include access to messaging content, since access to message content may conflict with other regulatory and compliance requirements.

Date	Time	Session ID	Control	UserID	IP Address		
20040622	074327	136	Close	jmyers	64.229.162.30:9610	Conference	Enhancement Suggestions
20040622	074333	136	Open	jmyers	64.229.162.30:9610	Conference	OTC Info
20040622	074337	136	Open	jmyers	64.229.162.30:9610	ConfItem	Outage - Bugs Database - Monday June 21 f
20040622	074342	136	Close	jmyers	64.229.162.30:9610	ConfItem	Outage - Bugs Database - Monday June 21 f
20040622	074342	136	Close	jmyers	64.229.162.30:9610	Conference	OTC Info
20040622	074347	136	Open	jmyers	64.229.162.30:9610	Conference	MailBox
20040622	074414	136	Open	jmyers	64.229.162.30:9610	Folder	HR
20040622	074416	136	Close	jmyers	64.229.162.30:9610	Folder	HR
20040622	074441	136	MsgDelete	jmyers	64.229.162.30:9610	How did it go?	0
20040622	074441	136	MsgDelete	jmyers	64.229.162.30:9610	Re: How did it g	52520710

Figure 13.5: Audit Trail of Messaging Content

Integrated Records Management

In a managed messaging environment, choices regarding message retention periods, message content destruction and message attachment handling must be policy-based rather than ad-hoc decisions made by the end user. In the same way that the MME provides role-based message content access, the MME must provide comprehensive role-based integrated content records management. Decisions on how long messages

> The Open University

The Open University, based in the UK, offers distance learning, including undergraduate and postgraduate courses, to approximately 200,000 part-time students that are spread all over the country and around the world. This gave rise to a formidable challenge: how to create an online community that takes the distance out of distance learning.

The Open University solved this challenge by deploying a network-based messaging and collaboration solution that provided the foundation with an easily accessible suite of asynchronous electronic forums for exchanging ideas and sharing knowledge.

"Our collaboration system enables our students to discuss course material, have queries answered and deepen their understanding through sharing perspectives," says the Head System Administrator at The Open University. "In addition, the social interactions facilitated by the system provide a mutual support network and a feeling of community for our users around the world."

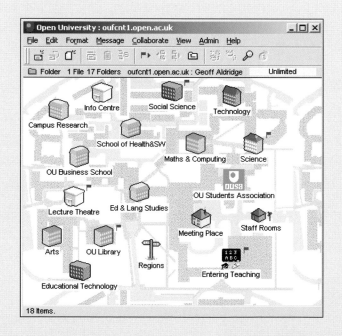

Figure 13.6: The Open University Collaboration Forum

are retained, how attachments are handled and when a message must be deleted may be centrally controlled by a records management system.

Email storage requirements and the number of email servers are growing as IT budgets shrink. With the introduction of an ECM-based infrastructure for MME, organizations can reduce the number and size of email servers and limit efforts for backup and recovery. Tight integration with records management provides a cost-efficient platform for the lifecycle management of messages.

Combining managed messaging and records management enables organizations to archive all email objects securely on optical media or on specific storage hardware. Using the system, companies can specify which emails and attachments to archive using defined rules such as size or date. Using records management to manage email messages ensures continued access to archived email. Users with appropriate access rights can find and retrieve specific messages. When linked to full text search facilities, the system can support the most demanding enterprise search requirements, regardless of format, location, language or media type. Archiving and records management is discussed in detail in Chapter 7, Document Lifecycle Management.

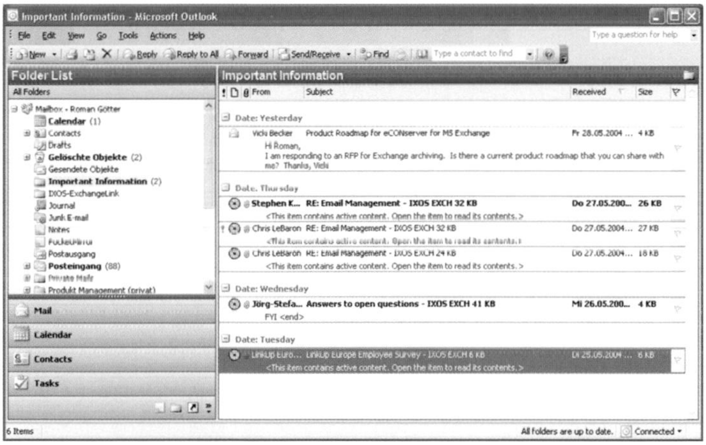

Figure 13.7: Records Management and Search Provides Access to Archived Mail

Immunity to Content Payloads, Including Viruses

Since the MME and, by extension, the ECM system will be called upon to retain all content, it is possible that some of the retained content may present a potential risk from viruses. It is critical that the MME put in place two important safeguards with respect to its content. It must ensure that all stored content is "wrapped" to prevent viruses from escaping. It must also guarantee that unauthorized access to content cannot be made by a rogue application run on an end-user machine. This last point is subtle but crucial. Viruses depend on being able to access messaging and contact content on local hard drives. Removing the ability to access a user's contact information renders most viruses impotent.

Support for All Messaging Services

We have established the fact that email is enterprise content that must be managed. To build a true content management system, however, we must take into account all of the messaging environments used inside an organization, including instant messaging, voice messaging, faxes and conference calls. A true managed messaging environment manages not only email messages but the content generated by these technologies.

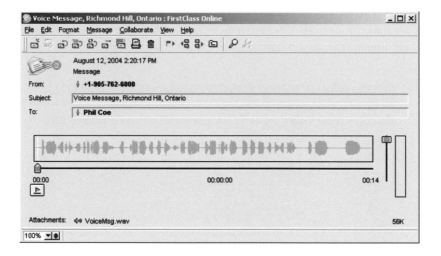

Figure 13.8: Voice Mail as Part of Managed Messaging

Messaging and Legal Compliance

As messaging technology has evolved to support more sophisticated collaboration, the business value of email and other messaging systems has increased. Today, for example, email is widely accepted as a standard business tool.

Standard Radio is the largest privately owned broadcasting company in Canada. A highly entrepreneurial company, Standard delivers winning performance through both AM and FM stations in major markets across Canada. As a company that depends on the spoken word, Standard knew that a simple text-based email system would not be suitable for its requirements.

"We needed a messaging system which encompassed all of the media types that we deal with," said the messaging specialist on Standard's national IT team. "While we needed a great email system, we also wanted to manage faxes and voice messages in a single integrated system." To meet their needs, Standard Radio chose a messaging system that included the ability to manage all voice and fax messages together with email and attachments.

In addition to these requirements, Standard's business model of centrally managed infrastructure meant that a network-based solution would deliver the benefits of managed messaging to their distributed group of broadcasting stations, while producing a total cost of ownership consistent with their entrepreneurial principles.

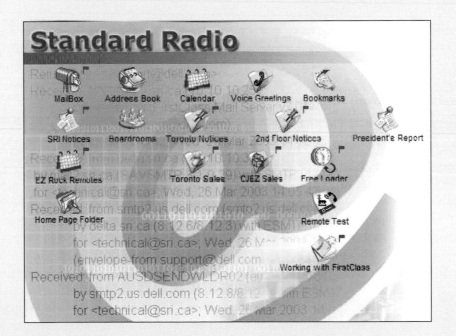

Figure 13.9: Standard Radio's Messaging System

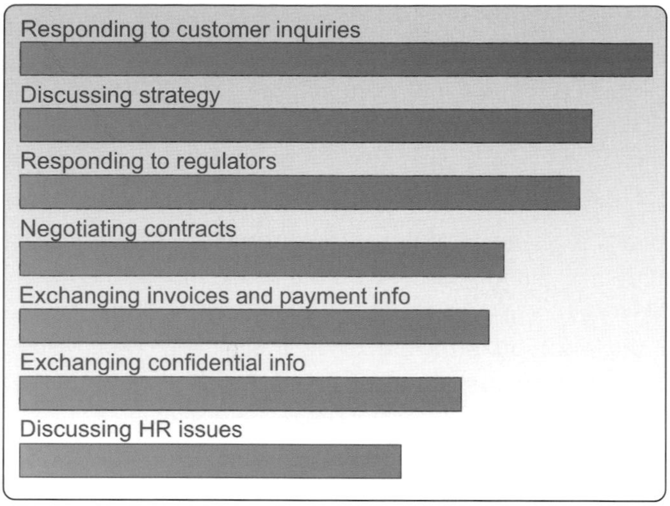

Responding to customer inquiries

Discussing strategy

Responding to regulators

Negotiating contracts

Exchanging invoices and payment info

Exchanging confidential info

Discussing HR issues

Figure 13.10: Managing Email

Content from various corporate messaging systems, including email and its attachments, represents business records that have to be retained and managed securely to support regulatory compliance, avoid legal fines or litigation costs and satisfy auditing requirements. Because it incorporates MME with archiving and records management, an ECM suite provides the functionality needed to protect information, reduce risk and achieve compliance.

ECM and the Managed Messaging Environment

The managed messaging environment is a critical component in any ECM strategy for the benefits it delivers. Beyond the security, compliance and productivity gains it delivers, an MME provides important additional benefits. Because an MME is network-based, users can access their messaging content from any computer. This greatly enhances worker mobility and provides a key foundation for effective disaster recovery planning. Integrated records management and search delivers access to corporate knowledge, improving productivity and the accuracy of information. Integration with ERP and business process management systems also leads to higher levels of productivity, as business processes typically triggered by an email are effectively managed. Finally, an MME is designed with built-in virus control to ensure that worker productivity is not compromised by virus attacks.

> # School Board of Broward County

The School Board of Broward County in Florida is the fifth largest school district in the United States, with an organization that includes almost 30,000 teachers and administrators spread over 250 locations. Broward's challenge was to find an advanced cost-effective solution that would replace a collection of different email systems that were slow, inefficient and difficult to manage.

A key additional requirement was the need for a solution that would provide flexibility and choice in the range of supported end-user personal computers. Broward has a large installed base of Apple® Macintosh® and Windows-based computers. Due to financial priorities, not all computers run the latest operating system releases, since that is costly and time consuming for such a large organization.

Broward ended up deploying a feature-rich, network-based managed messaging solution that handled the needs of the entire district on a single server. This provided tremendous cost savings over traditional email solutions.

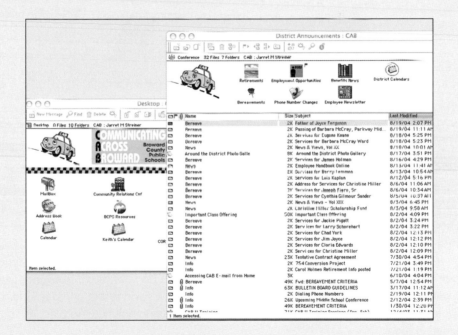

Figure 13.11: Broward County School District's Messaging Solution

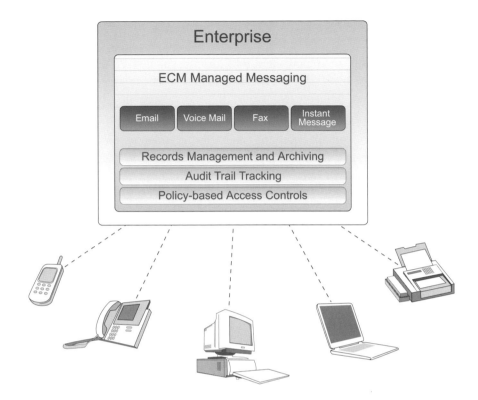

Figure 13.12: Managed Messaging

Managed Messaging: The Next Step

In any organization, messaging systems present risk and opportunity. A company is at risk if its messaging systems are unmanaged. If steps are taken to bring messaging into the sphere of ECM, opportunities are created for improving business operations. By deploying management tools for messaging systems, organizations can experience significant returns on investment, including increased compliance, expanded knowledge management and improved productivity. The investment in an integrated, network-based managed messaging environment typically pays off as cost savings are compared to the cost of running the disparate, dated single-function messaging solutions in place in most organizations today.

Other Chapters Related to Messaging

Messaging is the key component of collaboration. As such, many other ECM technologies that are synergistic to collaboration will increase the efficiency and effectiveness of most messaging solutions.

Chapter 4: **Search**	Search is typically used to access a knowledge base of documents and images in a messaging system.
Chapter 5: **Knowledge Management**	Knowledge management is used to organize, manage and provide access to an organization's knowledge base. As a critical part of an organization's knowledge base, messages should be incorporated into a secure ECM system.
Chapter 6: **Document Management**	A message or message text can be securely stored and managed as an object in a document management system.
Chapter 10: **Teams and Collaboration**	Messaging is one form of communication between people. Other forms of collaboration can extend the quality and effectiveness of a messaging system.
Chapter 7 **Archiving & DLM**	Many litigation and compliance systems require the long-term storage of information in an electronic archive that saves all messages securely with recall over decades of time. A records management system provides a full audit trail and recall of email and other types of messages to prove that critical information has not been tampered with.

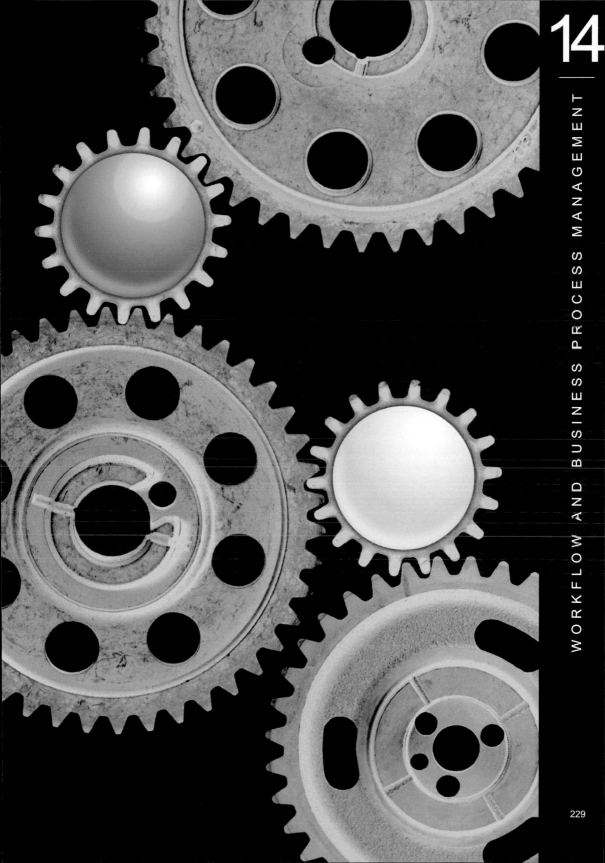

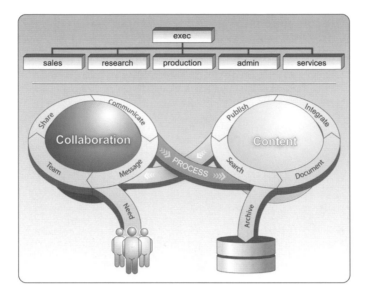

Figure 14.1: Business Process Management

Business Process Management (BPM) combines Content with Collaboration technologies used in ECM suites. This chapter explains everything you need to know about BPM; what it is and how it fits into the ECM equation. To demonstrate effective ECM, we profile a government agency using ECM to manage processes and connect cross-functional teams to drive new product development, from defining requirements to signing contracts.

WORKFLOW AND BUSINESS PROCESS MANAGEMENT

The challenges of today's business world are now forcing many organizations to focus on improving business processes to shorten cycle times and bring products and services to market more quickly, while reducing operational costs, increasing quality and meeting regulatory compliance. To stay competitive, many organizations are re-evaluating their approach to business processes and looking for ways to improve these procedures.

While organizations are examining the way they work, they are also reconsidering the technologies that drive the way they work. Over the past ten years, organizations have made significant investments in technologies like legacy systems and customer service systems. Optimization of these systems is a key consideration for development and Information Technology (IT) departments. These groups are tasked with creating systems that are both flexible and cost effective. This becomes more daunting as economic pressures force businesses to improve the operational effectiveness of their IT departments and technologies with less money.

IT departments are under constant pressure to deploy new technologies that automate and improve business processes within an organization. Due to this new focus on process, CEOs expect their Chief Information Officers (CIOs) to look beyond the domain of IT and think in cross-functional terms to problem solve across the organization. With this expanded role, CIOs are required to complete projects on time and under budget, while proving the value of proposed investments in technology. In today's world of economic pressures, accounting scandals and increased concern over security risks, this is not business as usual for most IT departments, where the focus has shifted from getting the project done on time to documenting and optimizing the controls and processes involved in completing the work.

Essentially, there are two issues here: improving the processes that drive a business and improving the technologies that run or support these processes.

What is Business Process Management?

We've all experienced the frustration and inefficiencies associated with paperwork and manual processes. Although working this way is becoming increasingly archaic, paper- and manual-based processes have traditionally involved high margins of error caused by processing bottlenecks, media interruptions, delays, duplications and inaccuracies. Computers promised to significantly change the way we work, but computers alone have not been enough. BPM defines a new approach that utilizes computing technology to automate and streamline processes by managing the flow of work throughout an organization.

Business process management does exactly what it says—it manages business processes. Business processes refer to any process, both ad hoc and structured, that take place within an organization to complete specific jobs or actions. At a basic level, business processes are transaction-based. When technology is added to automate processes, BPM describes how people interact with this technology, information and each other to get their jobs done.

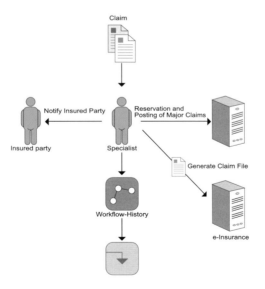

Figure 14.2: Claims Processing at an Insurance Company

> Shenandoah Life

Shenandoah Life, a life insurance company, was witnessing astronomical growth in new policy applications. The company decided to align technology with corporate strategy to manage growth and improve customer service. To do this without a large increase in staff, Shenandoah Life needed to reduce the time required to process policy applications.

Currently, document imaging and workflow technology drives all processes within the life insurance company and the workflow audit trail provides a flow reporting structure. A new department has been created, called the Digital Mailroom, where all incoming mail—including policy applications, claims and checks—is imaged and indexed, and then, using workflow technology, distributed across the company in electronic format.

Customer service representatives can now provide improved customer care, as they have immediate and direct access to case files. Process transparency has increased enabling managers to better meet service level metrics, redistribute workload, and minimize training costs. Within two months of solution implementation, Shenandoah Life realized a 50 percent reduction in application turnaround time in the automated areas.

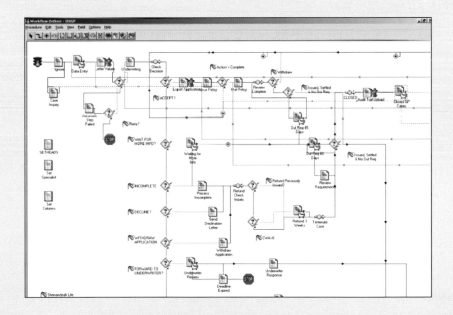

Figure 14.3: Shenandoah Life's Workflow Process

But why is BPM successful? Traditional attempts at process optimization have often delivered underwhelming results because they attempted to map the business to the technology. This is a restrictive approach that limits both the potential for and the degree of success; and it often follows that requirements are sacrificed in order to accommodate the technology.

BPM is successful because it understands that organizations, rather than technologies, define business processes. BPM enables organizations to leverage and extend their existing technologies to support the processes that drive the success of business. Furthermore, business processes are not isolated, one-time events within an organization. Each process is a connection of people and content, and as these connections span project teams, departments and entire organizations, we can see that BPM is a natural and indispensable component of an Enterprise Content Management solution.

Figure 14.4: Insurance Underwriter Process

To illustrate the effectiveness of BPM, let's examine claims processing within an insurance company. A typical insurance company receives approximately 10,000 claims each day. These claims are scanned, and meta-data such as customer number and claim total is added to each claim. These numbers are fed into a mainframe computer and this system uses a BPM workflow to apply some basic rules to the claim. For example, the workflow detects whether the claim falls within the assigned limits. If the data is complete and all business rules are satisfied, the claim is automatically processed and the customer receives payment. If there are exceptions to the business rules, for example, the total claim is too high, the system sends the form out to a team of claims processors for further examination. A BPM system enables the insurance company to capture and review an insurance policy in minutes and automate the flow of the policy through the required departments to improve throughput time and reduce cost per policy.

BPM solutions are increasingly becoming targeted to meet specific sector requirements. Examples of this include loan forms processing, mortgage application processing, accounts payable, complex order management in telecommunications, procurement and new product development.

From BPR to BPM

BPM has its roots in BPR, or Business Process Reengineering. BPR is the redesign of business processes to achieve dramatic improvements in critical measures of performance, such as cost, quality, service and speed. The basic tools that support BPR include process modelers and simulators that enable organizations to test run scenarios based on their key business processes. BPR was popular in the 1990s when Michael Hammer and James Champy published their best-selling book *Reengineering the Corporation*. The authors proposed that in some instances, a radical redesign of an enterprise was necessary to lower costs and increase levels of service and that technology could enable or drive these changes. In their groundbreaking book, Hammer and Champy suggested seven principles of reengineering to streamline the work process:

1. Organize around outcomes, not tasks.

2. Identify all the processes in an organization and prioritize them in order of redesign urgency.

3. Integrate information processing work into the real work that produces the information.

4. Treat geographically dispersed resources as though they were centralized.

5. Link parallel activities in the workflow instead of just integrating their results.

6. Put the decision point where the work is performed, and build control into the process.

7. Capture information once and at the source.

By the late 1990s, BPR had gained a negative connotation equivalent to "downsizing" and was abandoned as a concept. A new methodology emerged, called Enterprise Resource Planning (ERP).

So how does this all relate to BPM today? Business process management refers to transferring the results of business process re-engineering discussed above into production. In many instances, the term "workflow" is used to describe the technology that enables production.

From Documents to Processes

Workflow is the combination of tasks that define a process; it allows the flow of tasks between individuals, systems and departments to be defined and tracked. As previously mentioned, workflow was initially viewed as an add-on to document management capabilities. It defined approval processes that involved the circulation of documents in the right order to the right constituents for review and final sign-off. As the workflow industry matured, emphasis shifted from the document itself and the work it generated to the process that defined how work was generated. This change in focus, along with the growing complexities of organizational processes to include manual, automated and human transactions, prompted the growth in importance of a comprehensive approach and technology called business process management.

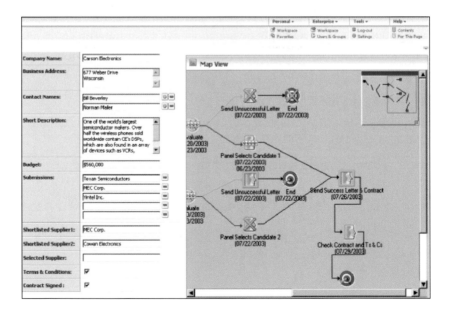

Figure 14.5: Workflow-Bid and Approval Process

BPM has not replaced workflow, however. Today, workflow technology has evolved into a very effective foundation for BPM solutions because of its open and standards-based technology. In fact, by providing an underlying IT infrastructure, workflows have enabled organizations to liberate themselves from their legacy systems to define and execute business processes independent of application and infrastructure limitations.

Processes describe the roles and requirements of an organization. If an organization uses both an ERP and a CRM system, it doesn't mean that these systems are streamlined or integrated. Understanding their business processes enables organizations to identify where systems need to be integrated and how users need these systems to interact.

Web technology has allowed further advancements in BPM. With the introduction and succession of Web-based open standards such as XML, SOAP or WSDL into process management, organizations can achieve a new standard of application integration, enabling the real-time information sharing that drives the success of daily operations and ensures business continuity. Instead of reconfiguring ERP as their commercial environment evolves, organizations can use BPM to build processes that adapt to new market conditions. Today, organizations insist on leveraging investment in existing applications to avoid reengineering the enterprise. Web services allow fast and simple integration between systems and drive the adoption of BPM systems.

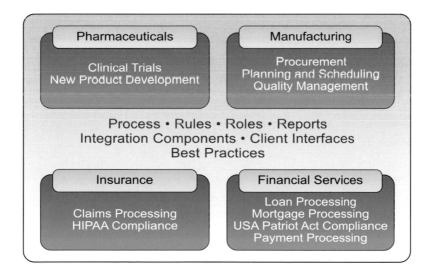

Figure 14.6: Business Process Management Applications

> **Genzyme**

genzyme

Ensuring careful management of information for FDA submissions is a major undertaking for life sciences companies such as Genzyme Corporation. To help it achieve this goal, Genzyme needed a solution that would help project teams work together, manage and share information, while providing processes and controls to ensure careful management of that information.

Virtual project areas provide the ideal secure environment to enhance project collaboration, preventing reinvention of the wheel and speeding time-to-market.

Genzyme's information library increases efficiency, while document management capabilities support the company's compliance with the FDA's mandate for electronic records requirements.

"ECM is becoming a fundamental part of the way we work at Genzyme. Developing innovative treatments directly affects the quality of people's lives, so time-to-market is always foremost in our minds in the pharmaceutical industry. Having key information immediately accessible online improves our efficiency and productivity, enabling us to fulfill the commitment we have made to patients that much sooner," says Genzyme Contract Associate.

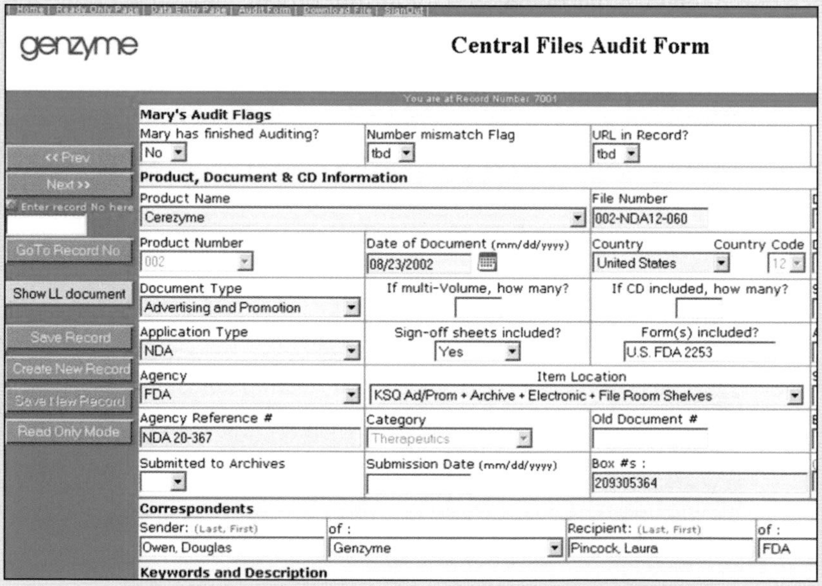

Figure 14.7: Genzyme's File Auditing

Bringing Together People, Process and Content

How does an organization effectively integrate the way people work together with information and technology?

This is a challenge when we consider that business processes are complex, dynamic and often implicit within an organization. In many cases, processes move beyond the firewall to involve customers, partners and suppliers. To manage these cross-functional processes, organizations are considering BPM because it enables processes to be modeled, refined and modified as business needs change over time. BPM is both a methodology and a technology that helps organizations continuously examine, understand and manage business processes that interact with people, technology and information.

From a technological perspective, BPM is the integration of various technologies, including process modeling and rapid application development (RAD) tools. BPM combines these technology components into a single and comprehensive solution that manages the entire lifecycle of a process.

Not only does BPM technology provide the tools and infrastructure required to define, model and track business processes, it delivers the tools needed to implement business processes in such a way that the resulting software "objects" can be analyzed from a business perspective to utilize the data for further process enhancements and reporting. In other words, BPM endorses a process-driven view of IT, where the management of processes (the business angle) is separated from the underlying infrastructure (the technology).

The real value of BPM is that it gives organizations the ability to define and execute business processes independent of applications and infrastructure. This transforms an organization into a knowledgeable enterprise because it provides a detailed explanation of all the activities required to complete a specific business process. An organization "in the know" can better manage the flow of work across applications, people and departments.

By separating the management of processes from the technology that drives them, BPM enables organizations to find the gaps between systems, identify which gaps are caused by human interaction with these systems, and connect these systems together more effectively to streamline process management. As a result, processes can be more clearly defined, controlled and monitored. In addition, best practices can be identified, modeled and distributed across the organization. Finally, because of its flexibility, processes can be modified or changed quickly without additional costs. BPM nurtures a process-centric and flexible approach that supports the continual evolution and optimization of processes across an organization.

> United States Air Force

The goal of the Business Solutions Exchange (BSX) process is to continually improve Air Force business practices and it involves uniting the members, processes and policies of Air Force service contracting. The Air Force was using a variety of client-server-based systems that were unable to manage this process across different geographical locations.

The deployment of an ECM solution has enabled the United States Air Force to use a unified system to manage BSX. A central knowledge library allows dispersed BSX teams to use workflow, tasks and version control to work together throughout the planning, execution and supplier management phases.

Processes are currently handled by a single system throughout the lifecycle of the project, from requirements definition to contract closeout. Using the consolidated solution, the Air Force has shortened the time spent between identifying point of need and completing a performance requirement document (PRD) from seven months to eight weeks, which is approximately 70 percent less time.

Figure 14.8: Business Solutions Exchange Project Workspace

Business process management has been around as long as business has. In fact, processes are often buried within a network of people and systems that has evolved over years within an organization, making them difficult to identify or "extract" and change. It is often difficult for organizations to understand exactly how their processes work and even harder to determine how to practically implement better processes.

What is driving the need for Business Process Management?

Clearly, organizations that have not implemented a BPM system suffer from the inefficiencies associated with inconsistent business processes. These inefficiencies result in delays in project cycles and late approvals, which negatively affect time-to-market and competitive advantage. They are exposed to significant legal, corporate governance and regulatory compliance risks because of an inability to route decision-centric information to the right people at the right time inside the organization, and the inability to reliably identify who performed a task or made a key decision. BPM alleviates these issues.

Organizations that have implemented their own, in-house business process management systems have their own set of obstacles to overcome. Most organizations are not in the software business and in-house development is not their primary focus or area of expertise. Using their own resources to create a BPM solution often involves taking on a development venture that spans across all business departments and systems. This can be difficult and challenging as costs escalate, knowledge or know-how about the proprietary system leaves the company and the system cannot accommodate or comply with emerging laws and regulations. Often, building a "home grown" BPM system requires a commitment that organizations are not realistically able to make.

Some organizations are currently using stand-alone BPM systems. These systems do not allow users from different departments to share information in a fluid and seamless way. Typically, people have to use two or three systems to find the information needed to complete a single business process. In many cases, these multiple content repositories and servers must all be administered and maintained independently. Companies in this situation suffer from the cost and complexity of managing multiple vendor relationships, wasted money on esoteric features that will never be used and the difficulties that non-technical people face when using BPM systems.

It is often the non-technical users who are the business owners of processes. The ability of these users to define and redefine processes and rules without having to depend on the assistance of IT resources provides a significant benefit and return on investment. In addition, BPM lets organizations better manage performance of tasks, more effectively handle process exceptions and automate repetitive tasks.

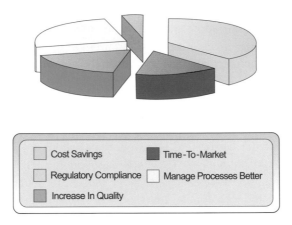

Cost Savings Time-To-Market

Regulatory Compliance Manage Processes Better

Increase In Quality

Figure 14.9: The Benefits of BPM

The Bridge Between Assets and Advantage

Successful organizations need to be knowledgeable enterprises. They need to track processes and measure their effectiveness. Senior management needs to know when deadlines are missed, why there are delays and the status of approvals and outstanding issues. It is only with this timely information that management can make informed decisions. And making fast, accurate decisions gives organizations a definite advantage. The ability to do this is directly related to optimizing operations by improving business processes.

From a content perspective, an effective BPM system enables organizations to eliminate paper-based processes, reducing print and paper costs. In addition, organizations can lower their total cost of technology ownership by integrating existing systems within a comprehensive and consolidated BPM system.

A BPM system also helps organizations comply with emerging government and regulatory requirements. BPM enables organizations to continually improve operational processes and align these processes within the context of laws and regulations, as well as with internal standards and policies. Organizations becoming familiar with Sarbanes-Oxley compliance are able to understand the effect that internal and external processes have on corporate integrity. The continual improvement of these processes is critical to the long-term success of not just Sarbanes-Oxley compliance initiatives, but those related to all other types of regulatory compliance mandates. The recent extension of the

The Royal Dutch/Shell Group of Companies have been finding and producing oil and gas around the world for over a century. With dozens of petroleum and natural gas exploration and production subsidiaries and approximately 90,000 employees in total, Royal Dutch/Shell recognized that it had to reduce duplication of exploration efforts and minimize overlapping skill sets.

Royal Dutch/Shell opted for collaboration technology to combine capabilities and expertise in order to manage the supply chain and improve efficiencies. Its British, Dutch and Norwegian exploration subsidiaries collaborate on exploring and developing oil and gas properties in the North Sea. A project for locating new oil fields requires the subsidiaries to work collaboratively and share key information such as geologic data. Most projects span six to nine months, although some can take as long as three years to complete.

ECM is used to share a wide variety of documents, from word processing files and spreadsheets to scientific data and CAD drawings. At any one time, there may be 30 to 40 projects in progress. ECM keeps all the documents of a particular project together in one place. When a project ends, the associated documents are easily accessible in the corporate knowledge base as a learning resource, and for reuse and reference on other projects.

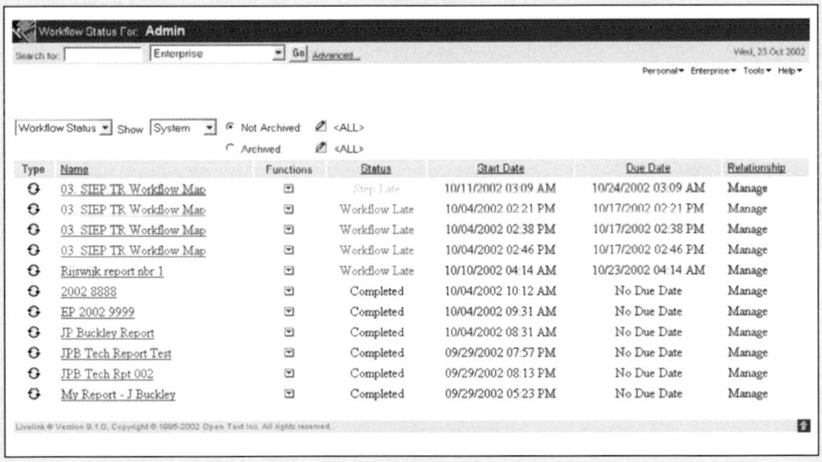

Figure 14.10: Managing Projects and Tasks at Shell

Section 404 compliance deadline also gives organizations an opportunity to take a more strategic, BPM-centric approach rather than a reactive, short-term approach to compliance. Regulatory Compliance as part of a comprehensive ECM solution is discussed in further detail in Chapter 3, Compliance and Corporate Governance.

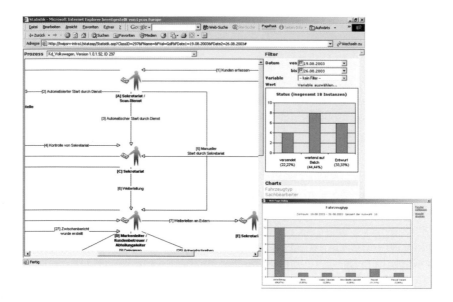

Figure 14.11: Online Reporting Based on Process Data—a Current Base for Management Decisions

BPM and ECM

BPM is evolving from simply being a tool to solve tactical, departmental-level problems to providing a strategic contribution to defining the enterprise infrastructure. This evolution means that the ability to cope with a wide range of different and often complex processes, and the need for high availability and increasing scalability are becoming key requirements.

BPM defines an emerging software category that delivers support for cross-functional business processes. It is built on a platform for collaboration and content management to support the transactions among people, processes and information. BPM is forcing organizations to map their business processes to their business objectives. Part of this process involves looking at how well an organization's underlying content supports these business activities. ECM solutions that provide document and records management, and full text search capabilities, integrate well with BPM systems to optimize business processes to improve performance. By linking processes with content creation, ECM enables organizations to exchange transactional information and respond more quickly to new or changing business requirements.

Other Chapters related to Business Process Management

If a company is solving only part of its content management problem, it will only realize a portion of the benefits. BPM technology as part of a comprehensive ECM solution extends the management of content across the enterprise to improve efficiency and reduce costs.

Chapter 6: **Document Management**	A process is only as good as the documents that define a sequence of events. A workflow is most effective when it processes documents that are contained within a comprehensive and secure document management system.
Chapter 7: **Archiving & DLM**	Many litigation and compliance processes involve the long-term storage of information in an electronic archive that saves all content securely with recall over decades of time. A records management system provides a full audit trail and recall of important documents to prove that critical information has not been tampered with or destroyed.
Chapter 9: **Transactions & EAE**	EAE extends content to all departments by incorporating the numerical data and tables contained in ERP systems into an organization's document repository, where it can be securely managed and integrated with key business processes.

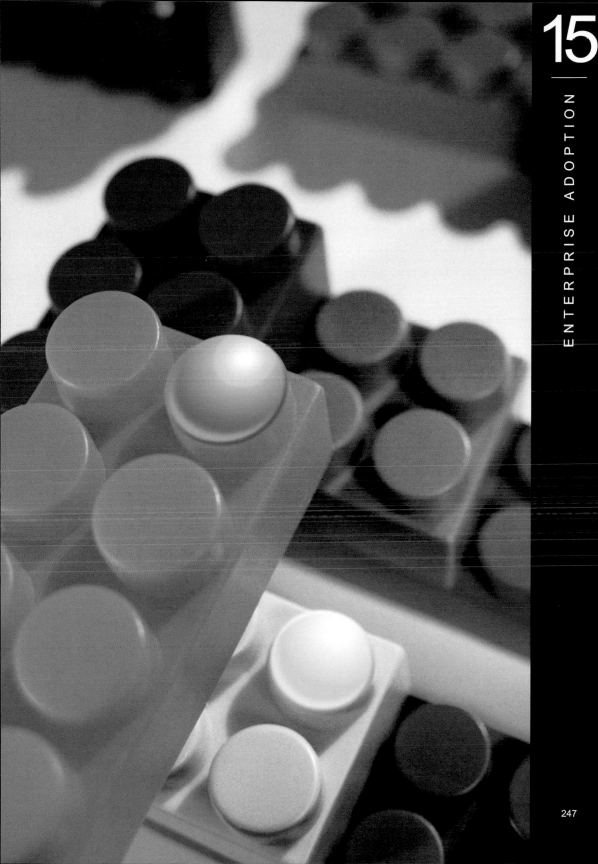

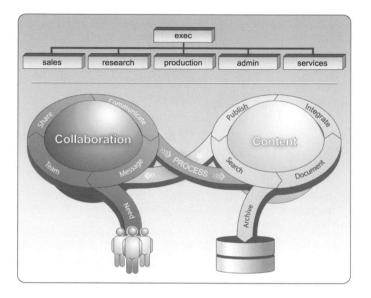

Figure 15.1: Enterprise Adoption of ECM

Enterprise deployments are delivered as inter-departmental applications within an ECM-driven organization. In this chapter, we examine how organizations adopt enterprise-wide strategies for implementing ECM to reduce the total cost of ownership (TCO) and to increase the effectiveness of existing ECM deployments. We explore the complexity of enterprise deployments and outline an architectural approach that enables organizations to scale ECM to set new standards and support the enterprise. To illustrate the issues encountered when installing ECM at the enterprise level, we describe a range of ECM applications, from internal administration to supply chain management, research and development and sales and marketing support.

ENTERPRISE ADOPTION

As more business applications are delivered using the same underlying technology, organizations will adopt enterprise-wide strategies for ECM to reduce the total cost of ownership and increase the effectiveness of existing deployments. In fact, ECM becomes more valuable as more people are exposed to the same data and can collaborate on it. This trend is described by Metcalfe's Law. Written more than a decade ago by Metcalfe, the founder of the Ethernet, it states that the value of a network grows exponentially by the square of the number of connections. Figure 15.2 below illustrates this law. Metcalfe's Law represents the inevitability of the growth of ECM deployments to an enterprise scale and beyond to encompass business partners and entire industries.

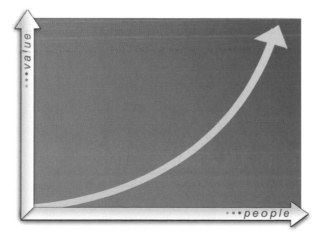

Figure 15.2: Metcalfe's Law

Enterprise Deployments by Early Adopters of ECM

After more than a decade of ECM adoptions, it is possible to identify trends in how large Global 2000 organizations implement ECM. Most organizations adopt ECM primarily to solve a departmental problem, such as accounts payable or customer support, which produces return on investment. This type of solution typically involves some 100 to 1,000 users in a department that produces and maintains a large number of documents, for example technical manuals in the customer support department. The departmental deployment is normally sought by the business owner of a department. The IT department becomes involved when the solution is installed, and this becomes their introduction to ECM.

As business problems emerge in other departments, the IT department identifies where ECM solutions can solve similar content management problems. As a result, ECM radiates from department to department throughout the company. As these department-level deployments expand, IT is tasked with increasing both the efficiency and the extent of ECM. This involves expanding document management systems to incorporate search and portal technologies to mine a document repository. Adding collaboration and business process management features increases the scope of the user's and system's ability to support more documents and processes.

After several ECM departmental deployments, IT finds new ways to efficiently manage all solutions to reduce total cost of ownership. This leads to the review and identification of similarities between applications to reduce the cost of administration and set new standards at the division level. At this point, a division level standard normally involves from 5,000 to 10,000 people in a Global 2000 company.

This process is repeated at the enterprise level, and the selection of an ECM platform becomes a strategic consideration that has far-reaching implications for an organization. The decision is normally made by "C-Level Management" (CEO, CFO, CIO, COO) and the rest of the executive management team. This is because competitive advantage often depends on selecting an effective and comprehensive ECM platform.

If we trace an adoption cycle that spans more than a decade and has grown from an initial departmental deploy to a full enterprise-wide application, Siemens provides an excellent example of the returns on investment realized from an ECM solution rolled out across the enterprise.

Siemens AG, headquartered in Munich, Germany, has more than 400,000 employees and a presence in more than 190 countries. Siemens has one of the most geographically complex and comprehensive ECM deployments in the world. The world leader's global solution extends to partners and customers while providing streamlined processes, collaborative workspaces and shared content to eight unique business areas:

- Information and Communications

- Automation and Control

- Power

- Transportation

- Medical

- Lighting

- Financing and Real Estate

- Household Appliances and Computers

Figure 15.3: Siemens' Web Site

"As a global company with employees all over the world, it is critical to provide our teams with tools for virtual collaboration and knowledge sharing across geographical and organizational boundaries. This system will serve as the backbone of the company-wide Siemens ShareNet and complementary divisional solutions, delivering these capabilities and supporting our ability to work faster, smarter and more efficiently," says Siemens' Corporate Knowledge Officer.

In the mid 1990s, Siemens began experimenting with ECM technologies within months of the public availability of a Web browser. Initial deployments of basic search and document management technologies were made to manage growing amounts of information in Web-based repositories. At the time, Siemens was experimenting and adopting Web-based search engine technology well before these tools were on the market. With this base of experience, Siemens' IT department introduced Web-based ECM technologies to various departments throughout the corporation. The following excerpts illustrate the evolution of departmental installs into an enterprise-wide deployment of ECM that occurred at Siemens.

Sales and Marketing

One of the most important early applications of ECM took place in departments related to customers in sales and marketing, as illustrated in the examples below.

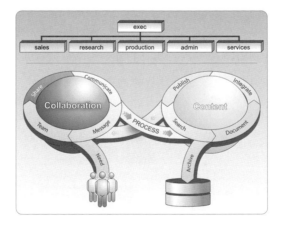

Figure 15.4: Sales and Marketing Deployment at Siemens

Siemens Industrial Solutions & Services (I&S) is a leading global supplier of electrotechnical equipment, drive systems, automation and IT solutions for the metals, mining and paper industries, oil and gas, infrastructure, marine engineering, airports and traffic control. To support the lifecycle of offer preparation and tendering, Siemens I&S created a customized workflow and project template. When users initiate a new offer tendering process, the system automatically creates a project and populates it with the framework for an offer in the form of a compound document. The workflow uses process steps and a dynamically generated address to send email notification to key people throughout the process.

Working on cross-divisional projects, **Siemens Netherlands** sells, manages and executes building projects, adding professional services and consulting value for customers. To reduce the amount of time spent setting up new projects and ensure that consultants and engineers were all working from the most current version of a document, Siemens Netherlands implemented technology to facilitate collaboration at the departmental level, within user communities and amongst cross-divisional project teams. Capturing knowledge gleaned through collaboration means that customers benefit from best practices, project time savings and improved productivity.

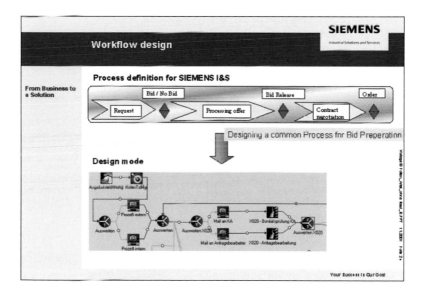

Figure 15.5: Workflow Design Drives the Bid Process at Siemens

Siemens Enterprise Networks has developed an application called EZA, which is an acronym for easy access to contracts and customer engagement information for solutions and services. EZA pulls together all Siemens activities for a single engagement with a customer, from the time a prospect becomes a lead, through installation and final confirmation of the arrangement. As a unique approach to sales and customer engagements, the solution aids the sales force in their ability to interact with customers, business partners and internal people.

Production

After sales and marketing, ECM was adopted at the production level within Siemens, specifically in areas where employees required quick and easy access to technical information in order to improve efficiency and effectiveness, both within and outside of the organization. By this time, the sophistication of ECM deployments increased and applications began to include workflow and business process management elements, closely integrated with document management. Collaboration began to take on a more important role in the deployments and early versions of knowledge management repositories with advanced search techniques were implemented.

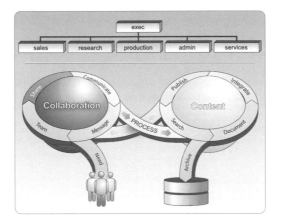

Figure 15.6: Production Deployment at Siemens

As the systems engineer for total solutions, **Siemens Building Technologies (SBT)** needed to collaborate and share information with seven locations and six divisions. Turning to an extranet solution, the organization today manages all information related to building and construction projects online. ECM technology has enabled SBT to address productivity and customer satisfaction challenges caused by time-consuming searches for documentation, data and images during building projects.

OSRAM, a subsidiary of Siemens AG, is one of the leading lamp manufacturers in the world. As customers grew highly knowledgeable about the sophisticated materials and technology they were using to develop lighting solutions, access to technical information became increasingly important. Using content management technology, OSRAM's marketing department developed a solution to support its sales force with detailed technical information on thousands of lighting products. Today, when a customer asks a technical question, the sales representative has immediate access to product-related documentation that provides the answer.

Research and Development

As the need to produce technical information in electronic format increased within Siemens, the next logical step was the deployment of ECM to research and development departments. As this happened, the use of more creative forms of collaboration like notification messaging and online meetings became more widespread to increase the effectiveness of teams as they worked in common document repositories.

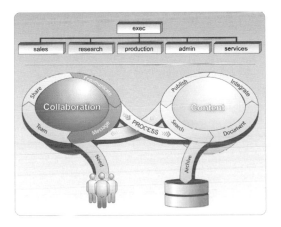

Figure 15.7: Research and Development Deployment at Siemens

Siemens Automation & Drives knows that world-class customer care is a critical part of the sales process—the winning and keeping of customers. To that end, the division built a knowledge management system that relieved its Customer Support Hotline staff of supplying daily routine answers to Frequently Asked Questions, leaving them free to aid customers with critical issues. The intranet was further designed to host answers in five languages for problem solving, downloadable software updates and technical documentation, such as end-user or service manuals.

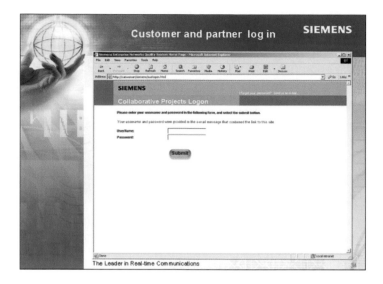

Figure 15.8: Collaboration with Customers and Partners at Siemens

Replacing 26 document management systems, **Siemens Enterprise Networks** developed a single, integrated knowledge management and Web publishing application for all of its product documentation, process and procedure materials—essentially all critical business documents. Keeping its internal people knowledgeable about the products and changes in processes and procedures in the organization, this solution for finding and disseminating key documentation is a critical part of Siemens' Web-based efforts for ongoing collaborative communication with partners and customers.

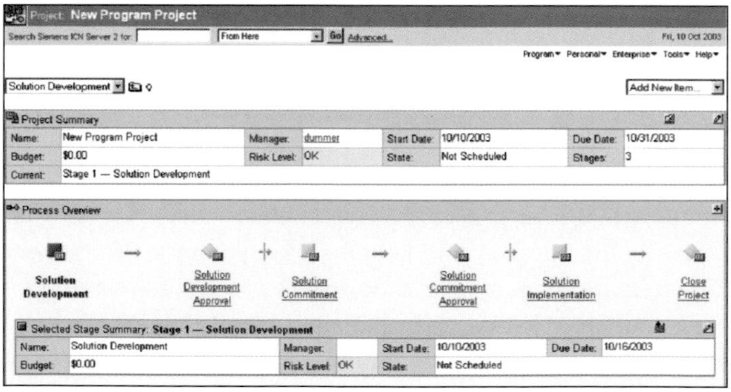

Figure 15.9: Program Management in Research and Development at Siemens

Administration

Administration was the last departmental area at Siemens to adopt an ECM solution. As more divisions and departments came to rely on the Internet for communications, the administration department followed suit and deployed an ECM solution to maximize their reliance on Web-based technology and the Internet. Company-wide, the need for compliance-driven documentation extended ECM applications to include records management and document lifecycle management technologies.

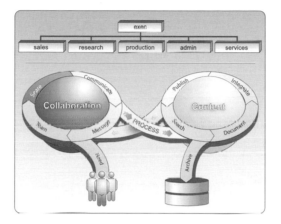

Figure 15.10: Administration Deployment at Siemens

Sharenet is the global intranet, project and knowledge management solution for **Siemens Financial Services (SFS)**. Based on ECM technology, Sharenet provides extensive business process support, from selling products and solutions to quickly responding to customer requests and finding experts across the organization. Building efficient processes across business units and regions based on best practices, SFS is able to set up new projects using predefined templates in minutes.

Using ECM technology, **Siemens Singapore** hosts a centralized standard solution, called Nexus, for the entire Siemens Asia and Australia region. Nexus is a completely Web-based, employee self-service solution that automates administrative approval processes, such as signature authority, travel booking, expense claims, leave management, training management, asset management, recruitment, separation, purchase requisition, business card ordering, timesheets and more. Tightly integrated with its ERP system, Nexus helps ensure adherence to business rules and policies.

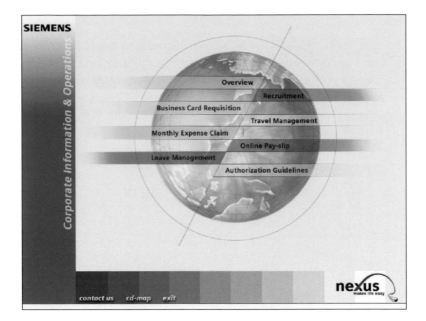

Figure 15.11: Siemens' Nexus Project

An Enterprise-Wide Platform

The final step in the ECM deployment cycle at Siemens began with a corporate-wide inventory and evaluation of ECM technologies and applications, as well as other applications that could be made more efficient with ECM. This resulted in the creation of a corporate-wide knowledge strategy at Siemens which was lead by C-Level Management. By this time, virtually all elements of an ECM system were in use at Siemens at various department and division levels. Cost reductions could be achieved by organizing these technologies into common standards across the enterprise.

Motivated by the desire to gain better returns on investment, implementing an enterprise-wide ECM system is key to achieving corporate memory. This is a concept that describes a corporation's ability to maintain a "memory" of all the documents and processes it relies on to function. ECM increases the stability of organizations that rely on intangible assets (people and knowledge) to create value.

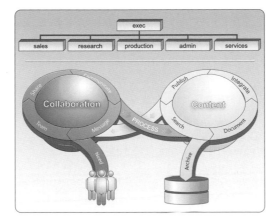

Figure 15.12: Enterprise-Wide Deployment at Siemens

We have illustrated how an initial ECM deployment occurs at the department level and expands to other departments and divisions after six to nine months. After consolidating several applications on a common infrastructure, organizations begin to consider a full enterprise-wide implementation of an ECM solution.

ECM Solutions Framework

Figure 15.13 illustrates how the different technologies of an ECM suite fit together. This illustration describes an ECM Solutions Framework that enables a variety of solutions to be delivered from one consistent data model. This model is easier and more affordable to maintain than a collection of disparate technologies.

The diagram below shows how different ECM solutions can be built on an ECM Solutions Framework. The ECM Solutions Framework provides a layer of software services that link corporate applications to repositories of information, no matter where they reside. The three key services are: Collaboration, Content and Process. For more detailed information, refer to Chapter 2.

The bottom layer illustrates the Enterprise Library, which is critical to achieving the benefit of a fully integrated ECM suite. The Enterprise Library enables content to be securely captured and stored. This is a critical feature for enterprise-wide deployments, since most enterprises have a large legacy of current and old data types. The collaboration service supports the rich human interaction that occurs among knowledge workers. The process service enables the use of business processes that span the enterprise and connect the ECM system with other leading ERP applications. The tight integration of these foundational services ensures that the right content can be located to fuel innovation, and that the by-products of team collaboration are recaptured with minimal effort back into the Enterprise Library.

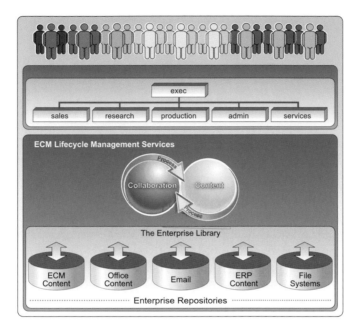

Figure 15.13: ECM Solutions Framework

This ECM Solutions Framework is completed by integrating these user interface and foundational services with business services such as document management, records management and Web content management. Competitive advantage is created because the Framework simplifies the deployment of ECM solutions that span the enterprise and extend into the supply chain. Solutions built on the ECM Solutions Framework provide a consistent view of content to the user regardless of where they may be, with access controlled by their role as defined for each process.

Scaling to the Enterprise

The evolution toward connecting more people with more computers places new demands on ECM technology; not the least of which is the burden placed on a system to accommodate an increasing number of users. Functionality within a system has to scale to accommodate each new user, their associated files and memory requirements.

For example, a search technology that can handle 1,000 people and their documents may not scale to handle 100,000 people and their documents. This is a key issue when considering the eventual usage profile and patterns of single departmental ECM deployment and how this will evolve over time within the enterprise. All of the component technologies for ECM must scale. If one component technology fails to scale, the entire ECM implementation will fail. The chain is only as strong as its weakest link. Therefore, a careful examination of the component technologies is critical to successful enterprise-wide deployments of ECM.

The key enabling technologies for the scale of deployments has been the cost of network connections, bandwidth, memory and CPU required to drive the applications. In the early days, the first Web site had very little data and required little CPU or memory. Since the data was light, it also required very little bandwidth. As the market evolved and intranets became more common, the industry started to require larger deployments to support people and information. Innovations in ECM have been driven by the enabling technologies of bandwidth and server performance. Today, deployments supporting 100,000 people or more and terabytes of data are possible. In the future, extranets between suppliers and vendors as members of e-marketplaces will become possible.

Consider Motorola's scaling requirements when they implemented a global collaboration and knowledge sharing solution. The system had to support 55,000 plus users and logins for guests, 4.6 million documents at 4.8 terabytes and 950k worth of transactions per day.

The following diagram illustrates the scaling challenges that Motorola faced.

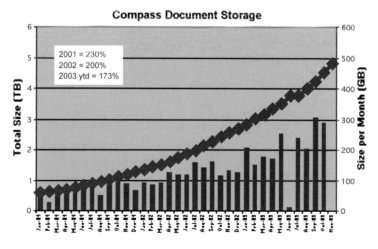

Figure 15.14: Motorola's Document Storage Requirements

Motorola is a global leader in integrated communications solutions and embedded electronic solutions. The telecommunications industry is fast-paced and technologies are highly dynamic. Motorola understands all too well that to maintain market leadership, it is imperative to capture its collective knowledge and leverage its intellectual capital.

A consolidated ECM system serves as the foundation for Motorola's COMPASS system, a global intranet that acts as a central repository for information and a place for small workgroup collaboration and general enterprise-level communication.

"COMPASS gives us a way to bring people and information together under one system. It's the primary location where people share information and collaborate. Improved communication and access to information are helping project teams work together more effectively and that, ultimately, has a positive effect on the way we serve our customers," says the Manager of Content Management and Collaboration Systems, Motorola.

The company's move to consolidate file servers and place more information in COMPASS will reduce costs and give Motorola a better handle on corporate knowledge scattered across numerous systems throughout the company. COMPASS already contains more than 4.6 million documents and is growing by some 40 gigabytes per week, a rate that is likely to increase with the file server consolidation. Motorola's plan to extend COMPASS as an extranet will help the company collaborate more closely with customers, improving communication and overall service. COMPASS will also be extended to Motorola's partners, increasing efficiency.

Since Motorola began using a consolidated collaboration and content management platform, the company has appointed a team of 250 knowledge champions, who educate users on features in COMPASS and help manage the library structure. Knowledge champions help users get the most out of COMPASS, which encourages knowledge sharing and collaboration across the company.

The COMPASS community spans the globe, with particularly active users in North and South America, Europe and Asia.

Although Motorola's requirements were straightforward, they were anything but simple. They needed information to be highly available, performance to be consistently reliable and support for the exchange of millions of items during peak traffic periods. Only a comprehensive ECM suite could support these requirements.

In general, they implemented an ECM system that supported their scaling requirements and allowed them to build project areas that could be extended to include their customers, suppliers and business partners in a secure extranet. In just the first month of implementation, 308 project areas and 833 external users were added to the system.

A large part of Motorola's success is due to their continuous monitoring of system availability and response time, as illustrated in the chart below. They have been able to make incremental changes to the system over several years in a highly controlled manner. Before any change is made, the effect on response time is measured to ensure that the new system will meet or exceed former service levels.

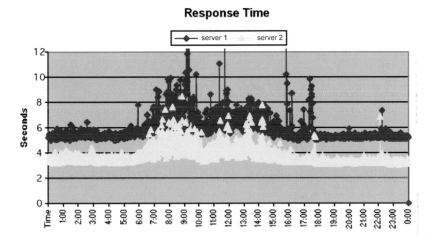

Figure 15.15: Server Response Times

Today, Motorola's system configuration includes a central cluster consisting of multiple tiers and a global network that also performs routing and caching functions so users receive optimal access regardless of their office location. The cluster architecture includes of a grid of load balancers, Web servers, front-end application servers, background process servers, database servers and storage servers that has expanded over time to meet growing usage requirements. Motorola provides extranet access to their ECM system with two additional tiers, which secure the central cluster from the Internet across three firewalls. The first tier provides global caching proxy services and the second isolates the Web servers supporting extranet users from the application services that must be shared with intranet users.

Planning Enterprise Deployment

How can you ensure success when deploying ECM technology throughout a large, multinational corporation and across its supply chain? It is obvious that such an endeavor requires careful planning and ongoing change management. An examination of large-scale ECM deployments, such as those highlighted in this book, reveals the following best practices. Organizations seeking to deploy an ECM solution across the enterprise should:

- understand and communicate the business needs that will be addressed by the ECM system;

- understand and address barriers that may affect adoption by new users, such as usability issues or needs for integration with other systems;

- identify those people who will provide a knowledge management network, and make sure they are able to commit time to the role;

- give knowledge managers the training and tools needed to build an appropriate information architecture and to support their end users;

- identify and communicate best practices;

- demonstrate corporate commitment to the ECM solution;

- plan ongoing activities that pull users into the system so that they are encouraged to contribute;

- establish quantitative success indicators and measures throughout the system's lifecycle;

- address performance issues that may affect adoption.

The following user story featuring the European Investment Bank illustrates the effective employment of these best practices.

> European Investment Bank

The European Investment Bank (EIB) finances capital investment in European Union policy objectives—the bricks and mortar that are constructing an integrated Europe. The bank also partially funds operations in approximately 150 countries outside Europe. This means that remote access to documents is operationally important, especially for countries with relatively weak telecom networks.

Over the last two years, EIB has been implementing an ECM solution called GED as part of a broader IT reengineering program affecting all of the major processes in the bank: borrowing, lending and administration. The integration of GED with the other systems and with the user's work environment is critical to its success. For that reason, GED is fully integrated other IT systems.

To ensure that users would adopt the ECM system, the project team planned how to market the system, developing an "elevator speech" to ensure that everyone understood that "all vital documents in the bank must be created, modified, signed, stored, indexed and available in structured folders" within the system. However, they soon realized that it was not practical for people to use the GED system for vital documents only. The system is in fact destined to receive all electronic documents in the bank, regardless of their importance.

Very early on in the GED project, the implementation team realized that a design is never finished and that iterative design is unavoidable. They adopted a system approach that relies heavily on process analysis and the interpretation of more than 550 varieties of documents produced by the organization.

"I call this practice corporate hermeneutics," says GED's Project Manager. "In the spirit of Gadamer, hermeneutics means looking at an answer to find the question that it responds to. This is a very interesting activity to carry out on corporate documents and one which has not been formalized anywhere yet."

In planning for the GED system, the EIB developed a bank-wide taxonomy, the most visible element of which is the file plan. The EIB taxonomy follows international best practice and more specifically the DIRKS methodology and is consistent with ISO 15489. An access control model was developed for the higher levels of the taxonomy. The taxonomy model has become the basis for knowledge management. The taxonomy fully describes the bank processes. In parallel, the permission model indicates who needs to have access to what to be able to work most efficiently. The combination of the two models and the mapping of the roles onto the file plan produces the knowledge map of the organization.

The GED project adopted a gradual approach over an eight-month period. In particular, training was carried out by two certified, inhouse trainers over a six-month period.

There is also a plan to give an internal official recognition to users who have reached a particular proficiency with the system.

Virtually everyone in the bank was trained, including senior management. There was a conscious decision to cater simultaneously, but sometimes with different means to all levels of the organization. It was essential not only to convince the top of the organization, but also to ensure that secretaries willingly adopt the new tool. Therefore, the project team included users from the start. In addition to the traditional steering committee, a high-level working group contributed directly to the design. This group, mostly secretaries, met every two weeks and was instrumental in keeping people at all levels informed of the status of the project. They contributed very significantly to the development of the taxonomy and continue to constitute a network of proficient users who help the system develop.

At the outset of the project, the team set quantitative indicators of the project's success. Two months into the launch of the GED system they were able to measure that their user adoption was 20 percent higher than expected. 100 percent of vital documents and new lending and borrowing operations were being supported and there were already 600,000 documents in the system—increasing at a rate of 100,000 documents per week.

Globalization

Enterprise deployments by their very nature also present another challenge when managing content: language. Unlike databases where one plus one equals two in any language, the subtleties of human language and culture play a role in the effectiveness in global deployments of content management systems. Every technology covered in this book is affected by language, whether it is searching for words in another language, or holding an online meeting over the Internet in multiple time zones with multiple languages. This is particularly true for symbolic languages which are generally found in Asia. Japanese and Chinese are examples of languages with symbolic character sets. This presents unique challenges in how an entire enterprise can make use of all information within it, regardless of source language.

Each ECM application may need to provide multiple user interfaces in the various languages of the individuals who participate in a global process. Content must be stored, searched and displayed regardless of the language in which it was originally written. If necessary, ECM applications can be designed to store content that is translated into multiple languages so that anyone can perform their tasks in their own language. Other globalization challenges that must be considered when designing ECM applications include: date formats, time formats, time zones, currency and advanced language-specific search features (for example, natural language query parsing, stemming and thesaurus).

ワークフローマップ: ワークフローマップ
移動 ...
マップエディタ
ワークフローマップ
スタート
開始者
評価
開発グループ
マイルストーン
グループ2
開発第一課
開発第2課
サブワークフロー
プロパティ
保存
名前を付けて保存 ...
開始

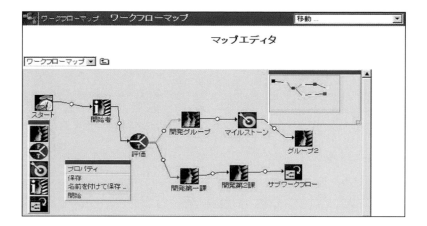

Figure 15.16: A Workflow Written in Japanese

A global consortium of interested parties has developed a universal character set, called unicode that supports every written language used on earth (and some that are not). The broad adoption of unicode across the various ECM technologies will make it easier to support global applications.

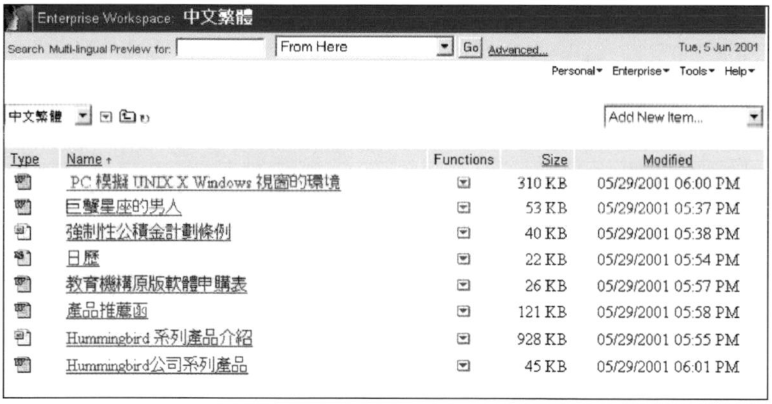

Enterprise Workspace: 中文繁體
Search Multi-lingual Preview for:
From Here
Go
Advanced...
Tue, 5 Jun 2001
Personal Enterprise Tools Help
中文繁體
Add New Item...
Type
Name
Functions
Size
Modified
PC 模擬 UNIX X Windows 視窗的環境 310 KB 05/29/2001 06:00 PM
巨蟹星座的男人 53 KB 05/29/2001 05:37 PM
強制性公積金計劃條例 40 KB 05/29/2001 05:38 PM
日曆 22 KB 05/29/2001 05:54 PM
教育機構原版軟體申購表 26 KB 05/29/2001 05:57 PM
產品推薦函 121 KB 05/29/2001 05:58 PM
Hummingbird 系列產品介紹 928 KB 05/29/2001 05:55 PM
Hummingbird公司系列產品 45 KB 05/29/2001 06:01 PM

Figure 15.17: A Collection of Documents Written in Traditional Chinese

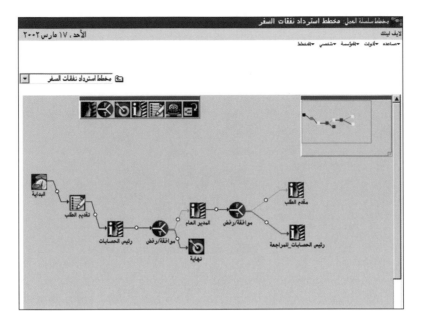

Figure 15.18: A Workflow Written in Arabic

A Platform for Enterprise Applications

Global organizations like Shell, Sprint and Unilever are using a consolidated ECM environment, one that combines collaboration with content management across the enterprise, to develop effective business applications for brand management, new product development, sales and marketing and supply chain management.

ECM at the Enterprise Level

In this chapter we reviewed how some of the largest organizations in the world are adopting ECM to increase productivity. We have also seen in previous chapters how ECM improves business operations by enabling organization to achieve compliance with various government regulations and quality standards. As ECM is adopted on a wider scale, the total cost of ownership (TCO) is reduced and further deployments gain increasing economic leverage to deliver applications. As we have witnessed with other technology adoptions from fax machines to email, organizations throughout the world will be driven to adopt ECM at the enterprise level in order to maintain competitiveness in the face of compliance and productivity pressures. As more and more industries adopt ECM applications, falling behind the curve on implementing ECM applications and technologies will lead to lost competitive advantage.

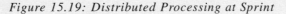

Sprint, a global communications company, required an infrastructure to consolidate the use of servers and centralize the storage of electronic documents—essentially, the telecommunications giant wanted to create a common path for "knowledge discovery" within Sprint.

Sprint deployed ECM in 1999 to create a Web-based knowledge repository to store customer circuit data in its Network Operating Center (NOC), allowing the company to move from a paper-based system to an electronic document management solution. ECM provides a Web-based repository for storing accounts payable invoices and managing Sprint employee expense report receipts linked to an intranet-based reimbursement system.

Today, Sprint is working to develop a Sarbanes-Oxley solution that is based upon an enterprise scalable platform for document management, project coordination and process improvement.

The ability to search and retrieve information online would empower Sprint employees to leverage the company's core competencies to efficiently solve business problems. According to Sprint's Intranet Team Manager, "Early indications show ECM will bring an immediate return on investment, improved efficiencies and better information sharing capabilities to our distributed workforce."

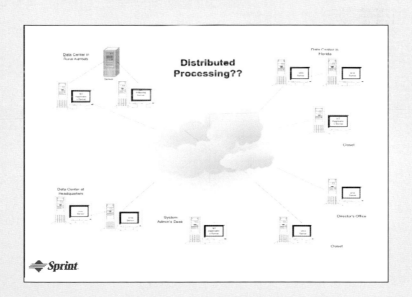

Figure 15.19: Distributed Processing at Sprint

> Unilever

Unilever is one of the largest international manufacturers of leading brands—such as Knorr, Becel, and Conimex—brands that are known and trusted by millions of consumers around the world. In order to align the daily business processes of several business units within Unilever Bestfoods Netherlands (UBF NL) with IT, the organization decided to implement a single digital platform across the organization.

The implementation within UBF NL includes key applications for brand/image management, recipe management, recipe marketing and a news-feed. These key applications are designed to generate user awareness and draw increased traffic to the intranet—a "pull" strategy that has been instrumental in encouraging users to use the system for document and knowledge management.

Every department can set up a localized information structure that completely addresses its distinctive needs to dynamically publish content. According to Unilever Bestfoods Netherlands' IT Manager, "This solution has helped Unilever Bestfoods Netherlands develop a unified way of working. It has improved internal communication and has helped create a stronger awareness of our new internal brand identity among our employees."

Figure 15.20: Content Management for Unilever Bestfood's Web Site

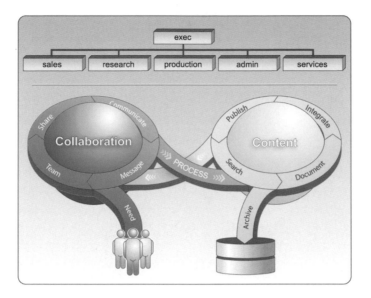

Figure 16.1: The Future of ECM Technologies and Applications

ECM in the future will require interaction among all components of current ECM technology. The value will lie in the combinations of components, not the individual technologies themselves. So now that you know something about ECM, what will tomorrow look like? Read on to discover how our future will be revolutionized by ECM, broadband and wireless technologies.

ECM AND THE FUTURE

In the future, all components of current ECM technology must be seamlessly integrated. The value will lie in the business solutions enabled by ECM technology, not the technology itself. The approach to these solutions will be revolutionized by advances in ECM, broadband and wireless technologies, and tighter integration with desktop productivity tools for information workers. In addition, the nature of ECM will change as content, collaboration, and processes begin to blur the traditional lines that separate applications.

When it comes to investing in technology, the rush to get on the Internet has been replaced by a more thoughtful and fundamental approach. Companies are asking themselves: What procedures must our company comply with to ensure that we can continue to do business as a trusted partner? Why is my company investing this much money? Where is the return on investment for this project?

These are valid questions that indicate the market is now entering a long-term, sustainable investment track for ECM-centric business solutions.

The future of ECM will also be driven by the growth and sophistication of enabling technologies such as rich media and mobile technologies. In the organization of tomorrow, creating a document will not happen in isolation and meeting with someone in an office on the other side of the world will be only a click away. In many ways, the combination of productivity applications is already occurring at the personal and group levels: content is currently being created and saved automatically to a company intranet and global meetings are coordinated from the desktop. By integrating the functionality required to create, share and distribute a document (or other forms of media), people can achieve the highest level of productivity and effectiveness.

Future Trends

All of these issues are driven by six fundamental trends that will greatly affect the future, not only in ECM but in computing and society as a whole:

Content Aggregation	Easy access to all enterprise information available in desktop productivity applications
Increased Legislation	Compliance and governance features as demanded by increased legislation and internal controls
Security	Server-based architecture models for safeguarding the quality, integrity and recoverability of intellectual property
Higher Bandwidth	Rich media collaboration made possible by increased bandwidth
Online Mobility	Presence-awareness within all ECM applications through "always on" online mobility

Content Aggregation

In recent years, enterprises have made large investments in IT infrastructure and enterprise applications, such as ERP, CRM, email and ECM. Information relating to core business processes is often spread across these multiple applications, but there is no single point of access. To streamline business processes, improve information worker productivity and reduce risk, there is increasing demand to provide easy access to all information from enterprise applications directly from desktop productivity tools and portals.

This aggregation of content is achieved through the ECM framework's "Enterprise Library." The Enterprise Library does not require content to be moved from its existing locations, but is a metadata layer that indexes and enables information workers to access content wherever it lives. The Enterprise Library layer makes it easy to retrieve information from multiple enterprise systems with a single search and to present the results in any interface, including Web-based portals and desktop applications. The Enterprise Library is connected to long-term storage devices to enable the use of records management rules to archive content for compliance purposes.

Increased Legislation

Perhaps the single biggest trend affecting ECM is the global increase in legislation. As discussed in the Chapter on Compliance and Corporate Governance, new legislation has had a profound impact on many industries. Regulators are seeking good governance and accountability through transparency. Such transparency is achieved by the diligent recording of all decisions made, including the collaborative processes and documents involved. We will see this diligence extend across every form of corporate communication—from email to instant messaging (IM) and recorded online meetings. Virtually everything will be digitized and recorded with a proper audit trail.

Most organizations will need to demonstrate that they are compliant with all regulations, both old and new. The amount of work required to comply is enormous. The Sarbanes-Oxley legislation, for example, has created an immense change in the way public corporations monitor and record decision making and reporting. Increased regulation means that organizations will receive more inquiries in the form of discovery orders, audits and so on. The information required for the response can span multiple applications and storage devices. The Enterprise Library provides a consolidated window into all enterprise content, enabling a timely and cost-effective response to such requests.

Regulations increasingly specify how organizations store information, and are particularly concerned with ensuring that it is tamper proof. The Enterprise Library enables organizations to automate the process of storing content relevant to a particular regulation appropriately. For example, most inland revenue regulations require a ten-year retention period for all cost or revenue-related documents on non-rewritable storage media, such as WORM (write once, read many).

Many industries are now subject to old and new regulations that regulate digitized content in the same way that paper-based content was regulated in the past. Going forward, this means that ECM will be mandatory for running a business. In the future, ECM deployments must assist an organization in meeting governance requirements, in addition to the basic requirements for higher productivity and a better return on investment.

Security

Security is another factor that will dramatically impact ECM and the rest of the computer industry. Intelligence theft, virus attacks and internal tampering are all threats to the quality and integrity of an organization's intellectual property. We all know that information on the desktop can be vulnerable to electronic attack and theft, but this information is also physically insecure—for example, when a laptop is stolen. With laptops containing more than 100 GB hard drives, the loss of content can seriously compromise an organization.

Organizations must also store backup copies of content in secure, offsite locations for disaster recovery. The Enterprise Library automates the process of storing vital or official documents on high-availability media servers that are located at a specified minimum distance from a main office.

These security issues can be addressed most cost effectively by a server-based architecture, which consolidates all active data on secure central servers, where it can be shared via a document management system. With heightened awareness of security issues, this type of architecture—content stored on central servers with user access via desktop GUIs—will become the standard in the near future.

A server-based architecture also makes it easier to control the information needed for regulatory compliance. Many regulations require an audit trail of information and actions. This involves enforcing higher levels of security for content storage and access.

Higher Bandwidth

Bandwidth will reach a satisfactory level once reasonable resolution (100x100 pixels) and VOIP (Voice Over Internet Protocol) can be delivered reliably. When this occurs, virtually all real-time collaboration, along with a substantial amount of asynchronous collaboration (email or blogging, for example), will advance from document to audiovisual formats. Instead of writing letters or sending emails, we will be sharing our ideas in face-to-face conversations hosted by rich media technology.

This evolution will improve productivity as the technology becomes more intuitive and easier to use. As a result, ECM technology will be available on a mass level, heralding the final stage of ECM adoption throughout the computing world. Because rich media places greater demands on bandwidth, storage and CPU power than other forms of media, it will become an increasing challenge for organizations to manage.

As rich media develops, ECM architecture will be required to integrate "slow zone" collaboration with "fast zone" bandwidths until the transition is complete. The ability to search on these objects will also require further advances to be made in retrieval algorithms. While this is achievable, it remains a growing challenge in the implementation of ECM solutions.

Online Mobility

Perhaps the most revolutionary of all future trends affecting ECM is the advent of "always on" computing. In its earliest form today, personal digital assistants (PDAs) or cell phones with SMS are letting users always be connected to the Internet. The next step in managing these online users is to enable collaborative groups to be aware of the presence of other members online. This presence-awareness creates a transition for users, from individual productivity tools such as writing a document to the ability to instantly initiate a dialog with other parties online.

Users can invite others into a real-time meeting area to review and discuss material as if they had just gathered physically around a whiteboard. In the virtual world, there will be as many hallways and whiteboards as there are users in the system, bringing Metcalfe's Law one step closer to the ultimate value of complete interconnectedness.

A Better Way to Work

Perhaps the most complex issue that ECM users face is the demand to achieve compliance via the transparency of content and action, while simultaneously supporting a security structure that restricts access. Balancing these conflicting requirements with the ability to deliver features and remain cost-competitive will be the true measure of success for future ECM implementations. Implementing a secure and scalable infrastructure in the context of a larger ECM strategy will determine an ECM solution's effectiveness over the long term.

As more transactions become Internet based, accounting will be faster and more precise. Transparency and compliance with such regulations as Sarbanes-Oxley will simply be built into the system and take place almost effortlessly.

Sales and marketing departments will receive critical information in record time, so they will be able to influence their markets at just the right moment. Direct mail information will be automatically collected and combined with individual consumer buying patterns to create customer profiles that can be used in email or targeted direct mail campaigns.

Research and development departments will be able to stay in tune with the changing needs of customers by having access to tailored information, sent along with each sale or Web search that occurs. Collaborating online using rich media will enable global teams to brainstorm ideas on a shared whiteboard.

Collaborative bid proposals and contract administration will streamline development cycles and improve time to market. Suppliers will add significant value by understanding the context in which a material is to be used if it is easily accessible.

CEOs will have incredibly accurate and timely information and make better decisions to pilot their enterprises. They will know that their teams have the right resources assigned and will be able to make the best decisions autonomously. They can be assured that their accounting practices and fiscal reporting are compliant. They will recognize how research and new product development meets regulatory requirements. They will know what their risks are and manage them effectively. Most importantly, they will know what their opportunities are and the precise moment to seize them.

Today, the ECM industry has taken the opportunity created by regulatory compliance to extend its leadership within the IT world. Leveraging the information within the organization has never been more important. Businesses today have to deal with large amounts of internal and external information—much of this brought about by the growing importance of the Internet. Organizations have to turn information overload into competitive advantage. Downsizing during economic hardship, the retirement of experts, the need for flexibility in the workplace and critical demand to better service customers are factors that drive companies to adopt an ECM strategy. Soon, the impossible will become an everyday reality as we log into a seamless system to find relevant information, meet online with colleagues from all over the world, collaborate on critical projects, share best practices, and effortlessly manage processes and the lifecycles of corporate information. ECM solutions will evolve in parallel with progressive Internet technologies. People will be more productive; companies will be more efficient. Because it defines a better way to work, the ECM industry will continue to expand the scope and scale of ECM solutions. In the future, millions of ECM users will become hundreds of millions of users as ECM solutions become commonplace.

So now you know that the next great idea, the next breakthrough, the next innovation, resides within the collective knowledge of connected people. This is the motivation that has driven ECM innovations from the start. By enabling great minds to work together across organizational and geographical boundaries, ECM unleashes potential and gives businesses room to grow. It ensures that companies evolve according to defined procedures and in accordance with standards and regulations. For this reason, ECM will be used by every sector of the economy, by all industries and by firms of all sizes. It will make global companies as nimble as start-ups and give small firms the global reach to deliver sophisticated, professional products and services using virtual networks.

GLOSSARY

Adobe Acrobat - A program that converts electronic files to Portable Document Format (PDF). PDF files can be viewed and printed via Adobe Reader on a variety of platforms.

Adobe Reader - A free program available for a variety of platforms that allows users to view and print Portable Document Format (PDF) files.

Advanced search - A variety of software tools that allow users to get more relevant search results. These tools include Boolean Operators, Stemming, Adjacency and Proximity Searches, Thesauri and Synonyms.

Application - Software or programs used to execute tasks on computers.

Application Service Provider (ASP) - A company that offers Internet access to applications and related services that otherwise would have to be present on users' personal or enterprise computers.

APQP - Advanced Product Quality Planning (APQP) is a quality framework used for developing new products in the automotive industry. It can be applied to any industry and is similar in many respects to the concept of Design for Six Sigma (DFSS).

Archive - Systematic transfer to alternate storage media of digital data that is no longer required to be immediately accessible. Often stored via Computer Output to Laser Disk (COLD) systems. Also a collection of historical records and documents, especially about an institution.

ASP - See Application Service Provider.

Bandwidth - The volume of information per unit time that a computer, person or transmission medium can handle.

BLOG (Web Log) - A Web site that provides updated headlines and news articles of other sites that are of interest to the user, also may include journal entries, commentaries and recommendations compiled by the user; also written Web Log.

Boolean operators - Logical connectors used within advanced search software to obtain more relevant results. For example, the query "apple OR orange" returns documents that contain either "apple" or "orange." The Boolean Operator in the example is OR. The basic operators are NOT, AND, and OR.

Broadband - Relating to or being a communications network in which the bandwidth can be divided and shared by multiple simultaneous signals (as for voice or data or video).

Browser - See Internet browser.

Business Applications - Software programs used to solve business needs such as word processing, accounting or customer relationship management.

Business intelligence - The focal point for improved end-user performance, enabling knowledge workers to synthesize many information sources (for example, data marts, real-time feeds, Web content, groupware, email).

Business Process Management (BPM) - Refers to aligning processes with an organization's strategic objectives, designing and implementing process-centric tools or architectures and determining measurement systems for effective process management. BPM also refers to automation efforts, including workflow systems and ERP systems.

Cadbury Report (Code of Best Practices) - A framework used for assessing Internal Controls issued by the Cadbury Committee of the United Kingdom.

Calendaring - Collaboration software used to schedule time on an individual, team or enterprise basis.

CCA - Commission de Contrôle des Assurances (CCA) Audit Board for Insurers.

CCITT - Abbreviation of Comité Consultatif International Téléphonique et Télégraphique, (France). An organization that sets international communications standards. CCITT, now known as ITU (the parent organization) has defined many important standards for data communications.

Central Processing Unit (CPU) - The part of a computer that does most of the data processing. The CPU and the memory form the central part of a computer to which peripherals are attached.

CFTC - Commodity Futures Trading Commission (CFTC) (USA). The mission of the CFTC is to protect market users and the public from fraud, manipulation, and abusive practices related to the sale of commodity and financial futures and options, and to foster open, competitive, financially sound futures and option markets.

Client Server - A system of sharing files and executing applications within a local or wide-area network. A two-tier architecture where the client (workstation) performs user interface and local data manipulation tasks while the server (host) provides data storage and network services. Typically, these systems feature rigid security and require significant hardware.

COCO - A framework used for assessing Internal Controls, branded as the Guidance on Control issued by the Criteria of Control (CoCo) Board at the Canadian Institute of Chartered Accountants.

COLD - See Computer Output to Laser Disk.

Collaboration Software - Programs that link processes and individuals across different locations and time zones to create an environment where team members work together to share ideas, experiences and knowledge.

Collaborative Knowledge Management (CKM) - Software that allows users within an organization to manage documents, projects and processes, and transparently store the by-products of collaboration into a knowledge base.

Compliance - Adherence to a body of regulations, government legislation or standards (for example, ISO 9000).

Compound Objects - Documents and images converted to a Web-viewable format and treated as a single object.

Computer Output to Laser Disk (COLD) - Archival storage of computer-generated data within an optical storage system.

Connectors - In database management, a link or pointer between two data structures.

Content Management - Storage, maintenance and retrieval of HTML and XML documents and all related elements. Content management systems may be built on top of a native XML database and typically provide publishing capabilities to export content not only to the Web site but to CD-ROM and print.

Contextual Information (Collaboration) - Smaller services/objects that can be embedded in business applications.

Control - A program module or routine that enhances program functionality. A control can be as small as a button on a user interface or as large as a complicated forecasting algorithm. The term is often used with regard to user interface functions such as buttons, menus and dialog boxes.

Converters - An application that converts data from one code to another.

Corporate Governance - The relationship among all the stakeholders in a company. This includes the shareholders, directors and management of a company, as defined by the corporate charter, by-laws, formal policy and rule of law.

COSO - Committee of Sponsoring Organizations of the Treadway Commission.

CPU - See Central Processing Unit.

Cross-platform - Refers to developing for and/or running on more than one type of hardware platform. It implies two different processes. The first is programming source code that is compiled into different machine environments, each of which has to be supported separately. The second method is with the use of an interpreter such as the Java Virtual Machine.

CRM - See Customer Relationship Management.

CRTC - Canadian Radio-Television and Telecommunications Commission (CRTC) (Canadian). Independent public authority in charge of regulating and supervising Canadian broadcasting and telecommunications.

Customer Relationship Management (CRM) - Enterprise-wide software applications that allow companies to manage every aspect of their relationship with customers. The goal of these systems is to assist in building lasting customer relationships and to turn customer satisfaction into customer loyalty.

DAM - See Digital Asset Management.

Data Mart - A subset of a data warehouse often created for just one department or product line.

Data Archiving - Enterprise applications store their transactional data in databases. Every business process produces additional data. Through this, databases grow, become encumbered and increasingly difficult and costly to maintain. Data archiving offloads historic data from the online database and archives it for future access on a secure media.

Data Warehouse - A database designed to support decision making in an organization. Data from the production databases are copied to the data warehouse so that queries and analysis can be performed without disturbing the performance or the stability of the production systems.

Database - A collection of data arranged for ease and speed of search and retrieval.

Desktop - The area of the monitor screen in a graphical user interface (GUI) against which icons and windows used to run applications appear.

Digital Asset - Describes any subdivision or collection of content and meta-data that holds value to the owner. Digital assets may include photos, video, audio, Web page, text document, Microsoft® PowerPoint or graphic.

Digital Asset Management (DAM) - A set of coordinated technologies and processes that allow for the efficient storage, retrieval and reuse of digital content files independent of the medium to which it may be deployed. DAM provides the business rules and processes needed to acquire, store, index, secure, search, export and transform these assets and their descriptive information.

Document - A piece of work created with an application, such as by word processor. A computer file that is not an executable file and contains data for use by applications.

Document Management (DM) - Involves the capture and management of documents within an organization. The term traditionally implied the management of documents after they were scanned into the computer. Today, the term has become an umbrella under which document imaging, workflow, text retrieval and multimedia fall.

Document Repository - A database that includes author, data elements, inputs, processes, outputs and interrelationships.

DoD - Department of Defense (United States).

EAE - See Enterprise Application Extensions.

Early Payment Discounts - Commonly, vendors give customers an optional early payment discount. If vendor invoices are being paid within a certain time frame, customers can reduce the payment by a certain predefined percentage.

ECM - See Enterprise Content Management.

ECM applications - Applications that are usually tailored to address line-of-business problems or customized for specific vertical markets. Core technology elements include an RDBMS, a suite of component services, and an access layer (Web browser or rich client). In addition to the platform infrastructure, solution components can encompass a combination of software, hardware, or even a process methodology.

Electronic Reports Management (ERM) - Accounting software that helps manage tax estimation/preparation, balance sheets and profit and loss statements.

Email - One of the first and most popular uses for the Internet, email (electronic mail) is the exchange of computer-stored messages by telecommunication. Email messages are typically encoded in ASCII text; however, files in non-text formats, such as images and sound files, can be included as attachments sent in binary streams.

EMEA - Similar to the FDA; related to compliance for pharmaceutical companies.

Engines - Software that performs a primary and highly repetitive function such as a database, graphics or search engine.

Enterprise Application - A computer program designed to perform specific functions, such as inventory control, accounting, payroll, material management.

Enterprise Application Extensions (EAE) - Combines business content (for example, documents) with business context (for example, transactional data in ERP, CRM systems), enabling organizations to extract the maximum value from content stored in enterprise applications. While enterprise applications provide the underlying business structure to support business processes, EAE provides the content. Typical solutions include Invoice Verification, Single Customer Folder, or Data Archiving.

Enterprise Content Management (ECM) - Systems that capture, store, retrieve, print and disseminate digital content for use by the enterprise. Digital content includes pictures/images, text, reports, video, audio, transactional data, catalog and code.

Enterprise Resource Planning (ERP) - Any software system designed to support and automate the business processes of medium and large businesses. This may include manufacturing, distribution, personnel, project management, payroll and financials. ERP systems are accounting-oriented information systems for identifying and planning the enterprise-wide resources needed to take, make, distribute and account for customer orders.

Extensible Markup Language (XML) - An initiative from the Worldwide World Wide Web Consortium defining an "extremely simple" dialect of SGML suitable for use on the World Wide Web. See also HTML and SGML.

Extranet - An IP network that provides secure connections between remote users and a main site, or among multiple sites within the same company, including connectivity to business partners, customers and suppliers.

FDA - Food & Drug Administration (FDA) (United States). FDA's mission is to promote and protect the public health by helping safe and effective products reach the market in a timely way while monitoring products for continued safety after they are in use.

FDIC - Federal Deposit Insurance Corporation (FDIC) (United States). Insures deposits and promotes safe and sound banking practices.

Firewall - A physical boundary that prevents unauthorized traffic crossing from one area into another.

FRB - Federal Reserve Board (USA).

FSA - Financial Services Authority (FSA) (UK). Independent body that regulates the financial services industry in the U.K.

Full-Text Retrieval - Software that allows users to search the entire text portion of digital information and retrieves files that match the user's search criteria. Document-retrieval systems store entire documents, which are usually retrieved by title or by keywords associated with the document. In some systems, the text of documents is stored as data. This permits full text searching, enabling retrieval on the basis of any words in the document. Reference-retrieval systems store references to documents rather than the documents themselves.

GICS - Government Information and Communication Service (GICS) (UK). The Government Information and Communication Service is a network of communication professionals working in government departments and agencies across the UK.

Graphics Interchange Format (GIF) - A filename extension used to describe digitized images.

Highly Scalable - Able to reach high-performance levels. Capable of being changed in size and configuration. Typically refers to the ability of a computer, application or system to expand.

Highly Structured - See structured data.

HIPAA - Health Insurance Portability and Accountability Act of 1996 (HIPAA) (United States). The goals of this legislation are to streamline industry inefficiencies, reduce paperwork, make it easier to detect and prosecute fraud and abuse and enable workers of all professions to change jobs, even if they (or family members) had pre-existing medical conditions.

Hosting - Maintaining a computer system and its applications at a third-party site.

Hypertext Markup Language (HTML) - A structured document format in which elements (commonly referred to as "tags") are embedded in the text. Tags are used for presentation formatting to delimit text which is to appear in a special place or style. HTML is an extension of SGML.

IMF (International Monetary Fund) - An organization of 184 countries working to foster global monetary cooperation, secure financial stability, facilitate international trade, promote high employment and sustainable economic growth and reduce poverty.

Index - In data management, the most common method for keeping track of data on a disk. Indexes are directory listings maintained by the operating system, RDBMS or the application. An index of files contains an entry for each file name and the location of the file. An index of records has an entry for each key field (for example, account number or name) and the location of the record.

Instant Messaging (IM) - Exchanging messages in real time between two or more people. Unlike a telephone, which requires that one entity contact another before making a connection, instant messaging (IM) requires that both parties be logged onto a network, such as the Internet, and their IM service at the same time in order for an exchange to be initiated. Instant messaging facilities also allow users to see if a contact is connected to the Internet; this is typically referred to as "presence."

Integrated Document Archive and Retrieval System (IDARS) - A consolidated system for storage, access, management, distribution and viewing of data that is often print-stream oriented. Often used in customer services support and electronic billing.

Integrated Document Management (IDM) - Full-featured programs supporting a large number of document and image types, including its specialty of creating extremely long documents (hundreds of thousands of pages). Other products in the family provide enhanced document control and workgroup operation, as well as document management, distribution and tracking.

Internet - An interconnected system of networks that connects computers around the world via the TCP/IP protocol.

Internet Browser - The program that serves as the client front end to the World Wide Web. Mosaic was the browser that put the Web on the map in 1993, but by the mid 1990s, Netscape Navigator (commonly known as Netscape®) had 80% of the market. Today, Microsoft® Internet Explorer, which is included with every Windows computer, has more than 90% of the market.

Intranet - An "internal Internet" configured behind a firewall, potentially connecting departments, customers and trading partners. A privately maintained computer network that can be accessed only by authorized persons, especially members or employees of the organization that owns it.

ISO - The International Organization for Standardization. A collection of more than 14,000 International Standards for business, government and society which provides a network of national standards institutes from 148 countries working in partnership with international organizations, governments, industry, business and consumer representatives.

JPEG, JPG - A file extension typically used for an image that appears within the body of a Web page. Most graphical Web browsers can display both GIF and JPG images online.

King II Code - A framework used for assessing Internal Controls branded as the 'King Report' of 1994 to promote the highest standards of corporate governance in South Africa. It advocates that companies develop risk management and internal control systems.

Knowledge Management (KM) - An umbrella term for making more efficient use of the human knowledge that exists within an organization. The major focus is to identify and gather content from documents, reports and other sources and to be able to search that content for meaningful relationships. Knowledge Management also concerns the ability to identify high-value individuals within an organization.

Knowledge repository - A database of information about applications software that includes author, data elements, inputs, processes, outputs and interrelationships.

KonTraG - Gesetz zur Kontrolle und Transparenz im Unternehmensbereich. German Business Monitoring and Transparency Act, which came into force in 1998, outlines requirements on detailed accounting information.

LAN - Local Area Network.

Legge 321 - Italian Law Number 321 on Corporate Governance.

LSF - Loi de Sécurité Financière (French Financial Security Bill, or the French equivalent to Sarbanes-Oxley).

Materials Management - A specific module within an ERP system used to process all material management related tasks.

Media Asset Management (MAM) - See Digital Asset Management (DAM).

Messaging-Based Collaboration - Messaging refers to a data set that is transmitted over a communications line. Messaging consolidation and standards consolidation are turning collaboration services from applications into middleware. For example, email is now a commodity and instant messaging (IM) and Web conferencing are emergent collaboration technologies.

Meta-data - Sometimes known as data about the data, meta-data describes, tracks and provides context for content.

Meta-data Tagging - Data that describes other data, including detailed compilations such as data dictionaries and repositories that provide information about each data element. May also refer to any descriptive item about data, such as the content of an HTML meta tag or a title field in a media file. Tags are a set of bits or characters that identify various conditions about data in a file. Tags are often found in the header records of such files.

Multimedia - Integration of text, voice, video, images, or some combination of these types of information. See also Rich Media.

NAIC - National Association of Insurance Commissioners (NAIC) (United States) Assists state insurance regulators, individually and collectively, in serving the public interest.

NASD - The National Association of Securities Dealers. An association of brokers and dealers in the over-the-current securities business. NASD acts to "adopt, administer, and enforce rules of fair practice…and in general to promote just and equitable principles of trade for the protection of investors."

OFCOM - (UK) Regulator for the UK communications industries, with responsibilities across television, radio, telecommunications and wireless communications services.

Online - Connected to or accessible via a computer or computer network. Typically refers to being connected to the Internet or other remote service.

Operating system - A computer's master control program that manages it's internal functions controls it's operation. An operating system provides commonly used functions and a uniform, consistent means for all software applications to access the computer's resources. Windows and Unix are operating systems.

Optical Character Recognition (OCR) - Recognition of printed or written characters by computer. Each page of text is converted to a digital image using a scanner and OCR is then applied to the image to produce a text file. Complex image processing algorithms are required and rarely achieve 100% accuracy, so manual proof reading is recommended.

OSHA - Occupational Safety and Health Administration (OSHA) (United States). The government agency that establishes protective standards and enforces them, and reaches out to employers and employees through technical assistance and consultation programs.

Patriot Act - The US Patriot Act was passed by Congress as a response to the terrorist attacks of September 11, 2001. The Act allows federal officials greater authority in tracking and intercepting communications, both for purposes of law enforcement and foreign intelligence gathering.

PDA - See Personal Digital Assistant.

Permissions - Management of who can access a computer or network. The Access Control List (ACL) is the set of data associated with a file, directory or other resource that defines the permissions that users, groups, processes or devices have for accessing it.

Personal Computer (PC) - A computer built around a microprocessor for use by an individual, as in an office, home or school.

Personal Digital Assistant (PDA) - A lightweight, hand-held, usually pen-based computer used as a personal organizer.

PIPEDA - Personal Information Protection and Electronic Documents Act (PIPEDA) (Canadian). An Act to support and promote electronic commerce by protecting personal information that is collected, used or disclosed in certain circumstances, by providing for the use of electronic means to communicate or record information or transactions.

Platform - The term originally concerned only CPU or computer hardware, but it also refers to software-only environments. A messaging or groupware platform implies one or more programming interfaces that email, calendaring and other client programs are written to in order to communicate with the services provided by the server.

PLM - See Product Lifecycle Management.

Portable Document Format (PDF) - File format used by the Adobe Acrobat document exchange system.

Portable Network Graphics (PNG) - An extensible file format for the portable, well-compressed storage of raster images. PNG provides a patent-free replacement for GIF.

Portal - Within the enterprise, software that provides access via a Web browser into all of an organization's information assets and applications. Portals provide a variety of services including Web searching, news, white and yellow pages directories, free email, discussion groups, online shopping and links to other sites. The term is increasingly being used to refer to vertical market sites for a particular industry such as banking, insurance or technology.

PRO - The Public Records Office of the United Kingdom of Great Britain. The national archives body of the U.K. PRO publishes a standard for records management systems designed to ensure interoperability with the national archive and promote records management best practices throughout the U.K.

Process management - The automation of business processes using a rule-based expert system that invokes the appropriate tools and supplies necessary information, checklists, examples and status reports to the user.

Product Lifecycle Management (PLM) - An enterprise application for product lifecycle management.

QS - FDA Quality System Regulation (21 CFR Part 820) (United States). Requires that domestic or foreign manufacturers have a quality system for the design and production of medical devices intended for commercial distribution in the United States.

Raster image - A graphic consisting of sets of horizontal lines composed of pixels.

RDIMS - Records/Document/Information Management System (RDIMS) (Canadian). As a concept, it is designed to provide a model for implementing information management programs and tools. The product and the concepts work together to allow the federal government to collect and store information, and to exchange information between government offices and with clients and partners.

Real-Time Collaboration - Tools that let people to collaborate simultaneously. The primary data collaboration tools are electronic whiteboards, which are shared chalkboards and application sharing, which lets remote users work in the same application together. Some form of human communication is also necessary, so either text chat, audio or videoconferencing becomes part of the total system.

Records Management (RM) - Refers to the creation, retention and scheduled destruction of an organization's paper and film documents. Email and computer-generated content also fall into the RM domain. Traditional data processing files are not considered part of RM.

Regulatory requirements - Overseen by various governmental agencies to ensure compliance with laws, regulations and established rules. Examples relevant to content management applications include: U.S. FDA 21 CFR Part 11, U.S. DoD 5015.2 Standard, U.S. Sarbanes-Oxley Act, Basel II and HIPAA.

Relational database - A database in which all the data and relations between them are organized in tables. A relational database allows the definition of data structures, storage and retrieval operations and integrity constraints.

Return On Investment (ROI) - Traditional financial approach for examining overall investment returns over a given time frame (supports indexing and scoring).

Rich content - See rich media.

Rich Media - Information that consists of any combination of graphics, audio, video and animation, all more storage- and bandwidth-intensive than ordinary text.

Rights & Permissions - Identifies the circumstances under which a particular asset may be used. For instance, indicates who legally owns the asset, in what mediums it may be used (Web, print, TV) and the financial liabilities incurred to include the asset.

ROI - See Return on investment.

Sarbanes-Oxley Act - Passed by U.S. Congress to protect investors from the possibility of fraudulent corporate accounting activities.

Scalability - Ability to reach high-performance levels.

SCM - See Supply Chain Management.

Search - To look for specific data in a file or an occurrence of text in a file or on a page. Implies sequential scanning of content or indexes in order to find the results, rather than a direct lookup. Search engines can differ dramatically in the way they find and index the material on the Web and the way they search the indexes from the user's query.

SEC - Securities and Exchange Commission. The SEC was established by Congress to help protect investors by administering the Securities Act of 1933, the Securities Exchange Act of 1934, the Securities Act Amendments of 1975, the Trust Indenture Act, the Investment Company Act, the Investment Advisor's Act and the Public Utility Holding Company Act.

SGML - See Standard Generalized Markup Language.

Short Message Service (SMS) - Text messaging sent using this service, which allows a short alphanumeric message (160 alphanumeric characters) to be sent for display on a mobile or cell phone.

SOAP - Simple Object Access Protocol, an XML protocol.

Software - The programs, routines and symbolic languages that control the functioning of a computer and direct its operation.

SOX - See Sarbanes-Oxley Act.

Standard Generalized Markup Language (SGML) - A language specification adopted by ISO (International Standards Organization) in 1986 as a means of defining and separating the structure, information content and presentation format of electronic documents. SGML is ISO standard no. 8879.

Storyboarding - The process of creating a rough outline of what your video will look like from a selection of video clips. This process helps the user visualize the whole video and how it will look when completed.

Structured data - Data that resides in fixed fields within a record or file. Relational databases and spreadsheets are examples of structured data.

Supply Chain Management (SCM) - An enterprise application for supply chain management.

Synchronous collaboration - Relating to computer systems or applications that update information at the same rate as they receive data, enabling them to direct or control a collaborative process in real time.

Taxonomic classifications - Laws or principles of classification; systematic division into ordered groups or categories.

Team Collaborative Applications (TCA) - Web-based software programs that enable groups of users, such as project teams to work together using a variety of applications.

Terabyte - A unit of computer memory or data storage capacity equal to one trillion bytes.

Thumbnail - A low-resolution small size rendition of an image asset; or, small size textual rendition of a text asset.

TPD - Therapeutic Products Directorate (TPD) (Canada). The Canadian federal authority that regulates pharmaceutical drugs and medical devices for human use.

Transaction - Synonymous with a specific business application, such as order entry, invoice information capture, etc. To create, change or display business information in an enterprise application, users have to call certain transactions in the system. See also: Transactional Data.

Transactional data - Orders, purchases, changes, additions and deletions are typical business transactions stored in the computer. Transactions update one or more master files and serve as both an audit trail and history for future analyses. Ad hoc queries are also a type of transaction but are usually not saved.

Transformation - An operation applied to one or more assets that result in the construction of a new asset, called a Transformed Asset. The transformation embodies business rules that are applied during this construction.

Turnbull Report - A framework used for assessing Internal Controls branded as "Internal Control: Guidance for Directors on the Combined Code." The Institute of Chartered Accountants in England and Wales has published the final guidance on the implementation of the internal control requirements of the Combined Code on Corporate Governance. This guidance has the support and endorsement of the Stock Exchange.

Unstructured data - Data that does not reside in fixed locations. Free-form text in a word-processing document is a typical example.

VERS - Victorian Electronic Records Strategy (Australia). Public Record Office Victoria (PROV) runs a compliance program to test systems and products against the Standard for the Management of Electronic Records (PROS 99/007) (the VERS Standard).

Virtual project (workgroup) - A group of individuals who work on a common project via technologies such as email, shared databases, threaded discussions and calendaring. Virtual workgroups are mandated by company policy and employment requirements.

Web - A shorthand way to refer to the World Wide Web and possibly its complementing technologies. For example, a Web authoring tool might be used to create documents that contain Hyper Text Markup Language (HTML).

Web browser - See Internet browser.

Web Content Management (WCM) - Systems designed to drive Web sites by separating content from presentation and providing the following capabilities: capacity planning, site design/layout, look/feel navigation, content development, production, delivery, session tracking and site evolution.

WSDL - Web Service Definition Language.

Web sites - A server process that provides access to Web pages and other data to client applications (for example, a browser).

Workflow - Using applications and technology to automate the execution of each phase in a business process. For example, a workflow may contain the automatic routing of documents and tasks to the users responsible for working on them. Documents and other data in a workflow may be physically moved over the network or maintained in a single database with the appropriate users given access to the data at the required times. Triggers can be implemented in the system to alert managers when tasks, documents or other operations in the workflow are overdue.

World Wide Web (WWW) - An HTML-based Internet system developed at the European Center for Nuclear Research (CERN) in Geneva. Also relates to the complete set of documents residing on all Internet servers that use the HTTP protocol. The Web is accessible to users via a simple point-and-click system.

XML - see Extensible Markup Language.

BIBLIOGRAPHY

Cain, Matt. *Mapping Collaboration Maturity.* META Group Report: ©October 16, 2003

Chapman, Merrill R. In Search of Stupidity: Over 20 Years of High Tech Marketing Disasters. Apress, ©2003

Cotton, Bob and Richard Oliver. Understanding Hypermedia. London: Phaidon Press Ltd. ©1993

Frappaolo, Carl. Knowledge Management. Oxford, UK: Capstone Publishing. ©2002

Hanser, Kathleen. *Amazing Technology Facts from Boeing Commercial Airplanes.* http://www.boeing.com

Hayward, Simon et al. *Hype Cycle for e-Workplace Technologies.* Gartner Report: ©June 6, 2003

Logan, Robert K., and Louis W. Stokes. Collaborate to Compete. Canada: Wiley ©2004

McGrath, Michael E. Product Strategy for High Technology Companies, Accelerating Your Business to Web Speed. New York: McGraw-Hill Book Co. ©2001

McLuhan, Marshall. Understanding Media. New York: McGraw-Hill Book Co. ©1964

Monks, Robert A. and Nell Minnow. Corporate Governance. 3rd Edition. Blackwell Publishing Ltd. ©2004

Moore, Connie and Robert Markham. *Market Leaders Emerging in Enterprise Content Management.* Forrester Research: ©August, 2003

Moore, Geoffrey. Inside the Tornado, Marketing Strategies from Silicon Valley's Cutting Edge. HarperBusiness: Reprint edition ©1999

Moschella, David C. Waves of Power, The Dynamics of Global Technology Leadership 1964-2010. New York, NY: American Management Association, ©1997

Open Text Corporation. Ten Years of Innovation: 1991-2001. Canada: ©2002

Open Text Corporation. LiveLinkUp Conference Proceedings. Volumes 1 – 7. Canada: ©1999-2001

Peters, Tom. *The Wow Project, Excerpts,* Fast Company. Issue 24. ©1999

Rao, Ramana. *Bridging Structured and Unstructured Data.* Knowledge Management Online. Line56 Media: ©April 01, 2003.

Saint-Onge, Hubert and Debra Wallace. Leveraging Communities of Practice for Strategic Advantage. New York: Butterworth-Heinemann. ©2003

Stewart, Thomas A. *The Case Against Knowledge Management,* Business 2.0. February 2002, Vol. 3, pp80-83

USER CASE STUDY BIBLIOGRAPHY

Air Liquide. *Air Liquide Selects Open Text's Livelink.* Press Release. Open Text © 2003. http://www.opentext.com/ecmbook/userstory/air_liquide

Airbus. *Visible ROI with IXOS Legacy Decommissioning Solution.* Whitepaper, IXOS SOFTWARE AG © 2003. http://www.opentext.com/ecmbook/userstory/airbus

Alaska Airlines. *Connecting A North American System.* Case Study. Open Text © 2003. http://www.opentext.com/ecmbook/userstory/alaska_airlines

Alte Leipziger. *Agent portal provides competitive advantage.* Case Study. IXOS SOFTWARE AG © 2003. http://www.opentext.com/ecmbook/userstory/alte_leipziger

Audi. *Automotive Giant, Audi, Utilizes Open Text's Livelink Enterprise-wide.* Press Release. Open Text © 2004. http://www.opentext.com/ecmbook/userstory/audi

Barclays. *Streamlining HR processes.* Case study. Open Text © 2004. http://www.opentext.com/ecmbook/userstory/barclays

BMW. *Hi-Tech Elegance.* Case Study. Open Text © 2002. http://www.opentext.com/ecmbook/userstory/bmw

British Council. *Saving With a Revamped Online Presence.* Case Study. Open Text © 2004. http://www.opentext.com/ecmbook/userstory/british_council

Broward County School District. *Open Text Secures Deal with Largest Fully-Accredited U.S. School District.* Press Release. Open Text © 2003. http://www.opentext.com/ecmbook/userstory/broward

BT. *ECM in BT – Vision and Realisation.* LinkUp Europe London 2004 Proceedings. Open Text © 2004. http://www.opentext.com/ecmbook/userstory/bt

CARE International. *Open Text Annual General Meeting Presentation 2003.* Open Text © 2003. http://www.opentext.com/ecmbook/userstory/care

Daimler Chrysler Financial Services. Open Text © 2005. http://www.opentext.com/ecmbook/userstory/daimler_chrysler

Dow Chemical. *Open Text's Live LinkUp Chicago Conference Draws Record Numbers.* Press Release. Open Text © 2002. http://www.opentext.com/ecmbook/userstory/dow_chemical

Electronic Arts. *Corporate Brand Management Brochure.* Artesia Technologies © 2003. http://www.opentext.com/ecmbook/userstory/electronic_arts

European Investment Bank. *Electronic Document, Records & Knowledge Management Solution for the European Investment Bank.* LinkUp Europe London 2004 Proceedings. Open Text © 2004. http://www.opentext.com/ecmbook/userstory/eib

Federal Ministry of the Interior. *Federal Government Procurement Goes Online.* Procurement Agency of the Federal Ministry of the Interior © 2003. http://www.opentext.com/ecmbook/userstory/fmoi

Fluor Hanford. Open Text © 2006. http://www.opentext.com/ecmtrilogy/solutionsbook/innovator/fluor

General Motors. *Data archiving at General Motors India.* IXOS SOFTWARE AG © 2002. http://www.opentext.com/ecmbook/userstory/general_motors

General Motors. *General Motors Selects Artesia Technologies' TEAMS 3.0 Digital Asset Management Solution To Extend Digital Brand Assets.* Press Release. Artesia Technologies © 1999. http://www.opentext.com/ecmbook/userstory/general_motors

Genzyme. *Records Management and Regulatory Affairs.* LiveLinkUp Orlando 2003 Proceedings CD-ROM. Open Text: ©2003. http://www.opentext.com/ecmbook/userstory/genzyme

HBO. *Artesia Technologies Presents Digital Asset Management - Simplified at the AIIM EXPO 2004 SolutionCenter.* Press Release. Artesia Technologies © 2004. http://www.opentext.com/ecmbook/userstory/hbo

ISO Central Secretariat. *Building a Worldwide Extranet.* Case Study. Open Text © 2001. http://www.opentext.com/ecmbook/userstory/ISO

Kerr-McGee. *Allen Hummel Interview.* LinkUp Europe London 2004 Proceedings. Open Text © 2004. http://www.opentext.com/ecmbook/userstory/kerr_mcgee

Kerr-McGee. *Using XML Skins to Enhance Usability and Time to Market.* LiveLinkUp Orlando 2003 Proceedings. Open Text © 2003 http://www.opentext.com/ecmbook/userstory/kerr_mcgee

Krispy Kreme. *Driving Growth Through Content Management.* Case Study. Open Text © 2003. http://www.opentext.com/ecmbook/userstory/krispy_kreme

Lockheed Martin. Chapman, Kimberly. *Lockheed Martin Takes Off With Livelink.* Network World. Copyright © 1999 from NETWORK WORLD CANADA. http://www.opentext.com/ecmbook/userstory/lockheed_martin

Lockheed Martin. Open Text Annual Report 1999. Open Text © 1999. http://www.opentext.com/ecmbook/userstory/lockheed_martin

M+W Zander. *Dr. Rudolf Simon Interview.* LinkUp Europe London 2004 Proceedings. Open Text © 2004. http://www.opentext.com/ecmbook/userstory/MW_Zander

Miller Group. *Integrated Invoice Scanning Solution.* LiveLinkUp Paris 2003 Proceedings. Open Text © 2003. http://www.opentext.com/ecmbook/userstory/miller

Mitsubishi Automotive Engineering. *Mitsubishi Automotive Engineering: Maneuvering the High Powered Roads of Technology.* Case Study. Open Text © 2001. http://www.opentext.com/ecmbook/userstory/mae

Motorola. *Consolidating Content and Collaboration Across the Enterprise. Motorola Compass: Availability, Scalability and Performance for the Enterprise and Beyond.* LiveLinkUp Orlando 2003 Proceedings CD-ROM. Open Text © 2003. http://www.opentext.com/ecmbook/userstory/motorola

Motorola. *Motorola Extends Use of Open Text's Livelink.* Press Release. Open Text © 2003. http://www.opentext.com/ecmbook/userstory/motorola

National Economic Research Associates. *NERA Consolidates Document Collection With Open Text Library Management Solution.* Press Release. Open Text © 2003. http://www.opentext.com/ecmbook/userstory/NERA

National Institute on Drug Abuse. *Fostering Nationwide Clinical Research.* Case Study. Open Text © 2003. http://www.opentext.com/ecmbook/userstory/nida

Northrop Grumman. *Livelink Management & Operations — Best Practices & Lessons.* Live LinkUp Chicago 2002 Proceedings. Open Text © 2002. http://www.opentext.com/ecmbook/userstory/northrop_grumman

Oral-B. *Real World.* Case Study. Open Text © 2002.
http://www.opentext.com/ecmbook/userstory/oralb

OSFI. *Case Management at the Office of the Superintendent of Financial Institutions.* LiveLinkUp Orlando 2003 Proceedings CD-ROM. Open Text © 2003.
http://www.opentext.com/ecmbook/userstory/osfi

Owens Corning. *Furthering its corporate-wide paper-free initiative.* Case Study. IXOS SOFTWARE © 2001. http://www.opentext.com/ecmbook/userstory/owens_corning

Roche. *Roche Streamlines Pharmaceutical Development with Livelink.* Press Release, Open Text © 2003. http://www.opentext.com/ecmbook/userstory/roche

Roche. *ShareWeb – Integrating Collaboration with Content Management.* LiveLinkUp Paris 2003 Proceedings. Open Text © 2003 http://www.opentext.com/ecmbook/userstory/roche

Samsonite. *Document Management Makes Good Business Case.* Case Study. Open Text © 2002. http://www.opentext.com/ecmbook/userstory/samsonite

Sasol. *Managing Regulated Documents with Livelink.* LiveLinkUp Orlando 2003 Proceedings CD-ROM. Open Text © 2003. http://www.opentext.com/ecmbook/userstory/sasol

Shell. Rapaport, Lowell. *Team Collaboration Unites the Workforce.* Transform Magazine. United Business Media Company © 2003. http://www.opentext.com/ecmbook/userstory/shell

Shenandoah Life. *Improving Service and Supporting Growth.* Case Study. Open Text © 2002. http://www.opentext.com/ecmbook/userstory/shenandoah

Shenandoah Life. *Melanie Sloane Interview.* LinkUp Phoenix 2004 Proceedings. Open Text © 2004. http://www.opentext.com/ecmbook/userstory/shenandoah.

Siemens Automation & Drives. *ADEBAR Delivers Documents Immediately.* Case Study. IXOS SOFTWARE © 2003. http://www.opentext.com/ecmbook/userstory/siemens

Siemens Enterprise Networks. *EZ-A: Easy Access to Customer Contracts, Engagement, Solutions, and Services.* LinkUp Orlando 2003 Proceedings. Open Text © 2003.
http://www.opentext.com/ecmbook/userstory/siemens

Siemens Financial Services (SFS). *Realizing a Paperless Office @ Siemens Financial Services.* LiveLinkUp Europe 2003 Proceedings. http://www.opentext.com/ecmbook/userstory/siemens

Siemens Netherlands. *Enterprise Content Management at Siemens Netherlands.* LinkUp Europe London 2004 Proceedings. http://www.opentext.com/ecmbook/userstory/siemens

Siemens OSRAM. *OSRAM GmbH: ROI 201%. Return On Investment Study.* Open Text © 1998. http://www.opentext.com/ecmbook/userstory/siemens

Siemens. *Global network of knowledge.* Live LinkUp Chicago 2002 Proceedings. Open Text © 2002. http://www.opentext.com/ecmbook/userstory/siemens

Siemens. *Integrating Livelink with SAP.* Live LinkUp Chicago 2002 Proceedings. Open Text © 2003. http://www.opentext.com/ecmbook/userstory/siemens

Siemens. *Supporting More than 80,000 Users.* LiveLinkUp Orlando 2003 Proceedings CD-ROM. Open Text © 2003. http://www.opentext.com/ecmbook/userstory/siemens

Sinclair Knight Merz. *Global Collaboration Using Distributed Livelink Servers.* LiveLinkUp Orlando 2003 Proceedings CD-ROM. Open Text © 2003.
http://www.opentext.com/ecmbook/userstory/sinclair_knight_merz

Sprint. *Improving Business Efficiencies: Livelink as an Intranet Hosting Environment.* LiveLinkUp

<u>Las Vegas 2001 Proceedings</u>. Open Text © 2002.
http://www.opentext.com/ecmbook/userstory/sprint

St. John's Hospital. *Building SaintsNet: An Enterprise Portal for Physicians.* Case Study.
Open Text © 2004. http://www.opentext.com/ecmbook/userstory/st_john

Standard Radio. Open Text © 2004. http://www.opentext.com/ecmbook/userstory/standard_radio

Sultex. *Building a flexible customer portal.* Case Study. Open Text © 2004.
http://www.opentext.com/ecmbook/userstory/sultex

The Open University. *Developing an Online Student Community.* Case Study. Open Text © 2002.
http://www.opentext.com/ecmbook/userstory/open_university

Time Warner. Open Text © 2004. http://www.opentext.com/ecmbook/userstory/time_warner

TransLink. *Increasing User Adoption.* <u>LiveLinkUp Orlando 2003 Proceedings CD-ROM</u>.
Open Text © 2003. http://www.opentext.com/ecmbook/userstory/translink

Turner Construction Company. *Using Technology To Blend Knowledge and Learning.* <u>Live
LinkUp Chicago 2002 Proceedings</u>. Open Text © 2002, pp237-238.
http://www.opentext.com/ecmbook/userstory/turner

UBS AG. *An Interactive Information Platform.* Case Study. Open Text ©.
http://www.opentext.com/ecmbook/userstory/ubs

Unilever Bestfoods. *A live link to a dynamic brand.* Case Study. Open Text © 2003.
http://www.opentext.com/ecmbook/userstory/unilever

Unilever Bestfoods. *Open Text Introduces Content Management Offering For Livelink.* Press
Release. Open Text © 2002. http://www.opentext.com/ecmbook/userstory/unilever

United States Air Force (Business Solutions Exchange). *United States Air Force Chooses
Livelink to Manage Outsourcing Operations.* Press Release. Open Text © 1999.
http://www.opentext.com/ecmbook/userstory/airforce

United States Air Force. Havenstein, Heather H. *In the Know.* Federal Computer Week. FCW
Media Group © 2003. http://www.opentext.com/ecmbook/userstory/airforce

United States Air Force. Schwartz, Karen D. *Getting Collaborative Systems to Walk the Talk.*
Government Executive © 2003. http://www.opentext.com/ecmbook/userstory/airforce

United States Army Reserve. *Selling a Records Management Solution to Your Organization.*
<u>LiveLinkUp Las Vegas 2001 Proceedings</u>. Open Text © 2001.
http://www.opentext.com/ecmbook/userstory/usar

United States Army. U.S. *Army Selects BearingPoint and Open Text to Deploy Worldwide
Training Portal for 42,000 Medics.* Press Release. Open Text © 2003.
http://www.opentext.com/ecmbook/userstory/usarmy

United States Patent and Trademark Office. Open Text © 2004
http://www.opentext.com/ecmbook/userstory/USPTO

Whirlpool Corporation. *Corporate Brand Management Brochure.* Artesia Technologies © 2003.
http://www.opentext.com/ecmbook/userstory/whirlpool

Whirlpool Corporation. *Whirlpool Corporation Selects the Artesia TEAMS Solution as its
Standard for Digital Asset Management.* Press Release. Artesia Technologies © 2004.
http://www.opentext.com/ecmbook/userstory/whirlpool

INDEX

K,L

M

N, O

P

T

Taxonomies: 50, 66, 77, 108, 109, 191
Team Collaborative Applications: 162
Team Members: 11, 75, 163, 165, 166, 177
Teamware: 163
Technical Documents: 13, 81
Technology Components: 22, 239
Text Search: 59, 221, 244
Time Warner Book Group: 209
Time Zones: 161, 165, 266
Time-to-market: 238
Total Cost of Ownership (TCO): 248, 268
Trading Communities: 173
Transactional Data: 15, 31, 136, 137, 149
TransLink: 119
Turner Construction Company: 75

U, V, W

UBS AG: 113
Unilever: 270
U.S. Air Force: 91, 240
U.S. Army: 189
U.S. Army Reserve: 111
U.S. Patent and Trademark Office
(USPTO): 68
Unstructured Content: 20, 33, 54, 137, 139, 154, 195, 208, 213
Unstructured Data: 21, 22, 138, 197
Unstructured Information: 20, 66, 140
Version Control: 86, 91, 92, 240
Virtual Project: 27, 31, 161, 165, 238
Vital Information: 81
Web Browser: 100, 128, 181, 183, 184, 259
Web Conferencing: 162, 163
Web Content Management (WCM): 26, 27, 50, 176
Web Master: 27
Web Page: 60, 125
Web Site: 27, 69, 125, 126, 127, 128, 130, 131, 132, 189, 261
Web Technology: 237
Web-based Extranets: 172, 173

Web-based Software: 28, 162, 188
Whirlpool Corporation: 205
Word Processing: 243
Work Environment: 30, 161, 265
Workflow: 10, 29, 33, 42, 47, 50, 52, 54, 74, 84, 92
Workflow Technology: 233, 237
World Wide Web: 26, 27, 56, 59, 60, 62, 123